THE WHEAT
MONEY

The Wheat Money

1865 – 2015

Kristl Tyler

For Jemima, Tolliver, Videlia,
Beatrice, Sampson, Bill, and Diane,
who deserved far better than
abandonment, disinterest,
and disdain.

CONTENTS

My larger-than-life great-grandfather, Ai Camp, flanked by my great-aunt Bertha, and my great-grandmother Eliza.

SESQUICENTENNIAL

My great-grandfather's name was Ai[1]. He was born in 1865, the same year victory was declared in the American Civil War. Eighteen years later, in 1883, Ai got a gift from the US government: he was given a free plot of land to farm. Although he'd been born into a poor family, he died a rich man with hundreds of acres of land, several houses, lots of cars, and a handful of businesses and investments.

The same year Ai was born, my husband's great-great grandparents had their natural-born rights to live freely, restored. Tolliver was ten years old and Jemima was five when they were most likely to have heard the news. The Thirteenth Amendment outlawed slavery and granted them a sort of *rebirth*. As Freedpeople, my husband's ancestors would finally have a chance to pursue their destinies—or so they must have thought at the time. They did *not* get a gift of land from the US government and they died penniless.

When I met my husband in 2005, I had a master's degree; a high-paying job; no dependent children; a modern, reliable vehicle; and I had just purchased a home.

He, on the other hand, was a homeless crack addict with a long felony record. I knew about the homelessness, and that he'd come out of prison about a year before, but I didn't suspect the crack addiction, and I didn't fully understand the weight of his rap sheet.

Could the homestead land our ancestors did or did not receive have anything to tell us about our own lives? American mythology admonishes us to take full credit for our failings. This admonishment is summarized in two words: personal responsibility. It also tells us that we should loudly

---

[1] That's pronounced aye-eye, by the way.

and proudly claim our successes. One word symbolizes this philosophy: bootstraps.

Personal responsibility and *bootstraps* are sacrosanct concepts in America. You're not supposed to question them but I wanted to do it anyway. I wanted to question my own bootstraps. Could I really take credit for all I'd achieved, and become? Furthermore, I wanted to examine personal responsibility in light of my husband's life. Was it *all* really his fault? And in the end, if I was willing to give up some credit, could he be allowed to escape some blame?

I started my exploration with pretty specific questions I wanted to answer for myself. For example, what might have happened if Tolliver and Jemima had made their way to Washington State and settled near my great-grandfather Ai? Would they have been allowed the opportunity to develop land, and therefore wealth, just as Ai had?

What had happened to those black families that did manage to acquire land in the US? Were there any parts of our country that allowed blacks to thrive as landowners?

Given that my husband's people stayed in the South until 1971, I decided to look at how decades of Jim Crow culture affected his family's ability to benefit from their hard work.

When I started the project, I thought I understood the history of racism in our country. As my research progressed, I was both disgusted and heartbroken by what I learned. Most of us know black families were subjected to more than a few injustices over the decades, but what I found was that things were so much worse than I had believed. What I now know, and what I hope this narrative manages to show others, is that those injustices have had a cumulative effect on the black community, such that when we take the whole story of the past 150 years we'll have no choice but to admit that current day black poverty and incarceration levels are not an accident, they are not a side-effect, and they are not an unintended consequence.

There've been more injustices than I could possibly cover, but I've tried to include summaries of some of the more institutionalized and wide-ranging oppressions.

For instance, way back in the late 1800s, right after the slaves' rights were restored, many Freedpeople were jailed on false charges so that they could be put on chain gangs and worked, literally, to death. I include details of this system in my chapter covering the period from 1910 to 1919.

Later, when social safety net programs were first created, my husband's ancestors were systematically and legally denied aid. This denial continued even during the Great Depression, when just about everyone, of all colors and backgrounds desperately needed help. You can read more about this discrimination in my chapters on the 1920s and 1930s.

I learned that while the GI Bill was revolutionizing US society and creating the vast middle class that made the US such a great country, blacks were being denied those same GI Bill benefits even though they'd been servicemen and servicewomen, too. You can read about this in the chapters on the 1940s and 50s.

I was shocked to learn how racist the Northern cities became as blacks arrived over the years. I hadn't been aware of the forced housing segregation in those cities. During elementary school I had been told that blacks lived in "black neighborhoods" because they preferred to be "with their own." I write about housing segregation starting in my chapter on the 1920s. Then, I write about the many ways housing segregation continued to be a method for oppressing blacks in every decade, even as recently as the 1990s.

Both my husband and I were born during the Civil Rights Movement. My husband was born in Louisiana the same year the Civil Rights Act of 1964 was signed. I was born in Texas in 1968, two months after the assassination of Martin Luther King, Jr. Starting in the chapter on the 1960s, I begin to write our own personal stories – my life and my choices, my husband's life and his.

I'd been taught about the *Brown*[2] school desegregation case in high school, and I'd believed that schools across the country had been desegregated around 1955, when my mom was in high school. Instead, I

---

[2] The Supreme Court case, *Brown v. The Board of Education of Topeka,* Kansas was the case that declared separate schools based on race violated the equal protection clause of the US Constitution.

learned that most schools didn't desegregate until after 1971. The Supreme Court had to rule on about four more cases before recalcitrant white officials finally complied.

In the early 1970s, when my husband's family moved from a small Louisiana town to Denver, Colorado, they were channeled directly into a ghetto Denver's whites had built expressly *for* them.

Denver's inner city had poorer schools, fewer jobs, higher prices, less stability, less clean soil, less clean air, and many other detriments. Learning that his neighborhood was all those things because whites purposely kept those neighborhoods poor, overcrowded, and dirty, was shocking. It had never occurred to me that banks would deny home loans to fully qualified black families just because they lived in a certain area of town; an area they'd been forced to live in because they were black.

Likewise, it had never occurred to me that banks would make sure the only businesses that would be able to operate there would have to be small, self-funded enterprises offering almost no jobs to local residents.

If that weren't enough, I learned that the US government, in the early 1980s, sent in both the crack cocaine, and the amped and eager police officers that would turn his neighborhood into a war zone.

I include details from the investigative work of journalist Gary Webb. His discoveries about the governments' role in cocaine trafficking are detailed in my chapter on the 1990s. I talk about those eager police officers when I share details of the work of Michelle Alexander in that same chapter.

As I recounted the history that I was learning, my husband poked fun at his side of the family for being so poor, while noting that my family had been "rich" for generations. He joked that my life of luxury had been waylaid when I married him.

Not so, I assured him. In every generation of my so-called rich family, the rich heir had married someone poor.

While many well-to-do families pressure heirs to marry only those of comparable wealth, that had never been the case in our family.

My great grandfather, Ai, had been born poor, and married a poor woman named Eliza. Together they increased their wealth year after year.

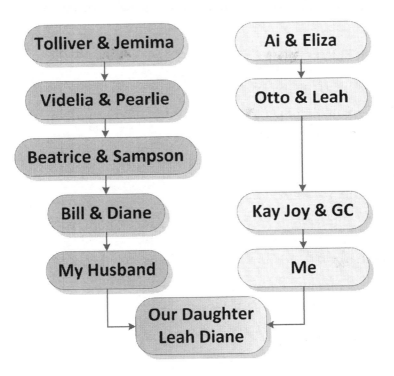

Figure 1: Leah Tyler's Family Tree

Their rich son, Otto, married Leah, a woman who grew up in a train depot with her railroad-employee father. Her entire life she joked about not being of the same class as my grandfather. Likewise, my grandfather often joked that she'd married him because "she got tired of livin' in the depot."

My rich mother, Kay Joy, married GC, an earnest, but poor, college professor. And now I had married my homeless felon, William. Yes, we could have doubled our wealth with each generation by marrying according to our station, but instead, we had all married, I guess, for love.

I also assured my husband that his family had not been poor because they were lazy; from what I'd been reading, they'd been poor because society had been designed to keep them poor.

He balked whenever I said things like this. He was quick to assert that he'd made his own choices, and reminded me that he takes full responsibility for his life's path. He doesn't consider himself a victim, and he won't let me paint him as one.

I told him that his attitude is commendable. I've met many, many blacks who have the same noble credo. I told him that my research was important because it would enable me to show Leah, our daughter, how the white side of our family had been lifted up, while the black side had been held down, even into the year 2005, setting each of us up in the life circumstances under which we found one another that day in the inner city.

As I learned details of the terrible treatment of blacks over the decades, I would try to share them with my husband, but he implored me not to. He gently (and sometimes not so gently) reminded me that knowledge of past injustices didn't help him live a better life; it only served to make him angry.

"I'll leave the outrage to you," he said. "You seem to enjoy it more than I do."

I planned my research and reading so that I learned the history in the order it took place. Since I was going one decade at a time, it took a while before I began learning about racism in our own lifetimes. Once I got to the research on the 70s, 80s, and 90s, I begged my husband to let me tell him how the War on Drugs, forced housing segregation, and educational channeling had directly affected his life.

"I promise this stuff won't make you feel worse. I'm almost certain you'll find it empowering," I said.

Little by little, he relented and allowed me to bend his ear. As he accepted my claim that he had the right to set down some of the guilt and shame he'd been carrying, I saw him open up and I heard his view of himself change. Maybe, he wondered aloud on several occasions, he wasn't such a bad person after all.

He'd once said to me, in the first few weeks we knew one another, *I ain't shit and I ain't got shit.*

He'd come a long way since uttering that phrase to me, but learning the history and accepting my claim that "personal responsibility" only held so much sway in his life, helped him come even further forward.

Obviously, the facts of systemic, institutional racism in the United States are not something I personally discovered. Anyone who has studied the dark side of Black American History is aware that these things happened. The seminal works that provided me with these details are known to many. Unfortunately, those who know the history tend to be black and brown people and a few progressive whites. That's why this book is not for black and brown people. It is aimed squarely at whites.

Sometimes whites and blacks need to learn about the history of the United States differently. Generally speaking, when blacks look at Black History it makes sense that they might want to celebrate those who achieved things and overcame obstacles during the bleakest of times. Conversely, it is my conviction that white people need to look unflinchingly at the worst things whites did, and accept that whites benefitted—and continue to benefit— from denying blacks opportunities, fair wages, respect, and dignity.

Recently, our family went to see the movie 42. It's the story of Jackie Robinson, the first black man to play Major League baseball. It was an uplifting story. My husband left the movie theater in a great mood. I was happy to explain a bit of history to our daughter. But I hold some reservations about the movie we all enjoyed together. The movie was carefully crafted to tell the story without reopening old wounds for older blacks or slashing fresh cuts into the psyches of younger ones. Unfortunately, these presentations of history, by protecting blacks from the assaultive truth, often coddle and salve the psyches of whites[3].

I believe we, as whites, owe ourselves a little more exposure to the truth than to see movies like *The Help* and 42. We walk out of the theater, (perhaps dabbing our cheeks with a tissue) and we say or think things like, "It's just so terrible how those people were treated. Thank goodness all that is in the past," and then, "I am so glad that *Good White People* took a stand and put an end to that nonsense."

---

[3] These versions even lead us to believe ridiculous fiction about white heroism such as the idea that were it not for some 11th hour pep talk by Branch Rickey, Jackie would have chosen to be footnote instead of a legend.

These movies have happy endings, and that's fine, unless we allow them to blind us to the fact that whites continue to benefit from unearned advantages that are not enjoyed by black and brown people.

If you are a white person who truly wants to end racism (and there are lots of us), it is vitally important to learn what has happened over these last one-hundred-and-fifty years. That way, when we see a movie like 42, we will be able to enjoy the uplifting message, but we won't indulge in the belief that the movie scratches the surface of what it was really like to be Jackie or Rachel Robinson.

There were, and are, very real consequences to racism. It was not, and is not, just about hurt feelings. High school history books try to boil down the hundred years of Jim Crow to a picture of a sign about separate drinking fountains. As the proverbial Good White People in charge of moving white people forward today, we (you and me) can't let other whites lose sight of the fact that those signs represented a system wherein drinking from the wrong fountain could get you murdered.

At certain points in this book I depart from the historical narrative and delve into research from the fields of economics, sociology, and social psychology. I present information from these fields because it's important to understand not only what has happened, but also how, why, and when we humans are most susceptible to manipulation by others.

Some whites might say, *you had a rich great grandfather but I did not, so your story is worthless as an example for me*. In fact, the descendants of poor whites have plenty to regret and take responsibility for. In a section called "The Racial Bribe" I note the role poor whites played in keeping blacks down and the benefits they gained from doing so.

In several sections of this book, I share the work of a well-known social psychologist who has spent over thirty years studying good people who did horrible things as they participated in systematic atrocities like the Holocaust, the Rwandan genocide and Abu Ghraib. Social psychology research can help us understand the past and avoid future atrocities.

When you read my section called, "Last Place Aversion" you'll learn about recent research by economists that can help us understand how people respond when they fear they might be falling into last place. In ancient times "last place" might have involved being eaten by a predator but in modern times it might involve being a poor immigrant who doesn't like being at the bottom of a social hierarchy.

Finally, as my last area of inquiry, (this one a much more inward-facing exploration) I asked myself why, starting very early in life, I'd chosen to buck Southern taboos against race mixing.

Am I just a really great person who was willing to sacrifice myself by doing the right thing in the face of entrenched racism? Of course not. I gained something (or lots of things) for dating across color lines. What exactly did I gain? In other words, what were my short-term and longer-term rewards for pissing off so many white people?

I learned a lot about myself during the writing of this book. For example, when I started writing, I truly couldn't explain how and why my husband and I had come together. By the time the book was finished, our courtship and marriage made perfect sense.

The exercise of writing has also helped me understand how our race and class differences have led to our most consistent area of disagreement. My husband and I have struggled most mightily over the question of which child-rearing and disciplinary techniques we would use. He's always been raising her so she'd be able to make it in *his* world. I've always been teaching her the lessons she needs in order to get by in *mine*. Our disagreements have repeatedly required serious negotiation because we both believe that raising our child to meet life's challenges is our most important job.

I enjoyed capturing several key arguments about childrearing we've had in the past. While we took them very seriously at the time, we've learned to laugh at ourselves in retrospect. I hope you will enjoy reading about those arguments. In the end, you'll see that we learned to respect each other's lessons as valid, functional, and vital and we vowed to exercise patience and stand respectfully aside, each for the other, when teachable moments arise, even if we don't understand what's being taught.

I am not a trained historian, genealogist, social psychologist, or economist so I'm certain I've made errors. I continue to worry that some errors may exist in this writing due to my lack of expertise, my willful oversimplification, or my need to filter information in ways that serve my ego.

I've tried to acknowledge those possibilities when they might be applicable. I hope that even where I've made errors, I will pique an interest that will encourage you, my reader, to explore some of these topics further.

The sesquicentennial of the Emancipation Proclamation took place on January 1, 2013. Many other events relative to the Civil War and the Freedpeople will be discussed and celebrated between 2013 and 2015.

Some will say, *Look how far blacks have come over these 150 years! Isn't it great?* Others will say, *It's been over a hundred years! What's wrong with them?*

I hope that by reading this book, you will be prepared to acknowledge, as I am, that the real questions should be:

Look how long ago whites pretended to stop oppressing blacks! and, *How are we going to fix the mess we made?*

Perhaps you'll even agree that the most pressing questions of all are:

Who is still benefiting from driving a wedge between poor whites and poor blacks? and, *How can we expose them and put a stop to it once and for all?*

1865

In 1865, slavery became illegal in the United States.

Slave masters were instructed to read a statement to "their" slaves informing them that they were free.

My husband's second-great grandparents, Tolliver and Jemima, were children when that statement was read to their parents and themselves.

What must that news have felt like for Tolliver, who was ten years old?

Tom Robinson[4] was a child and a slave in 1865 and he told this story:

One day I was out milking the cows. Mr. Dave come down into the field and he had a paper in his hand.

"Listen to me," he said. "Listen to what I read you." And he read from a paper all about how I was free.

You can't tell how I felt. "You're joking me," I says.

"No, I ain't," says he, "You're free."

"No," says I, "it's a joke.

"No," says he, "it's a law that I got to read this paper to you. Now listen while I read it again."

But I still didn't believe him.

"Just go up to the house," says he, "and ask Mrs. Robinson. She'll tell you"

"It's a joke," I says to her.

---

[4] See the appendix entitled *Primary Sources and Usage Notes* for information about "Slave Narratives" and "Jim Crow Narratives." Tom Robinson's Slave Narrative is available from the Library of Congress.

"Did you ever know your master to tell you a lie?" she says.

"No," says I, "I ain't"

"Well," she says, "The war is over and you're free."

By that time I thought maybe what she was telling me was right.

"Miss Robinson," says I, "can I go over to the Smiths?"

They was a colored family that lived nearby.

"Don't you understand," she says, "you're free. You don't have to ask me what you can do. Run along, child."

And so I went. And do you know why I was a-going? I wanted to find out if they was free, too. I just couldn't take it all in. I couldn't believe we was all free alike.

Was I happy? You can take anything. No matter how good you treat it — it wants to be free. You can treat it good and feed it good and give it everything it seems to want — but if you open the cage — it's happy.

I smile when I read Tom's account and imagine that my husband's great-great grandfather Tolliver Young might have, as a ten year old in 1865, experienced a similar exuberance.

The woman he would someday marry, Jemima Bouton, had been born in 1860, in Alabama. She was five years old when the news came, and was probably too young to have later recalled her feelings.

We can read the *Slave Narrative* of Annie Mae Weathers who was around five years old at the time *her* family heard the news. When Weathers was asked about her recollections of that day she could only repeat the story she remembered her father telling:

I remember hearing my pa say that when somebody come and hollered, "You [slaves] is free at last" say he just dropped his hoe and said in a [strange] voice, "Thank God for that." It made ol' miss and ol' massa so sick they stopped eating for a week. Pa said ol' massa and ol' miss looked like their stomach and guts had a lawsuit and their navel was called in for a witness, they was so sorry we was free.

THE WILD AND CRAZY 1860S AND 1870S

The 1860s were crazy; almost as crazy as the 1960s.

The 1860s weren't wild because of hippies, free love, and weed, but because of a different set of tumultuous social changes.

Throughout the previous decade (the 1850s), slavery was on just about everyone's mind.

Rich white Southerners wanted slavery to expand out across the open frontier.

Rich white Northerners didn't like the Southern slave owners so they wanted slavery confined to the existing slave states.

Poor whites in the South were told by rich whites that they, too, should want slavery to expand into the West. So, even though it wouldn't be likely to benefit them, they agreed to fight (and die even) so that the plantation owners' wealth might be expanded.

Finally, there were the poor whites of the northern US. They wanted to escape the Northern factories

Figure 2: Lincoln signed a lot of stuff that made our ancestors happy. Both our black ancestors who had their freedom restored, and our white ancestors who wanted affordable land were Lincoln fans.

and fan out across the frontier.

Those Americans who were anti-slavery and wanted the frontier land to go to common people were called Free-Soilers. My white ancestors were very likely Free-Soilers and they almost certainly voted for Lincoln in the 1860 election because of that.

As soon as Lincoln was declared the winner of the presidential election, unhappy leaders from the Southern states started making plans. They left Washington DC and went home to their state capitols. Once there, they wrote up documents[5] announcing their reasons for leaving the United States and forming a new, pro-slavery nation. Mississippi leaders mentioned slavery seven times in their document. Texas included 22 references to slavery. Georgia's declaration mentioned it a whopping 34 times.

With all the Southern congressmen gone from Washington DC, the legislators who remained seemed to have had a Free-soiler extravaganza. They passed all kinds of stuff that benefitted my poor white ancestors.

They passed the Homestead Act of 1862 and therefore approved giving 160 acres of free land to anyone who would stake a claim and follow a few simple guidelines.

They passed the first of five Pacific Railroad Acts and thereby gave land to railroad companies and let those companies raise money[6] to build the rail lines that would go all the way from the Atlantic Coast to the Pacific. Those train lines would make frontier life a lot less harsh for the pioneer families.

Everything my pioneering, homesteading ancestors needed from the East would arrive much more quickly by train: mail, food, tools, seeds, cloth, etc.

---

[5] The documents are called Ordinances of Secession. Many people today claim the Confederate States did not secede because of slavery. Documents of that time period make it very clear that slavery was absolutely the issue that drove states to secede. Historians also outline that prior to secession, slave states had repeatedly asked the federal government to rule against "states' rights" when Northern states used it.

[6] The railroad companies raised money by issuing federal bonds.

Southern Life: The Immediate Aftermath

The Civil War ended in the spring of 1865. Since Tolliver and Jemima's families lived in conquered states, they were considered "free"[7] as soon as Lee surrendered to Grant at the Appomattox courthouse.

As amazing as this news must have been for the Freedpeople, it's easy to imagine that it might also have been pretty terrifying.

In his *Slave Narrative*, W.L. Bost describes the anxiety at least some of the Freedpeople felt:

> *After the war was over, we was afraid to move. [We were] just like the tarpins or turtles after 'mancipation. Just stick our heads out to see how the land lay.*

In addition to the insecurity of this sudden freedom, the former slaves were also at risk of being targeted by furious and frustrated whites.

As quoted in the *Slave Narrative* of Tines Kendricks:

> *When my race first got their freedom and begin to leave their masters, a heap of masters got raging mad and just tore up truck. They say they going to kill every [black] they find. Some of them did do that very thing...I'm telling you the truth. They shot [blacks] down by the hundreds. They just wasn't going let them enjoy they freedom. That is the truth.*

The Freedmen's Bureau was responsible for keeping records of crimes committed against the former slaves[8]. Browsing the website today, one can find entries that illustrate just how random and ruthless whites were behaving after the war ended.

Freedman Assaulted: *ANDREW PRICE.*

Date: *May 15.*

Injuries: *Stabbed.*

Cause: *"For not bringing WESTMORELAND a cup of coffee immediately when asked for."*

Attacker: *R.W. WESTMORELAND (student, white).*

---

[7] The Thirteenth Amendment wouldn't be ratified until December. Once ratified, all slaves, even those in non-rebelling states, were free.

[8] The Freedmen's Bureau website has a number of documents listed under the heading "Murders and Outrages." The two sample entries are from a document entitled "1867 Report of Freedmen Murdered and Assaulted in the Sub-District of Athens, Georgia"

Disposition: WESTMORELAND *was tried by J.D. PELLARD,*
Intendant, Athens, Georgia. He was fined $50.00 and costs.
WESTMORELAND is at large, place unknown.

Name of Person Murdered: *NANCY WRIGHT (colored).*
Place: *Camden.*
Supposed Murderer: *DR. WM. WRIGHT (white).*
Date of Killing: *5 May 1866.*
Remarks: *The deceased was about 14 years old and was shot by DR.*
WRIGHT when he was drunk. A bill was found against the doctor. He
made his escape before being arrested.

The New *Not-Slavery*-Slavery

No sooner than they read those "you're free" statements to "their" slaves, former slave owners seem to have asked themselves, "*Well, now that we can't technically have them as slaves, is there some way we can just treat them like slaves, getting rich off their labor, but call it something else?*"

In other words, whites were looking for a *Not-Slavery*-Slavery.

Michelle Alexander, writing in *The New Jim Crow*, presents the compelling case that ever since slavery was outlawed, whites have consistently replaced one system of control with another— even through the present day.

Back in 1865, their first big idea was to create work contracts for blacks that were essentially slavery contracts. White landowners were planning to scare blacks into signing these "voluntary" work agreements. These work contracts stipulated that blacks would have to refer to their overseers as "Master"; the workday would be sunup to sundown; and workers would be whipped if they did not perform quickly or efficiently enough. Any black person who didn't sign a work contract was going to be thrown in jail. The rules around these mandatory work contracts were called *The Black Codes* because they specifically listed blacks as the people who had to have a work contract.

When federal laws were passed that made The Black Codes illegal, whites were sent scrambling once again, as they tried to conjure up their

United States Oppression of Blacks

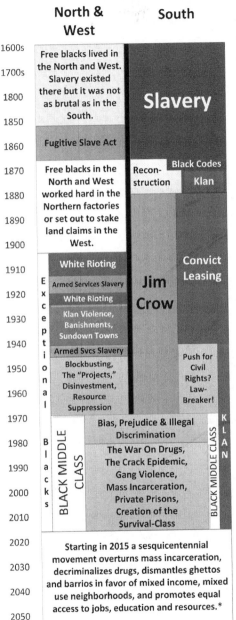

Figure 3: As one system is destroyed, another is invented in its place.

* Wouldn't that be awesome?

next *Not-Slavery*-Slavery.

The next big idea was to pass what I call the wink-nudge laws. These laws didn't mention race, but all the important white people understood that these laws would only be applied to black people. There were wink-nudge laws against trading goods after sundown or being unemployed.

Blacks should have been able to survive in the war-ravaged South much like the Western pioneers did – by hunting, fishing, growing crops and trading goods with one another.

Blacks should have been allowed to choose a life of working sunup to sundown on behalf of their own families, but whites called this lifestyle "vagrancy" when a black person did it. Under the enforcement practices of the wink-nudge laws, if you weren't working for a white person, you weren't working.

With this so-called anti-vagrancy law in effect, white landowners had successfully created a system that forced blacks to agree to work for them.

The white landowners sectioned off their holdings and assigned each of the black families their own portion. This arrangement, known as sharecropping, gave white landowners almost complete power over black families' lives.

Harriet A. Washington, writing in *Medical Apartheid,* manages to summarize the hopelessness of sharecropping and tenant farming in just a few sentences:

> *Trapped in the usurious cycle of tenant cotton farming, they were chained by debt and forced to work the same land as had their enslaved grandparents... they owned nothing, not even the crumbling shacks they lived in.*
>
> *These sharecroppers, including children, were weighed down by hundred-pound bags of cotton, living and working under the orders of white landowners who kept them in economic thralldom by paying low prices for their crops and charging inflated prices for food, seed, and other necessities.*
>
> *Those blacks who tried to flee the land were arrested, punished, and returned—or worse—just as their enslaved grandparents would have been. Beatings, lynchings, and murders that were never investigated enforced black serfdom.*

This *Not-Slavery*-Slavery would start taking hold in the late 1860s and tightly control blacks for a hundred years in the South. It lasted well into the 1960s.

When that system finally ended, another *Not-Slavery*-Slavery would be developed that continues to the present day.

Leah Tyler's White Ancestors: 1865 through the 1870s

During this period of tumult for the black side of our family, there were also upheavals for poor whites in the North and Midwest.

There's no doubt my poor white ancestors were aware of the Homestead Act very soon after it was signed in 1862. They were living in Ohio and working for wages. They did not own land and they knew that owning some could be key to creating stability for the family. They were willing to move almost anywhere to find that stability.

My great-grandfather Ai was born in Ohio two years after the Homestead Act had been passed. Shortly after his birth, Ai's family packed up and left Ohio, moving 700 miles west, to Iowa.

By 1870, they'd moved another 200 miles, south and east, to Olathe, Kansas.

In the last months of the 1879 they'd made their way another 200 miles south and west and were re-grouping near Wichita, Kansas.

Certainly those years must have been hard for the white side of our family. They traveled by covered wagon and, as pioneers, went through all the things history tells us the pioneers endured.

The website of the National Archives, in an article about the Homestead Act, states:

> Physical conditions on the frontier presented...challenges. Wind, blizzards, and plagues of insects threatened crops. Open plains meant few trees for building, forcing many to build homes out of sod. Limited fuel and water supplies could turn simple cooking and heating chores into difficult trials. Ironically, even the smaller size of sections took its own toll. While 160 acres may have been sufficient for an eastern farmer, it was simply not enough to sustain agriculture on the dry plains, and scarce natural vegetation made raising livestock on the prairie difficult. As a result, in many areas, the original homesteader did not stay on the land long enough to fulfill the claim.

These harsh conditions are probably why Ai's family kept uprooting itself. Perhaps Ai's parents worried that they might never find the right place to put down roots. The further they pushed West, the harder life became. Still, westward they went.

THE 1880S AND 1890S

Union troops left the South in 1877 and white men eventually regained all positions of power. Even with a monopoly on legal power they weren't altogether sure how to organize their new society so that rich whites could continue to get richer based on the exploitation of black labor.

They had the wink-nudge laws and those kept the sharecropping system righted, but they still had one major issue: mixed-race babies.

Blacks and whites spent an awful lot of time together but the shared space and time was supposed to be limited to situations where blacks were doing work for whites.

Sometimes a work situation resulted in two people finding themselves alone together, just one black person and one white.

White man and black man: no problem.

White woman and black woman: no problem.

White man and black woman: as long as the black woman accepted her fate, white men saw no cause for alarm, even if mixed-race babies proliferated.

But woe to the community if the pair turned out to be a black man and a white woman. All hell's fury, and nothing less, would ensue if a white man learned of it, or if a mixed-race baby popped out forty weeks later.

Mixed-race babies threatened the Southern system of black labor exploitation because these neither-nors scuttled the strict system of classification.

"Okay," they said, "One drop of black blood makes you black."

That really meant, "If I know your momma, and she's black, well, you're black too, no matter what you look like."

Additionally, it meant, "If I know your momma and she's white, but you're not, then I know for a fact your momma was raped, and a black man will die a gruesome and public death because you exist. Doesn't much matter which man, because it's not about justice, it's about keeping the system intact."

Blacks (as well as the mixed-race babies) would be rigorously trained to behave one way, while whites would be trained to behave another. The rules of behavior were layered into existence and became a labyrinth of unwritten social rules that blacks and whites would follow in order to remind both, every day, in every possible way, that whites were supreme and blacks were little more than pack animals.

Whites would walk with their chins high and their backs straight. Blacks were expected to tuck their chins into their chest and avert their eyes. Eye contact, improperly exercised, could result in a death sentence[9].

Whites could have a confident stride. Blacks needed to strike a balance between lackadaisical ambling and up-tempo ambling, depending on whether they had just received an order from a white person.

Whites could dress as formal and fancy as they desired. Blacks were expected to dress for field work at all times. This meant sharecropper overalls and dresses made of sack cloth. Blacks caught wearing "white folks clothes" would be told to go home and change; and warned not make that mistake again.

Whites were allowed to speak any way they pleased, from the Queen's English to a backwoods dialect. Additionally, whites could use their voices to command attention and direct the actions of others. Blacks were never allowed to speak with any intellectual confidence in the presence of whites. They had to express themselves using a limited vocabulary and a slave-style grammatical structure. Likewise, they could not acknowledge an understanding of anything beyond the simplest logic and could not show interest in anything but the most rudimentary topics.

In reaction to being forced to play dumb all the time, fooling whites into unwittingly meeting black's needs became a bit of a game for blacks. Trickster tales had long been part of West African culture, so the tradition

---

[9] For more information on the social rules of Jim Crow see the work of Leon Litwack.

continued through slavery and then throughout Jim Crow. A good trickster tale ended with a self-satisfied master character who walked away from a situation believing in his superior intelligence, while the servant character was the only one who fully understood what had happened, because they, by pretending to be dumb, had outsmarted everyone.

Since self-satisfied whites made life so much easier on them, many blacks allowed, even encouraged, whites to believe in black intellectual inferiority.

In her *Jim Crow Narrative*, Wilhelmina Griffin Jones told the story of a time when she and a male friend were driving through a small rural town and were stopped by a policeman. They were ordered to appear before the sheriff and the mayor the following Monday. Though Jones and her friend were both educated and had professional occupations, her friend chose to pose as a simple-minded person, in a sort of trickster ploy, because he knew the meeting would go more smoothly if he did:

> *When my friend came back with me on Monday he came dressed for the occasion. He had on overalls with one suspender hanging to the side, and a cap with the bill turned in the back, some old dusty shoes without strings and his sleeves rolled up, that sort of thing, collar open.*

> *[My friend] did this because he felt like doing this kind of thing would certainly make [the mayor] be more lenient, which he was.*

> *He would have charged us a with whole lot more if he didn't act the way he wanted him to react you see. I dressed like I was on Saturday, the same way. I was well dressed, and as I talked to him I didn't change my language at all. He wasn't very pleased with me at all, but he was very pleased with my friend because of the way he reacted and the way he had come dressed and that sort of thing.*

> *[The mayor turned] to the sheriff and he said, "Let's see what this boy over here's got to say for himself." So he looked over at my friend and said, "Boy!"*

> *And the moment he said that my friend popped up and started sort of fidgeting with his trousers and that just pleased [the mayor] to no end. So he said, "Boy, what's your name?" And [my friend] told him his name.*

Jones goes on to explain that her friend lied about his occupation when asked.

"What [work do] you do, boy?"

He said, "I's the janitor, sir."

And oh, that brought a big smile when he said he was the janitor. So the mayor looked at him, and then he turned around to his deputy. And he said, "Now, you see, he looks like a good boy. We're going to be real lenient on them."

We laughed about it afterwards and he wasn't angry at all. But it would have been a whole lot harder for me to have done that though. I just couldn't have done it. But knowing my friend who did this sort of thing, he can shift from one personality to another very easily.

Poor, Dumb and Ugly

I grew up in Texas. When I was a senior in high school I met a white girl from a nearby rural high school who told me that she considered herself superior to all black people.

I asked her why she believed that was true.

"Because I'm white," she said.

"I know, but why does being white mean you're better than any and all black people?" I asked.

"Because whites are superior," she said.

I was looking for her to tout some ridiculous monkey theory or cite the results of some bogus testing paradigm. "Yes, I know you're white, but why does that make you better than any black person?"

"Because they're black," she offered.

My confusion must have revealed itself in my expression.

She slowed down for me. "I can be dumb...ugly...poor...doesn't matter. I'm white and that means I'm better than any [black person]."

As it began to sink in, my voice leaked out of my face, low in tone and volume at first. The sound wasn't a word or words, but a slowly increasing gurgle of disgust and rejection.

"EwwwwwwwWWWWWWWW!"

As my voice grew louder, my face contorted into a sour, twisted mess; my nostrils flared and my eyebrows came down and together. My head shook *no* with greater and greater desperation.

I wheeled a hundred and eighty degrees away from her and took off, almost running, trying to get as far away from her as I could.

At that point in my life, I was accustomed to whites laying out a collection of personal observations about differences between the races and announcing, in a self-congratulatory tone, that, as much as they regretted their conclusions about the innate superiority of whites, they had to stand by them.

I'd heard them say that they opposed interracial marriage on the grounds that it created such a terrible life for the children who were stuck in the middle, never accepted as black or white.

I'd feigned patience as white people contorted themselves, working hard to present to me the case that they were not racist just so they would feel licensed to say something racist to me immediately afterwards.

But this was new and it was shocking.

What this girl was telling me was so foreign, it took me days, if not weeks, to process it.

When I finally unraveled what she'd said to me, I realized that her logic was a rejection of personal responsibility for her own failings and weaknesses.

For some whites, to let go of racism would require facing the reality of their own capabilities, accomplishments and prospects for the future. That reality is sometimes something some people don't want to face.

White skin has no trade value – you can't exchange it for food – but rich whites have managed to trick poor whites into thinking it does.

During slavery, rich whites had said, "Let's stick together. You'll never be rich like me, but you'll be white, and that alone is more valuable than money, isn't it?"

Rich whites had progressively sweetened the deal by hiring poor whites and putting them in charge of keeping blacks in line. Poor whites were hired as slave supervisors. It was the poor whites who often did the beatings. They were also hired as patrollers for escaped slaves. This gave poor whites license to harass any and all blacks who were given passes to walk the roads from plantation to town, or from their plantation to another.

These privileges meant the poor whites would not only accept the system but they would fight to keep the system alive because it served them financially as well as psychologically. Had the attempts to divide poor blacks from poor whites failed, rich elites would have lost the power to write all the laws and gather so much wealth.

Even after slavery was deemed illegal and blacks were given the label of "free," the celebration of white skin value continued and drove the deep wedge between poor whites and blacks. No matter how much poor blacks and poor whites had in common, and no matter how much they could have benefitted by coming together, they saw each other as the enemy.

Frederick Douglass wrote about this racial bribe in his 1881 biography, *Life and Times of Frederick Douglass*, saying simply, "They divided both to conquer each."

Later, in 1935, W.E.B. Du Bois, in his book *Black Reconstruction in America*, called out the technique the elites were using:

> It must be remembered that the white group of laborers, while they received a low wage, were compensated in part by a sort of public and psychological wage.

> They were given public deference and titles of courtesy because they were white. They were admitted freely with all classes of white people to public functions, public parks, and the best schools.

> The police were drawn from their ranks, and the courts, dependent on their votes, treated them with such leniency as to encourage lawlessness. Their vote selected public officials, and while this had a small effect upon the economic situation, it had great effect upon their personal treatment and the deference shown them.

> The newspapers specialized on news that flattered the poor whites and almost utterly ignored the Negro except in crime and ridicule.

Michelle Alexander, discusses the racial bribe in her book *The New Jim*

Crow: Mass Incarceration in the Age of Colorblindness:

> *Deliberately and strategically, the planter class extended special privileges to poor whites in an effort to drive a wedge between them and black slaves.*
>
> *White settlers were allowed greater access to Native American lands, white servants were allowed to police slaves through slave patrols and militias, and barriers were created so that free labor would not be placed in competition with slave labor.*
>
> *These measures effectively eliminated the risk of future alliances between black slaves and poor whites. Poor whites suddenly had a direct, personal stake in the existence of a race-based system of slavery. Their own plight had not improved by much, but at least they were not slaves.*
>
> *Once the planter elite split the labor force, poor whites responded to the logic of their situation and sought ways to expand their racially privileged position.*

Klan members, especially those who did the dirty work, were often the poorer members of the community, inanely carrying out tasks that served the rich and not themselves.

In John Harrison Volter's *Jim Crow Narrative*, he explains:

> *The Ku Klux Klan was not set up by the lower class of Caucasians. The lower class of Caucasians were recruited into the Ku Klux Klan by former rich plantation owners who saw a way to gain some of their property back. And they used prejudiced ideas…on these ignorant low-class Caucasians. The act of giving each free slave so many acres of land and then the Ku Klux Klan scared them off it, you know. These poor whites that was the body of the Klan didn't gain nothing. The land went back to the rich owner, you know, it didn't go to them. It's just showing you how [they] manipulated their own people.*

When one hears the diatribes of some whites today claiming that blacks love welfare because they like to relax in front of big screen televisions while *us white people* work hard and have our paychecks savaged to support them, one is hearing the same narrative that has been circulating for 150 years now.

It all boils down to the rich selling a message to poor whites, "Whites work hard and blacks are freeloaders."

The funny thing is, rich whites started selling this message in 1866.

Figure 4: Racial Bribery Propaganda

This flyer was posted in public in 1866. It was designed to encourage poor whites to see blacks as freeloaders. I have blurred the face of the cartoon because the features depicted are exaggerated versions of some West African groups' features.

The poster reads: "The Freedmen's Bureau! An Agency to Keep the Negro in Idleness at the Expense of the White Man."

On the fence next to the man chopping wood it says, "The White man must work to Keep his Children Fed and Pay his Taxes."

Just above the lounging Freedman, there is a quote saying, "Whar is de use for me to work as long as dey make dese appropriations?"

When whites posted notices that showed a black man lying on the ground, relaxing, while a white man chopped wood, they were selling a caricature that differs little from the welfare caricature of today.

Take a moment, if you will, and consider how completely ludicrous it was, in 1866, to accuse blacks of being freeloaders.

In 1866, nearly every black in the US had *just* been released from a bondage within which they had worked long and hard their entire lives, for no pay, little food, and under frightening brutality. How did these whites manage to call blacks "freeloaders" while maintaining a straight face? Weren't rich whites[10] the real freeloaders after all?

Sub-Human? Or Inhumane?

So the racial bribe explains how poor whites were encouraged to engage in the system of white supremacy, but what about the rich? Were they all in on the secret plan to exploit the labor of blacks by making poor, angry whites into their unwitting minions?

Such a vast conspiracy would be hard, if not impossible, to maintain. Besides that, weren't there any white people who had a conscience that needed to be coddled?

In fact, there were plenty, and a quote from a French Baron illustrates the dilemma those conscientious white folks faced. Charles-Louis de Secondat, Baron de La Brède et de Montesquieu, writing in the early 1700s, noted:

It is impossible for us to suppose these creatures [African slaves] to be men; because allowing them to be men, a suspicion would follow that we ourselves are not Christians.

Montesquieu's observation related to the institution of slavery was clever, apt, and very much applicable to the position taken by white slave owners in the United States both during and after slavery.

---

[10] The concept of a middle-class has a short history. In most of human history people were either laborers or landowners and there was little in between. For the purposes of this book the middle-class will be ignored because it is notoriously complex to define and utilize those definitions. Rather than write a book trying to define what "middle class" mean, I will gloss over it so as to make larger points about racism.

Put another way, Montesquieu was saying that either Africans were sub-human, or Europeans were inhumane. Not surprisingly, when faced with this dilemma, most white Southerners chose to believe that blacks were sub-human.

It was the less inconvenient conclusion of the two.

Dehumanization turns out to have its own special "perks." Research in social psychology has shown that the process of dehumanizing others prior to victimizing them makes the task less unpleasant for the perpetrators of the violence. By characterizing blacks as subhuman, whites could assure each other and themselves that there was no reason to feel guilty about the violent punishments that were carried out. *Would they feel guilty about whipping a horse? Of course not! A horse was a beast of burden; A work animal who had to be prodded in order to get things done. Blacks, likewise, were beasts of burden* (or so the justification went).

The Bible, in the book of Genesis, chapter 1, verse 26 says:

> *And God said, Let us make man in our image, after our likeness: and let them have dominion over the fish of the sea, and over the fowl of the air, and over the cattle, and over all the earth, and over every creeping thing that creepeth upon the earth.*

Many a Southern preacher explained that whites were made in God's image and blacks were creeping things that creepeth-ed upon the earth.

But dehumanizing blacks wasn't the only game in town. Many so-called *Good White People* acknowledged blacks as human, but in the same breath espoused the idea that those of African descent would never reach full maturity. In other words, they thought of blacks as "simple" people, perpetual children, who benefitted from their guidance. In other words, they believed blacks of all ages *had* to be held under white authority just as white children were.

It's easy to see how corporal punishment of black workers then became in their minds, not cruelty, but "for their own good." Like the proverbial parent who stands ready with a belt tightly gripped in their hand and announces, "This is going to hurt me much more than it hurts you," being a self-appointed pseudo-parent to blacks was something whites regularly held up as supremely philanthropic.

And much like parents who admonish children to smile, be polite, and have a cheery disposition, whites demanded that blacks have a sunny attitude toward them at all times. Blacks were not allowed to show frustration, anger, irritability, or disappointment in the presence of whites.

Before long white Southerners could proudly proclaim that blacks were immature simpletons (*"I's the janitor"*) who were endlessly happy, cheerful people who gratefully accepted their role in society.

Ai's Family Arrives in the Washington Territory

As Ai's parents moved him from place to place he must have been exposed to many of the chores, tools, and techniques frontier life required. Homesteading was an ongoing experiment in ingenuity and tenacity. Ai's family probably supported themselves along their journey by working for other homesteading families. This wage labor would have created opportunities for them to learn frontier adaptations to farming, animal husbandry, hunting, fishing, lumbering and carpentry.

Ai's mother and sisters would have learned the many skills necessary to be successful and supportive homesteading women. They would have developed skills in gathering wild food, cooking without the benefit of modern kitchens, sewing without modern machines, mixing herbal remedies that could be used in lieu of medicine, and many other skills.

In short, Ai's family, because they were white, would have repeatedly been welcomed into various frontier communities. We can speculate that they would have been paid fair wages in cash or trade and would have been able to learn from the experience of other white homesteaders, therefore greatly increasing the chances that they would do well when they later staked claims of their own.

Each time they opted to move on from a place, they would have known a little more about what items they should carry onward and which items they could leave behind.

In 1883, Ai's parents, along with Ai and all his siblings, took what locals called "The Immigrant Train" to the southeastern portion of the Washington Territory. This would be the place they'd been seeking all along; the place they would call home.

The Racial Climate of the Washington Territory in the 1880s

So we know that the 1880s were bad for blacks in the South, but what might things have been like for Jemima and Tolliver if they'd left the South? Specifically, what would life have been like for them in Washington, where my white ancestors were living?

My research turned up some anti-black sentiment in the Oregon Territory just to the south of the Washington Territory.

HistoryLink.com[11] outlines how Oregonians came to oppose black settlers:

> [S]ettlers in Oregon Territory…feared the arrival of blacks who might marry Natives and thus pose a threat to what was still a small white population. The issue was put to public vote. Oregon voters … excluded African Americans—as well as Hawaiians—from Oregon when it became a state. Hawaiians had made up a large portion of the territory's work force, and most soon returned to the islands.

Unlike the anti-black sentiment in Oregon, in the earliest years of the Washington Territory, blacks were welcomed. In fact, the western cities of Seattle and Tacoma, allowed blacks to flourish[12].

For example, in 1883, black pioneers John and Mary Conna arrived in Tacoma. John became a wealthy real estate agent and the first black appointee to the Washington Territorial House of Representatives.

Black residents Nettie Craig and Henry Asberry were married in Tacoma in 1895. She founded a music school that was attended by whites and blacks. He operated a barbershop in a prestigious hotel, also catering to whites and blacks alike.

In 1886, a black couple, Horace and Susan Clayton, arrived in Seattle. By 1894, they were publishing a newspaper called *The Seattle Republican*. The Claytons' newspaper became, for a time, the second-largest in the city. It was read by whites and blacks alike.

---

[11] HistoryLink is a free online encyclopedia for studying Washington State History.

[12] Two books provided me with details about early Seattle and Tacoma black families: *Calabash* and *Seattle's Black Victorians*, both by Esther Hall Mumford and *The Forging of a Black Community* by Quintard Taylor.

In 1889, Robert O. Lee, a black man, began practicing as a lawyer in Seattle. That same year, a black entrepreneur named Robert A. Clark arrived in Seattle. Clark operated a drayage and delivery service.

In short, blacks in Washington, in the 1880s, were truly free.

Why was this? Didn't the whites of the Pacific Northwest need someone to do their (literal) dirty work? And didn't it make sense for them to use non-whites for their selected underclass?

It did, and they did.

The servant class in Washington State was filled with Chinese immigrants and American Indians. Sadly, the same kind of racial scapegoating and racial cleansing that happened in the South against blacks was being perpetuated in the Northwest against American Indians and Chinese immigrants.

For example, according to *HistoryLink*, in 1884, a white shopkeeper was killed and two white men came forward to testify that the shopkeeper had been murdered by a fourteen-year-old Indian named Louie Sam. Louie Sam was a member of the Sto:lo tribe.

Louie Sam was lynched. The leaders of the lynch mob were the two men that had identified Louie Sam as the murderer. After some investigation, it was learned that the two accusers had lured Sam down from Canada with an offer of work. They then killed the white shopkeeper in an attempt to frame the young man. The ploy was constructed so that the real murderers could take over the dead shopkeeper's lucrative general store.

This is just one of many instances in which whites terrorized Native Americans in the Northwest.

The Chinese were also targeted with violence when it served the needs of whites.

Chinese immigrants had been brought to Washington to work on the railroads. Many of them stayed and began to participate in a thriving Chinese community.

Patricia Long, writing for the *HistoryLink* website:

Chinese [residents in Tacoma] worked as waiters, as servants, and in the logging industry. They did the town's laundry and collected its garbage. A few entered business as labor contractors or merchants, at first selling goods to fellow Asians, and then to the whites in town. They fished and grew vegetables in large gardens and raised pigs.

The more established Chinese had been in Tacoma as long or longer than the anti-Chinese mayor.

Figure 5: Tacoma poster, 1885 Courtesy Washington State Historical Society (Image 1903.1.4)

Whites wanted the Chinese to live in Tacoma and serve only as laborers for white needs; They did not want them to build businesses and gain wealth.

Long writes:

On November 3, 1885, a mob, including many of Tacoma's leading citizens, marches on the Chinese community and forces everyone out of their houses and out of town. Tacoma mayor Weisbach..deemed the Chinese a "curse" and a "filthy horde." The Tacoma Ledger, the carpenters' union, and many workers and business people had spewed racist rhetoric against the Chinese for months.

This would not be an isolated incident. Less than a year later, Seattle's residents would perform a similar expulsion.

Another article on *HistoryLink* notes that, in 1886, Seattle residents forced most of their Chinese population onto a ship bound for San Francisco. The ship couldn't accommodate all of the Chinese residents in a single trip. The police tried to escort the remaining Chinese back to their homes so they could wait for the next ship to arrive but the angry white mob wouldn't allow it. Seeing the Chinese returning to their homes, they opened fire on the Chinese.

The Chinese then fled back to the shore and were forced to wait there six days until the next ship arrived.

So in answer to my question about how Jemima and Tolliver's families might have been treated in Washington State, they might have been very happy there, at least during the last two decades of the 1800s.

Newlyweds: Two Marriages of 1888

In 1888, Jemima Bouton and Tolliver Young were married in Ashley, Arkansas.

That same year, Ai Camp married a young woman named Eliza George. Ai and Eliza were married in Pampa, a small town in the southeastern part of the Washington Territory.

While the year of the two marriages was the same, the net worths of the two couples were not. Though all four of them had started life in families with no property, Ai, by 1888, was a landowner.

He'd staked a land claim under the Homestead Act when he was just nineteen years old. The rules of the act said he had to build a dwelling on the land and work to improve it for five years.

The year before he married Eliza, he was able to file the final paperwork to officially make the land his own.

And just like that, Ai was on his way to becoming a wealthy man.

The 1890 Census: A Tale of Two Farmers

Two years after their respective nuptials, the 1890 census was taken, and both men listed their occupation as "farmer." Despite this match, their lives were strikingly different.

Both couples were working hard. But their opportunities to work their way out poverty were grossly unequal.

THE SHARECROPPING LIFE

Tolliver and Jemima were sharecroppers. This meant a white

landowner was allowing them to raise crops on a piece of his land. In exchange for providing the land, the landowner kept the ledger containing a list of their expenditures and earnings.

At the end of each crop season, Tolliver would have met with the landowner to settle the books.

From the *Jim Crow Narrative* of Thomas Christopher Columbus "Bud" Chapman:

> [W]hen we had gathered our crops and sold all the money crops like tobacco, peanuts, and cotton, my father told me that Saturday, "Let's go and settle up so you can get ready to go to school."
>
> I said, "Okay."
>
> And so we went up to Mr. Thomas's house, to the backyard as usual, and he came out onto the back porch.
>
> "Well John, I guess you and Bud came to settle up today."
>
> He said, "Yes sir."
>
> [Mr. Thomas] got his book out. I had kept a record myself of everything we had gotten from that man that year and I know we didn't owe him, and we were supposed to clear good money. So he came out on the porch and he started thumbing through his book.
>
> Finally he looked up at my father and said, "John, you don't have any money coming, but you cleared your corn."
>
> Well, when he said that I reached for my book and my daddy stepped on my foot because he knew them crackers would kill you if you'd dispute their word.
>
> The first thing that went through my mind was "How could this man take all our money when my father had six other children down there, raggedy, no money, winter was coming and he's going to take it all."
>
> So my father said, "Mr. Thomas, we don't have any money coming?" He said, "No, John, you don't have any money coming, but you're going to clear all your corn."

So we said, "Okay," and we started back to the house. We lived about four or five blocks from him on a country road. This was the second time I'd ever seen my father cry. He started dropping tears, so I told him, "Papa, don't worry about it. I'll make it. I'll go back to school. I'll make it somehow."

When me and my father got back to the house I went in and pulled a pillowcase off my pillow, the little clothing I had I put in that pillowcase. I looked at my [deceased] mother's children and I hated to leave them. I was just like a second father to them, and I started walking. It was 12 miles from where we lived to Ocilla.

But anyway, I had ordered me a suit of clothes and the suit was in the post office there in Ocilla. That's where I went to school. And the suit was $17.25 to get out, and my father told me, he insisted that I take a load of corn. I had a friend of mine to come out there and pick up and take a load of corn and that's how I got my suit out.

[T]hat night [landlord Thomas] stopped by the house...[M]y daddy came out and he asked my dad, "Well where's Bud?" My daddy said, "That boy's gone."

"Well, tell Bud when he comes back, come on, and I'll let him have some money."

My dad told him, "He ain't coming back."

And I was a good plow hand, see, because I love farming. "Is he really ain't coming, John?"

"No, that boy ain't coming back."

"Well I bet if I let him have some money.... "

"Naw, he ain't coming back."

My father would come to town every Saturday and bring the kids and I would see them, and I would give them money.

I got a job working in a dry goods store, department store in fact you call it now. We called it a dry goods store. And I had a job picking up at the cleaners. I had three jobs and went to school every day and I was able to still help my father while going to high school.

According to census records, both Tolliver and Jemima were able to read and write. This surely would have improved their lives in many ways, including being able to keep their own books just as Bud Chapman had. Even still, their literacy likely had no effect on their to ability dig their way out of poverty.

Just as it was with Bud Chapman and his father, challenging their white landowner would be too dangerous and there was no court in which a black person's claim of unfair treatment would be heard by whites and rectified.

THE HOMESTEADING LIFE

The Homestead Act had been incredibly significant in the fate of the white side of our family. It meant that Ai, his parents, and his siblings were able to develop wealth almost out of thin air. Our government gave them free land and a railroad service that would bring all the goods and materials they might request.

Ai and Eliza certainly worked hard, just as Tolliver and Jemima did. They milked cows before sunrise. They raised chickens, pigs and goats. They planted and tended to vegetables and some grains.

But planting, tending, and harvesting crops in the crisp Washington climate was nothing like the crushing labor of picking cotton or tobacco in the hot, depressingly humid Southern states. Tobacco required stooping, and cotton picking shredded the skin on the fingers and palms.

One of the railroad companies hired Ai to clear the land on both sides of the railroad tracks and this enabled him to develop cash resources. Cash was something most of his fellow homesteaders did not have.

He used those cash resources to buy a team of horses, which he lent to his brothers and parents when they needed them. He also rented them out to others in the community, for a fee.

Ai and Eliza owned their labor, their time and their proceeds. They could stay in bed on the days they felt ill. They could break for water or food any time they wanted. When Eliza got pregnant, she and Ai could decide how little or how much she should continue to work.

Under no circumstances were either of them whipped, tied up by their thumbs, or forced to stand so close to a fire that their skin formed blisters.

If anyone had cheated them, that person would be called in to the local court or a community hearing so that the dispute could be settled. In short, they were living the kind of life citizens of the United States were proud to claim and promote. Their hard work, and the benefits they accrued are a case study in *The Great American Bootstraps*.

Go West, Young *Black* Man?

So what about this homestead thing? Could blacks take advantage of the Homestead Act? Could they head West and live out their own bootstraps story?

Yes! And many did.

Writing in *Sundown Towns*, James W. Loewen notes:

> Blacks moved everywhere in America between 1865 and 1890. African Americans reached every county of Montana. More than 400 lived in Michigan's Upper Peninsula.

Blacks headed west for the same reason that whites did. They wanted a parcel to call their own; a place they could pour their labor into that might eventually become something they could pass to their children and grandchildren.

But would they be treated in a neighborly way by the whites they settled near? Or was neighborly treatment reserved for those who *looked* a certain way?

Loewan goes on to note that Michigan's Upper Peninsula (the UP) jailed most of its black residents by the 1930s and surely must have driven many others away.

Loewen writes:

> Between 1890 and the 1930s, however, [black populations in the UP] changed. By 1930, although its white population had increased by 75 percent, the Upper Peninsula was home to only 331 African Americans, and 180 of them were inmates of the Marquette State Prison. Eleven

Montana counties had no blacks at all.

This change in complexion did not happen by accident. Whites all over the United States worked to ensure that blacks did not reap the rewards of land-ownership.

Later, Loewen declares:

> *Whenever the census shows that a town or county has been all white or overwhelmingly white for decades, we do well to investigate further, since across the nation, most all-white towns were that way intentionally.*

Loewen's book skillfully details how, over the decades, no matter where blacks put down roots, if they got land they almost always had it taken back from them by whites, sometimes through trickery; often times through violence.

THE SOUTH: A FREEDPEOPLE'S UTOPIA?

I ponder Tolliver and Jemima's decision to stay in the South. Didn't they at least consider leaving? Why didn't they head North or West, where it seems like the odds of escaping poverty would have been so much better?

Why would *any* blacks have chosen to stay?

As it turn out, many believed that because black people formed an overwhelming majority in the South, they would have their best chance at success in the South.

Blacks knew how to work the land better than any other group. They had the fortitude to work it, and were excited about the opportunity to use their hard-won skills and knowledge. Because of that belief, many felt they had no reason to go West.

In his book *In Search of The Racial Frontier*, Quintard Taylor writes:

> *Most freedpeople in the late 1860s saw their destiny, economically and politically, in the "reconstructed" South. The promise was so alluring that it briefly drew some [black] westerners back East. San Francisco minister John Jameson Moore, former* Mirror of the Times *editor Jonas H. Townsend, and Mifflin W. Gibb, British Columbia's first black officeholder, all moved to the South, casting their lot with the freed people.*

There were legitimate reasons for former slaves to believe they would be given forty acres and a mule. Nearly all of the rumors swirling around at that time were based on real programs that were proposed in Washington, DC[13], but that ended up being thwarted by legislators unsympathetic to the plight of blacks.

The forty-acres-and-a-mule program was actually instituted but was later rescinded. After President Lincoln was shot, the ten thousand black farmers who were farming land along the east coast of Florida were ordered to give the land back to the former white owners.

Rumors spread throughout the South that slave pensions would begin paying out any day. Slaves who had joined the Union troops during the war were told not to file for soldier's pensions but to file for slave pensions instead. Their service as slaves had lasted a lifetime and it seemed logical that these pensions would generate greater compensations.

In his *Slave Narrative,* Boston Blackwell notes:

> *That old story about the forty acres and a mule, it make me laugh. They sure did tell us that, but I never knowed any person which got it. The officers told us we would all get slave pension. That just exactly what they tell. They sure did tell me I would get a parcel of ground to farm. Nothing ever hatched out of that either.*

Blackwell had joined the Union Army during the war. After the war he went to work for a railroad company, digging grooves for railroad ties.

> *I get one dollar a day. I felt like the richest man in the world! Always I was a-watching for my slave pension to begin coming. Before I left the Army, my captain, he told me to file. My file number, it is 1,115,857. After I keeped them papers for so many years, white and black folks both telled me it ain't never coming—my slave pension—and I reckon the children tored up the papers. That number for me is filed in Washington.*

Though there were "Back To Africa" movements and some groups actually moved back and settled in Africa, many chose to stay close to their old homes so that families separated by slave owners could now re-group.

---

[13] W.E.B. Du Bois, writing in *The Souls of Black Folks,* in his essay "Of the Dawn of Freedom," details all the various programs that were put forward. Likewise, he details when, how and why they failed or were voted down.

From Sarah Gudger's *Slave Narrative:*

> *Lots of men want me to go live in a foreign land, but I tell 'em I go live with my pappy, long as he live.*

In fact, Tolliver and Jemima did leave the *Deep* South. They went to Arkansas. From the *Slave Narrative* of Tines Kendricks:

> *One day I heard some [Freedpeople] telling about a white man what done come in there getting up a big lot of [Freedpeople] to take to Arkansas. They was tellin' about what a fine place it was in Arkansas, and how rich the land is, and that the crops grow without working, and that the 'taters grow as big as a watermelon and you never have to plant them but the one time, and all such as that. Well, I decided to come.*

Once in Arkansas, Tolliver and Jemima managed to avoid trouble. We know this because, as far as we can tell, they weren't murdered, sent to the convict work camps, or put on chain gangs; the fates that befell so many.

THE 1900s

Leah Tyler's Black Ancestors During the 1900s

By 1900, Tolliver and Jemima had lived most of their lives free from the label "slave."

Some former slaves had begun to romanticize the past. Those who had lived on plantations and had less-than-cruel masters reminisced about slavery as a time when things weren't much different in terms of workload, but at least they'd always had food to eat.

Tolliver and Jemima might have listened to the old folks banter and wondered what all the fuss had been about "freedom" some thirty-five years before. After all, blacks who'd stayed in the South were still, for all intents and purposes, enslaved.

Whites controlled every aspect of black lives as they continued to develop techniques for discouraging black voting, closing down black schools, barring black collective bargaining, burglarizing black property, and generating creative new schemes for further impoverishing and undermining blacks.

While many white groups existed that oppressed and terrorized blacks, the Ku Klux Klan name has become the generic label for white extra-judicial violence against blacks in the South.

In his *Slave Narrative*, Boston Blackwell recalled the terrible deeds of the night riders:

> *Them Ku Kluxers was terrible—what they done to people. Oh God, they was bad. They come sneaking up and runned you outen your house and take everything you had.*

In Mingo White's *Slave Narrative* he recalled:

> *We kept movin' and makin' sharecrops till us saved up enough money to rent us a place and make a crop for ourselves. Us did right well at this until*

the Ku Klux got so bad, us had to move back with Mr. Nelson for protection.

In his *Slave Narrative,* Pierce Harper explained:

After us colored folks was considered free and turned loose, the Klu Klux broke out. Some colored people started farming and gathered old stock. If they got so they made good money and had a good farm, the Klu Klux would come and murder 'em.

The government builded schoolhouses, and the Klu Klux went to work and burned 'em down. They'd go to the jails and take the colored men out and knock their brains out and break their necks and throw them in the river.

There was a colored man they taken. His name was Jim Freeman. They taken him and destroyed his stuff and him 'cause he was making some good money. Hung him on a tree in his front yard, right in front of his cabin.

The message night riders sent to Tolliver and Jemima was that they were allowed to sharecrop, and they might even be allowed to rent land as tenant farmers, but if they were too successful, they would be putting themselves in grave danger.

The 1900 Census: Infant Mortality

When the 1900 census data was collected, women were asked how many children they'd given birth to, and how many were currently living.

The census tally columns tell us that Jemima had given birth seven times, but only three had survived; two boys and a girl. The first surviving child was a boy they named General Sherman Eugene. The second survivor was named William. William's middle initial shows as "H" on the census and family recollections have his middle name as "Howard." Tolliver and Jemima named their third, a baby girl, Videlia.

Videlia was my husband's great grandmother.

Certainly childbirth in the early 1900s wasn't modern by any definition; still, less than a 50/50 chance were the perilous odds Sherman, William and Videlia had been up against as they grew from infants to toddlers, and forward from there.

The Whitman County, Washington, census shows Ai and Eliza with six living children. As of 1900, Eliza had given birth seven times and six had survived.

My grandfather Otto had come along in 1899. He was the baby brother to Cleon, Oscar, Gerna, Lena, and Bertha. His mother would give birth three more times and two of those would also survive. Eliza's babies' overall survival rate was, in the end, 80%.

The chasm between Eliza and Jemima's personal infant mortality rates looks less like two women in the same country during the same era, and more like a comparison of two women living in completely different countries or decades apart.

Childrearing: Rich versus Poor

My grandfather Otto was still a baby in 1900, but he was born into a family that could provide him with nutritious food, a warm bed, medical attention, and a mother who was available around the clock to cater to his needs.

Eliza may have even participated in mothering study groups that were becoming more and more popular for rich white women.

Julia Grant, in *Raising Baby by the Book*, writes about the influence of childrearing books on middle- and upper-class women beginning in the 1800s. As part of her review, she introduces us to two models of mothering documented by historian Laurel Ulrich.

Ulrich's first model is called "extensive mothering." Ulrich, as quoted in Grant, defines extensive mothering as "generalized responsibility for an assembly of youngsters rather than concentrated devotion to a few."

Ulrich labels the opposite mode of mothering, "intensive mothering."

A trend toward intensive mothering had been building in America's East Coast cities since the late 1700s.

In response to the trend toward intensive mothering in the US, pamphlets and books about the best methods for childrearing proliferated. The increase in published advice then led to more mothering anxiety and created the vicious cycle that some claim continues even today.

By the time Eliza started raising children, interest in studied and deliberate mothering techniques would have been an important mark of refinement. As the wife of a rich man, Eliza's labor was no longer needed on the farm. According to the norms and expectations of the time period, her only concerns should have been caring for her husband and children[14]. To prove her capabilities she would have been expected to run her home efficiently and be able to trot out impressive children on cue.

Black mothers of relative wealth were not exempt from the pressure and anxiety. In *Growing Up Jim Crow*, Jennifer Ritterhouse notes that black publications managed to put the same kind of pressure on middle-class black mothers:

> "Child-culture and mother-culture are the demands of the age for the race," the Atlanta-based Voice of the Negro *editorialized in 1904, in one of many articles about childrearing that appeared in the black press in the early twentieth century."[I]n a day of freedom we must have children who are reared and trained in home duties, home obedience, and who are trained in heart to know that virtue makes heaven, and that immorality is the mother of death.*

Though the anxiety of intensive mothering wasn't restricted to white mothers, it's unlikely to have reached Jemima. For one thing, she was too poor to have subscribed to a journal like Atlanta's *Voice of the Negro*.

Grant notes that plenty of mothers were not hand-wringing over childrearing "best practices." Instead, these mothers were still in full-on *extensive* mothering mode:

> Certain mothers ... [during the 1800s] continued to engage in extensive mothering: those who were living in slavery, raising large numbers of children, struggling to make ends meet, caring for children alone, or working for wages outside the home.

Jemima, no doubt, was forced to practice extensive mothering. She likely worked in the fields all day beside her husband, Tolliver, and then returned home to cook, sweep the floors, wash dishes and clothes along with all the other duties most women were expected to fulfill.

---

[14] She didn't have voting rights and it was considered un-ladylike to care about business dealings, politics, or the news.

In his *Jim Crow Narrative*, Leroy Boyd recalled how hard (and continuously) his mother worked:

> *Well, my mother, Lilly, she was the mother of 10 children. And she would cook for us. Get up and cook breakfast, get us off to the field.*
>
> *Then she'd come to the field, and she would quit around ten, eleven o'clock, come home, cook dinner, and we'd come home at twelve; we'd eat dinner. Then she'd be able to come back to the field maybe about two o'clock after she got the house straightened out.*
>
> *If [a sharecropping woman] had any girls, well, they would help wash the dishes. Then you head back to the field, chop cotton, pick cotton. During the first of the season it was chopping time. She would be the last one to come to the field, the first one to quit to go to the house, prepare dinner. And sometimes she'd put a dinner on that night.*
>
> *She'd cook them peas and whatnot, put the pot on. She wouldn't have that much to do then. She come to the house, just cook some bread.*
>
> *My mother worked right with him. That's one thing I can say, they was a team.*

Tolliver and Jemima would have shown their love toward their children by working hard in the fields and keeping a roof over their heads.

Videlia's care, when she was a baby, might have amounted to laying her under a shade tree while her mother worked the fields.

Alternately, her care may have been left to an older community member who "tended" the children of multiple families. Her caretaker would most certainly have practiced extensive parenting and probably would have found it hard to meet the needs of many children at once. A communal caretaker would most likely have been physically disabled in some way because otherwise they, too, would have been working in the fields.

From the *Slave Narrative* of Georgia Baker:

> *I 'members Grandpa Stafford well enough. I can see him now. He was a old man what slept on a trundle bed in the kitchen, and all he done was to set by the fire all day with a switch in his hand and tend the chillun whilst*

their mammies was at work. Chillun minded better them days than they does now. Grandpa Stafford never had to holler at 'em but one time. They knowed they would get the switch next if they didn't behave.

While Grandpa Stafford trusted his switch, intensive mothers were spending endless hours reading, discussing, and pondering the effects of one disciplinary technique over another.

Grant tells of a white, upper-class mother's group that was formed in 1878:

> *Club members had read Jacob Abbot's* Gentle Measures in the Management and Training of the Young *(1871), an immensely influential book, which attempted a compromise between religious and scientific thinking about children.*
>
> *Abbot was quite clear about the need for obedience but argued that it was to be gained by systematic and reasonable discipline rather than severe punishments.*
>
> *One member said, "What is known as 'blind' obedience should never be demanded of children, because it banishes all originality and spirit."*

Beginning in the late 1800s and continuing throughout the 1900s, baby books became essential reading for middle-class and upper-class, white, American mothers.

Conversely, during this same time period, poor mothers more than likely parented on auto-pilot. They weren't likely to have given much thought to their particular words and actions. They had much more important things (things directly related to their survival), that they needed to focus on.

Research[15] shows that if parents don't willfully focus on carrying out a chosen parenting pattern, they are most likely to parent in a way that prepares their children for the jobs those children will have if they follow in their parents' footsteps.

---

[15] The book *Meaningful Differences* by Betty Hart and Todd R. Risley is covered in more detail in the chapter on the 1990s. The book is about research Hart & Risley carried out that exposed major differences in the parenting styles of different social classes.

We can't know for sure how Tolliver and Jemima parented, but we can presume that anyone raising future sharecroppers would need to teach them to obey orders without question, show extreme deference toward authority figures, and learn to accept disappointment as an immutable fact of life.

In fact, perhaps as a sharecropping black parent in the 1900s, teaching your child *not* to have hopes, *not* to have dreams, and to *never* expect justice might have been the kindest lessons you, as a parent, could have conveyed to your children.

Schooling: Black versus White

The census shows us that all of Ai and Eliza's children, who were old enough, attended school. Conversely, none of Tolliver and Jemima's children were listed as being in school.

Perhaps the local Wilmot, Arkansas school for black children was burned down by night riders.

Over the hundred years that Jim Crow ruled the South, disrupting black schooling was always a priority for whites. They managed to create a number of obstacles that hindered blacks' attempts to get an education.

For starters, black school years ran on a shorter schedule than white school years. From Cleaster Mitchell's Jim Crow Narrative:

> You see, they had a seven months school. The white had seven months. The colored had five months, but out of these months, you did not go to school those five months. In all, you might have went three.

> And then we couldn't go all the time. Some days you went a half a day. Some days you didn't go at all. You know how it was? See, you might go twenty days out of this month. The next month, you go fifteen.

Another stumbling block for blacks was the fact that their families needed their help in the fields.

From the *Jim Crow Narrative* of Willie Harrell:

> I didn't go to school but once or twice out of the year. That's right. I was in the first grade. I can't read and write now, because I didn't have the chance to go to school like children got now.

Back there then, there wasn't no school like it is now. You had to walk seven or eight miles to the school. When it rained and you couldn't do nothing in the field or you couldn't do no other kind of work, that's when you had a chance to go to school, but as soon as the sun comes out and dry off, you in the field.

Never did have no chance to go to no school in them days. You always doing something, cutting wood or cross ties or sawmill or doing something, in the winter. I bet you I didn't go two days out of a month or a year.

White farming families in the South didn't need their children to help in the fields, they had black people toiling on their behalf instead.

If black sharecropping parents didn't keep their children out of school, the white landlord might step in. Ann Pointer, in her *Jim Crow Narrative* recalls:

[I]f you got a child and the man want him to work, he go and tell the teacher that "this boy can't come to school right now because he working for me." He'd go there and get him out of school and make him go to the field.

White children might be ferried to school, but black children almost always had to walk to get to theirs, regardless of how harsh the weather might be.

Cleaster Mitchell:

About seven or eight miles to school, and that was children was going to school that was four and five years old. The oldest ones a lot of times have carried them. You leave early and you walk to school and you walk back. And when it was cold and bad, they make you a thing what they called a little fire bucket, and the two olders carried them. When you get too cold, you stop and warm your hands. You had some coals and stuff in it to warm your hands over.

The teachers might not be chosen for their teaching abilities. The *Jim Crow Narrative* of Stine George:

The white superintendent always picked the least of the evils of all the blacks. In other words, he never picked the blacks who he thought would do a good job of teaching and educating the black kids. He got the ones who were strong and [mean], who he thought would keep the kids in place.

Additionally, the educational materials were significantly different. Leon Litwack, writing in *Trouble in Mind*, includes details regarding the disparity of funding for black schools:

> *South Carolina... in 1915, spent $23.76 on each white child in school [and] $2.91 on each black child.*

> *In Alabama some $22.96 was spent annually for each white child's education, but only 98 cents for each black child.*

Because of the differences in funding, the desks, books, heating system, and the buildings for black schools were inferior in every way to the white schools.

The *Jim Crow Narrative* of Merlin Jones:

> *Outdated textbooks, untrained teachers, overcrowded classrooms, I've been in many classrooms in which we had 36, 40 children. They had the old-fashioned seats, with the desk in it, which was designed for one child. With the inkwell. They were designed for one student, we sat two on a seat. When you wanted to write, I always tried to find me a left-handed buddy, so we would have no problem.*

The *Jim Crow Narrative* of Ralph Thompson:

> *We did reading and writing, but we didn't go beyond that. And I guess that was part of [segregation]. And, to see [white] kids that could play baseball and had baseball diamonds and things like that and we were denied. We didn't have it and nobody could furnish it for us including our families and all.*

If a black family was having trouble making ends meet, the child might make it to school but not be in the right frame of mind to learn. Ann Pointer:

> *I'm going to tell you, if you [are] a child, and you get up in the morning time, and there is no food in the house—no kind of food nowhere, I mean nothing, just the cupboard is bare—and you've got to get up and go on to school and act like nothing's happened, you cannot say a word or let anybody know that you haven't had anything to eat, and didn't know when*

you were ever going to get anything else, that is a horrible experience for a small child. A child seven or eight years old and you don't have food to give them, that child carries a heavy burden. My mother was proud. We could not tell people that we didn't have anything.

Many black parents tried to shield their children from interaction with whites so that they would not have to suffer racist treatment. Unfortunately, sending them to school exposed the children to miles of roads upon which they might encounter whites as they walked there and back each day.

Ralph Thompson:

When we would walk home in the evening down a gravel road and when the white bus would come, the driver would get up in the center, you know. The gravel would pile up in the center and the wheels would cut tracks in the road and it would pile it up. And he would get up in the center for those rocks to shoot out from under the wheels.

And I can remember having to turn our backs in case a rock might come out and hit you in the eye. And if you were walking home from school and it rained and there's a low spot and you happened to be coming by that low spot and you could hear the motor on the bus rev up because he's going to speed up cause he's going to hit that water as hard as he can.

How can a person be so cold? And we would run, and we would turn our backs. And I'd say how can a person be so cold that would try to wet us down and try to put our eyes out and things like that? And those are some of the things that when you look back today and you see how mean people could be to a kid.

That's what it was like and you didn't have nobody that you could turn to help you say, "Hey, bus driver, don't do that." See? And going home telling your parents, you can imagine how frustrating that is.

They'd tell you to turn your head and little things that they could tell you to do, but you couldn't fight back because you didn't have no way of fighting.

Because of the poverty black families were kept under, black children often had to drop out so they could earn money. Leon Alexander, in his *Jim Crow Narrative*:

> *When I finished ninth grade in school, I had to come out and had to go to work because my mother and father had separated, and she had all of the children. Back in those days black women would wash and iron for white families. Mama would wash them and iron them. My job was to deliver them back to the families that she was washing for. I came out of school at 13 years of age and that was the end of ninth grade.*

The long list of factors that degraded the quality of black education, from the 1870s to the 1970s, is the reason race-based affirmative action policies were added to college admissions. People often talk about ending affirmative action "when the time is right."

Some argue that the end is already overdue. I would argue the opposite and say that a hundred years of undermining calls for a hundred years of making up for it. That would mean the descendants of the Freed People should receive education benefits based on their heritage at the very least until 2070.

Ai's Increasing Wealth and Power

Around 1902, Ai bought a hotel in Pampa. He moved Eliza and the children into town and they began to live in their hotel. Later that year he started up a livery stable. Anyone needing to rent a team of horses from the livery stable would pay Ai for the team's time. The trains required water and wood. Pampa Pond supplied the water. Ai worked out a deal to supply the trains with wood.

The land in Whitman County still wasn't being used for commercial wheat farming in the early 1900s. People were predominately using it for subsistence farming and livestock grazing. No one was making much money, and few could figure out how to make more. Locals called it "bunchgrass land" and some were coming to see it as almost worthless.

For whatever reason, Ai believed that buying up lots and lots of bunchgrass land was a sound plan.

Decades later, his son Otto (my grandfather) recalled that most people in town thought Ai had lost his mind when he started buying up acres and acres of land that others considered useless.

Ai's gamble would pay off mightily when people figured out the land and climate were hospitable to commercial wheat farming.

In 1905, Ai took over the Pampa General Store. As the new store owner, Ai was able to get his own supplies and wares at wholesale prices, thereby increasing his farming profits.

He had also now become the de facto town banker.

Douglas Blackmon, in *Slavery by Another Name* writes:

> *Merchants…were as much bankers as retailers. Nearly every purchase was made on credit to be repaid when a farmer's crop was sold at the end of a season. More often than not, the store owner would be the buyer of the crop as well, meaning that the man who had plowed the fields… might never actually see hard currency. His debts, payments, and profit or loss were recorded only in the ledgers of the store.*

In buying the general store from the previous owner, Ai took on the debts of everyone in the region. Having all those people indebted to him would have been a highly strategic move for a man who wanted to increase his land holdings.

Looking into the store's accounting ledgers, he was able to see who in the area was most in arrears. He could offer these deeply indebted farmers an easy way out of their debt miseries.

"What if I forgave your debt and gave you some traveling money in exchange for your land deed?" he might have said. "You'd have enough money to go back East and see your people. Get the wife a new dress and the kids some candy before you go? They'll be happy to pack up and move on."

Perhaps instead, he appealed to their wanderlust, "You could try again in another area. I hear western Washington still has some great unclaimed land. Think of the riches that might still await a clever man like you!"

According to *HistoryLink.org*, it was in about 1903 that commercial wheat farming began to perform well for others who were planting and harvesting it in the western part of the state. Over the next few years, there was a ripple effect across the counties as people began converting their grazing land to commercial wheat farming enterprises. Ai might have heard murmurings about wheat farming just enough earlier than others in his area to take advantage of the leverage this information provided.

Then again, maybe the promise of commercial farming was widely discussed but conversion to commercial farming wasn't something the average debt-ridden landowner could manage. To farm wheat on a commercial scale, a farming family needed a team of horses and a horse-drawn harvest combine[16].

Figure 6: This picture from my grandmother's album is dated November 5th, 1911. The number of horses needed for pulling commercial farming equipment is astonishing to me. Clearly commercial wheat farming would not have been possible without some level of wealth or the extensive cooperation of other community members. Black farmers would likely have found a lack of cooperation from white farmers.

Ai already had the horses because of his livery stable business. He had a credit account established with suppliers on the East Coast, due to

---

[16] The piece of farm equipment called a harvest combine is a combination of header and thresher. Harvester combines are often referred to simply as a "combine" by farming families. The emphasis is on the first syllable so that it is pronounced COM-bine.

his position as owner of the general store. Therefore, Ai was in position to convert his land to commercial farming quite easily.

As for other farmers in the region, it would almost certainly be at Ai's whim whether they would be able to take advantage of commercial farming's promises of wealth. If Ai decided not to support a certain farmer in the transition, that farmer probably wouldn't have succeeded.

Voting and Political Influence

As we've already seen, Ai's position as the owner of a general store and other businesses gave him a great degree of power. He would have been able to develop his power and influence further by discounting his prices for area farmers if he found that he needed something from them in exchange. In fact, if Ai had been interested in a political career, he would have been in a good position to curry favor.

Instead of running for public office, my research revealed that many of his brothers, uncles and cousins served in various political positions. Ai had the right to vote, and I feel safe assuming that he voted for his brothers and other close allies.

Down in Arkansas, Tolliver also had the *legal* right to vote, but Southern lawmakers were unabashedly intent on restricting voting rights to rich white men. Poll taxes, property requirements and even tests that required advanced education worked to make voting a rich man's game.

In the *Jim Crow Narrative* of Leon Alexander, he states:

> Now, when you hear me talking, it sound like I'm talking, or I'm saying that only blacks had a difficult time of registering to vote, but that is not so. It was a whole lot of white had a difficult time. Whites in Walker County, whites in St. Clair County—especially in these mining counties. Whites had a difficult time because the coal operators didn't want them— black nor white—only those people that they controlled and wanted to vote.

> Those were the people, whether you white or black. If the operator wanted a black to be qualified to vote, he just send him down there and called down there and they qualified. If he didn't want to pass, whether he's white or black, he didn't pass. Now it just wasn't a black versus a white thing. This

was the coal steel barons and the big coal operators in this state; were the people who controlled the voting in this state.

In modern times, we often talk of voting in somewhat romantic terms. In spite of our idealistic musings, does one vote *really* count in a national election these days? The answer isn't simple. In some ways one vote matters; in other ways it doesn't.

When it comes to local elections, however, each vote matters much more. This was especially true during that era, with its much smaller populations. In those days, people were voting for (and against) neighbors, relatives, and friends.

Today, even on a local level, those of us who live in large towns or cities are not likely to meet the people we vote for. We are not likely to see our elected officials at the local market or go to the same church as our town's mayor. Back then, many more voters (especially whites who were wealthy like Ai) had personal relationships with the officials they voted to elect. Because of this, votes could be leveraged much more easily as an exchange of favors. In short, if you could vote for the guy that ended up winning, you could count on things going your way, more often than not.

Blackmon writes about the immense power of elected county judges to make or break the farming operations of others:

> The power of the county judge's position whenever it intersected the life of a specific individual was almost boundless…which roads and bridges to rebuild after each year's spring downpours, in what order, and by whom among the small coterie of local men who lived primarily off the odd jobs of the county were the judge's most consistent questions and demonstrable executive power.

> They were mundane decisions but often were the determining factor between which farms would thrive and which would wither in isolation. A passable road was critical to the primitive task of moving to market a five-hundred-pound load of cotton—the sole goal of most small-acreage farmers. A washed-out bridge, unrepaired, might be insurmountable.

Ai's voting rights provided him with friends and relatives in high places. If he needed a particular decision to go his way, he could likely just ask, and he'd have things worked out on his behalf. If asking didn't get the job done, perhaps a padded handshake would, and he had plenty of money to use for padding.

Diversity in Ai and Eliza's Community

We've already noted that the cities of western Washington were open to black success in the 1880s, but we haven't yet explored the racial climate of the more rural, less developed, eastern part of the state. Namely, we haven't looked at the racial climate of Whitman County.

Would a black family who saved the money to board that same "immigrant train" bound for eastern Washington have found welcoming neighbors when they arrived in Pampa?

To answer my question, I opened a book my mother gave me a dozen years ago. It's a spiral-bound volume, written by locals in 1996. It details the history of a cluster of towns that included Pampa, Washington.

The book's authors used local newspapers and other documents in their research. This book provided me with a lot of details about Ai, his brothers, his children, and even my mother's generation.

The authors of the history book state that in those early days, the area was "no place for a tenderfoot," and then go on to say:

> [T]here were those settlers who took a chance coming to the area without enough money for food or supplies…for shelter, they turned the wagons on edge, placed a temporary roof on top, and covered it with the canvas from the wagon tops using the canvas as a roof and doorway. A stove and living area was on a dirt floor.

The authors explain that some of the early settlers died because frontier life was so full of challenges, but for those that survived, a bond was forged between them:

> As the settlers faced these and other common hardships, they developed the feeling that they and their neighbors were more or less equal. Food and help were shared between neighbors when necessary. A man's ability to overcome hardships and problems facing him and his family made it easier for these persevering people of many backgrounds to have pride in their

accomplishments and in their new country, and if they were immigrants, eager to become Americans.

I wanted to know more about these "people of many backgrounds" and their *kumbaya community,* so I looked a little more carefully at the census of 1900. In fact, I looked at every single family in the Whitman County ledger and noted their race and their birthplaces.

As I expected, the community was almost exclusively white. I counted whites with birth origins from over twenty different US states. I also noted immigrants from Germany, England, Canada, Scotland, Sweden, and Norway—all white.

The only non-whites were three Japanese men. They worked for the railroad. Two of the men were married, but their families did not live with them. Presumably, their families were back in Japan. One man had been married for twenty-one years and had very likely relocated away from his wife for this job with a US railroad company. The other married man had only been married three years, a relative newlywed, but was also a half a world away from his wife.

When it came to "people of many backgrounds," what the town never had as residents were blacks, Jews, Irish, people with Spanish surnames, American Indians or any other group that, during that period, were considered by white Protestants to be undesirable as neighbors. They did tolerate their Catholic neighbors, but later, during the 1920s, would look to deny them the right to vote.

The most suspect line in the paragraph waxing about community was when it states that food and help were given "when necessary." This line disappoints me because I know how forcefully subjective perception comes into play when one decides whether help is "necessary."

Surely sometimes these subjective decisions about the necessity of neighborly help missed the mark.

For example, the same winter the newspaper reported that Ai built a "large modern dwelling," another Pampa resident froze to death in a cave dwelling on his homestead land nearby.

The Clansman: An Historical Romance of the Ku Klux Klan

A book called *The Clansman: An Historical Romance of the Ku Klux Klan*, written by Thomas A. Dixon, was released in 1905 and became extremely popular.

The Clansman begins by introducing the reader to a noble family of former-Confederates, the Colemans. The Colemans are trying to avoid having themselves put to death for fighting against the Union during the Civil War.

Next, readers are introduced to a Yankee family called the Stonemans. The father character is a politician named Austin Stoneman. He's a radical member of Congress who supports giving blacks the right to vote. Readers are told that he lists a mixed-race woman as his servant but privately he treats her as his wife. The relationship causes a scandal in Washington, DC. Stoneman's daughter, upon visiting him, is offended by the mixed-race woman's level of power over her father's household.

Stoneman's daughter begins volunteering at a hospital for recuperating Confederate soldiers. The Confederate soldiers and the Yankee daughter begin to realize just how much the former Civil War enemies actually have in common.

Dixon paints a picture of the South during Reconstruction that portrays blacks with unchecked power:

> [A] Negro electorate controlled the city government, and gangs of drunken negroes, its sovereign citizens, paraded the streets at night firing their muskets unchallenged and unmolested.
>
> A new order of society sprouted in this corruption. The old high-bred ways, tastes, and enthusiasms were driven into the hiding-places of a few families and cherished as relics of the past.

In the story, the radical Stoneman has to relocate to South Carolina so that he can recoup his health. While there, he enlists a mixed-race man to lead an uprising of blacks. Stoneman encourages the mixed-race man, in a secret meeting, to lead blacks toward more proud and strong behaviors:

> Your first task, as I told you in the beginning, is to teach every negro to

stand erect in the presence of his former master and assert his manhood. Unless he does this, the South will bristle with bayonets in vain. The man who believes he is a dog, is one. The man who believes himself a king, may become one.

Stop this sniveling and sneaking round the back doors. I can do nothing, God Almighty can do nothing, for a coward. Fix this as the first law of your own life. Lift up your head! The world is yours. Take it.

Beat this into the skulls of your people, if you do it with an axe. Teach them the military drill at once. I'll see that Washington sends the guns. The state, when under your control, can furnish the powder.

Later in the story, a Southern white doctor talks to Phil Stoneman, son of Austin Stoneman. The doctor's daughter has fallen in love with the young Yankee son. The doctor talks to his potential son-in-law about the current state of the South:

Delicate and cultured women are living on cowpeas, corn bread, and molasses—and of such quality they would not have fed it to a slave. Children go to bed hungry.

Droves of brutal negroes roam at large, stealing, murdering, and threatening blacker crimes. We are under the heel of petty military tyrants, few of whom ever smelled gunpowder in a battle. At the approaching election, not a decent white man in this county can take the infamous test-oath. I am disfranchised because I gave a cup of water to the lips of one of my dying boys on the battle-field.

My slaves are all voters. There will be a negro majority of more than one hundred thousand in this state. Desperadoes are here teaching these negroes insolence and crime in their secret societies. The future is a nightmare.

Phil Stoneman, leaves the doctor's home and contemplates his new affection for white Southerners:

As Phil hurried home in a warm glow of sympathy for the people whose hospitality had made him their friend and champion, he encountered a negro trooper standing on the corner, watching the [doctor's] house with a furtive glance.

Instinctively he stopped, surveyed the man from head to foot and asked:

"What's the trouble?"

"None er yo' business," the negro answered, slouching across to the opposite side of the street.

Phil watched him with disgust.

The text then goes on to describe the black man's features and equate them with that of an animal. There are a number of passages in the book that talk about the physical features of blacks in dehumanizing ways.

As the story proceeds, every manner of injustice and humiliation is heaped on the white people. The police troopers are depicted as former slaves who abuse their power and seek to subjugate whites at every turn.

Dixon's message in writing the book was clear: Reconstruction turned blacks into despots, and whites were brutally victimized by them. The further message to

"Take dat f'um yo' equal——"

Figure 7: An illustration from the book *The Clansman*. The caption, translated out of the dialect, is, "Take that if I am your equal."

Northerners was: *If you let them gain a foothold, they will take over your towns and make you into their slaves!*

There are also scenes of whites' humiliation and intimidation. In one scene, a white man is arrested. This white prisoner is being transferred to the state capitol by a white police captain who is in cahoots with blacks.

A crowd of black men begin to follow while the white captain in charge of the transfer announces to the crowd:

"Fellow citizens, you are the equal of any white man who walks the ground. The white man's day is done. Your turn has come."

As the white prisoner is walked past the home of his most loyal servant, the black servant steps out and asks his former boss if they are equal. The white prisoner replies that, yes, they *are* equal. The former servant punches the white man and says, "Take that if I'm your equal."

The white captain stands by as the white prisoner lays face down after the black man's punch.

Power is not the only thing blacks seem to have going for them in Dixon's story. Throughout the book blacks are also depicted as having plenty of money while whites have none and are scraping by.

As if Dixon's portrayal of white subjugation wasn't enough to scare whites into banning blacks from their towns in the North and West, the author included lots of imagery related to the idea that the main goal of black men was to have sex with white women.

In one scene, he shows the black lieutenant governor speaking to a crowd of blacks at a meeting hall:

[F]ive thousand negroes, as one man, were on their feet, shouting and screaming. Their shouts rose in unison, swelled into a thunder peal, and died away as one voice...

"Within five years," he cried, "the intelligence and the wealth of this mighty state will be transferred to the Negro race. Lift up your heads. The world is yours. Take it. Here and now I serve notice on every white man who breathes that I am as good as he is. I demand, and I am going to have, the privilege of going to see him in his house or his hotel, eating with him and sleeping with him, and when I see fit, to take his daughter in

marriage!"

The book goes on to tell of black policemen who show up at the home of a white widow and her daughter, tie the older woman up, and rape the daughter.

The text stops short of spelling out the rape; it instead uses the flesh of the throat to imply rape:

"We ain't after money!"

The girl uttered a cry, long, tremulous, heart-rending, piteous.

A single tiger-spring, and the black claws of the beast sank into the soft white throat and she was still.

It would seem from this passage that the younger woman was killed, but we see her in the next scene, plotting to commit suicide:

"No one must ever know. We will hide quickly every trace of crime. They will think we strolled to Lover's Leap and fell over the cliff, and my name will always be sweet and clean—you understand—come, we must hurry—"

Next, we see the white men gathering to strategize the creation of a guerilla force. They revive the name of the Ku Klux Klan, a group that had dwindled years before, and use it for their new group. Local whites join up in droves. They create uniforms, come up with their edict (spelled out in the book for the convenience of readers who want to set up their own real life chapter), and ride around the region confiscating guns from blacks through intimidation.

Through the course of the story, up until this point, we've seen one Yankee after another apologizing for the actions of the Union and for the torture they brought upon the "good" white people of the South. These repentant Yankees then ask to serve as allies with the former Confederates.

Still, Stoneman, the one stalwart white supporter of black rights, remains opposed to white rule in the South. Finally, in an emotion-wracked confession/reversal, Stoneman states the source of his support for black rights:

"Three forces moved me—party success, a vicious woman, and the

quenchless desire for personal vengeance.

When I first fell a victim to the wiles of the [mixed-race] vampire who kept my house, I dreamed of lifting her to my level. And when I felt myself sinking into the black abyss of animalism, I, whose soul had learned the pathway of the stars and held high converse with the great spirits of the ages—I'm done now," Stoneman went on, slowly, fumbling his hands. "My life has been a failure. The dice of God are always loaded."

His great head drooped lower, and he continued: "Mightiest of all was my motive of revenge. Fierce business and political feuds wrecked my iron-mills. I shouldered their vast debts, and paid the last mortgage of a hundred thousand dollars the week before Lee invaded my state. I stood on the hill in the darkness, cried, raved, cursed, while I watched his troops lay those mills in ashes. Then and there I swore that I'd live until I ground the South beneath my heel!"

Stoneman's admission ends with his conversion. He joins with the former Confederates in their all-white solidarity movement. The final dénouement of the tale is when rich whites and poor whites, Southern and Northern, fully unite to overthrow blacks and restore whites to their "proper place" in society.

Of course, Reconstruction had been nothing like what Dixon's book presented, but few Northerners had any experience with the reality of the South during Reconstruction.

Dixon's book was wildly popular in both the North and South and was quickly staged in playhouses. The play was extremely popular as well.

Whites read the last page of the book or came away from the play convinced they had perfectly valid reasons to drive blacks away if possible, or to restrict their rights and movements if they were important laborers in the local economy.

Sundown Towns and Banishments

Dixon's cautionary tale changed everything. He became famous as an author and, when interviewed, he regularly stated that Northerners should understand that residential segregation was essential for controlling blacks.

Whites heeded the message. Sometimes gently, but more often forcibly, whites moved blacks into enclaves. In common parlance, these areas were called, "Darktowns" or worse.

In *Sundown Towns*, James Loewen details the sad history of how Northern and Western towns went from being integrated to being segregated. The South had never been based on segregated neighborhoods. Whites lived side-by-side with blacks because the rural layouts had been built with big plantation houses, surrounded by slave quarters. After slavery ended, the configuration stayed the same only now the master's house was called the landlord's house and the surrounding dwellings were not referred to as slaves' quarters but as sharecropper's homes.

The Northeast had also been, up to that point, integrated. Blacks of the northeast had integrated comfortably over the centuries as free blacks arrived in the original colonies or freed blacks took up residence in the northern cities. The West, on the other hand, had been settled so quickly and furiously that people landed wherever they landed.

Loewen chronicles the various ways blacks were moved into isolatable areas outside of town or city limits. In many cases, the details of the isolation are lost to local folklore. Time has glossed over the details and allowed them to be replaced them with more genteel fables.

In any event, once blacks were re-situated, and the black area was given its own name, town officials would declare that blacks were not allowed to be in the white town once the sun set. Many towns had signs posted warning "N****r Don't let the sun go down on you in <our town>".

Sundown towns act as the rural version of the inner-city ghetto where officials are able to keep resources like good schools, job opportunities, and housing equity extremely low and use the suppression of those resources as a way to keep blacks oppressed.

In other areas, entire counties were racially "cleansed." The book *Buried in the Bitter Waters: The Hidden History of Racial Cleansing in America*, details twelve incidents of racial cleansing during the first part of the 1900s. The book was written by journalist Elliot Jaspin.

Jaspin used census records to identify towns where cleansing seemed statistically plausible. He then followed up by searching the town records for reports of massacres or mob actions that would have caused blacks to flee, leaving their land, homes, and property behind.

Jaspin's book includes detailed narratives of racial cleansings in Lawrence County, Missouri in 1901; Atlanta in 1906; Springfield, Illinois and Marshall County, Kentucky in 1908; Boone County, Arkansas in 1905 and again in 1909.

Jaspin's book also includes other racial cleansings before and after the first decade of the 1900s.

The movie *Rosewood*, released in 1997, tells the story of a racial cleansing in Rosewood, Florida that took place in 1923. When watching *Rosewood*, try to keep in mind that the basics of the cleansings took place in hundreds, if not thousands of communities during the early 1900s.

The Sundown Town era began in the 1890s. Their end still hasn't been realized. Loewen tells of various dismantlings across the decades. He also admits that while signs have come down in most localities, actions are still taken to discourage black settlement in many rural areas and even some city suburbs.

I worked in Birmingham, Alabama for a few months in 2011 and asked several Nigerian taxi drivers to share any first-hand racist experiences they'd had, as well as any stories they'd heard from others. Several told me of present-day sundown towns in Alabama, Mississippi and Georgia. One told me of an actual sign he'd seen, still posted in 2011, warning blacks not to enter at all.

Attack of the Giant Negroes

Dixon wasn't the only writer scaring white people with his tales of black licentiousness. Just before the turn of the century, in New York, two newspaper owners[17] began sensationalizing the news in an attempt to put each other out of business. Later, two additional New York newspapers

---

[17] Joseph Pulitzer owned the *New York World* and William Randolph Hearst owned the *New York Journal*.

would join the highly competitive environment of New York newspaper competition[18] The intense competition led the editors to move toward sensational, attention-grabbing that were so far from factual events their trade came to be known as Yellow Journalism.

David Mills, writing in 2007 on his *Undercover Black Man* blog, recounted Yellow Journalism's particularly curious phenomenon of Giant Negroes.

Figure 8: Giant Negroes made the headlines of Northern newspapers on a regular basis in the first half of the twentieth century.

In Mills' post titled "Attack of the GIANT NEGROES!!!" he explains:

The Times first acknowledged the existence of these fearsome creatures on August 5, 1897. The headline was "Insane Negro Giant in Newark."

Over the next four decades, the New York Times provided all the news that was fit to print about "giant negroes." Articles with headlines such as

---

18 Adolph Ochs' *New York Times* and Horace Greeley's *New York Tribune*.

these:
"Giant Negro Attacks Police." [Sept. 24, 1900]
"Negro Giant Guilty." [July 28, 1905]
"Armed Negro Giant Goes Mad on Liner." [May 15, 1916]
"Giant Negro Disables 4 Policemen in Fight." [June 12, 1927]
"Posse in Gun Battle Ends Giant Negro's Reign of Terror..." [March 6, 1932]

And it wasn't just the New York Times. Rampaging black giants were a nationwide phenomenon. Naturally, headline-writers at major newspapers were all over this:

"Officer Is Hurt By Giant Negro." [Atlanta Constitution, April 2, 1906]
"Giant Negro, a Walking Arsenal, Believed He Was To Be Burned Alive." [Los Angeles Times, October 15, 1908]
"Giant Negro, Trapped, Seizes and Throws Officer." [Los Angeles Times, March 28, 1911]
"Wife of Hotel Proprietor and a Giant Negro Sought." [Chicago Tribune, January 23, 1916]
"Giant Negro Gambler Flees After Shooting Two on Windsor Street." [Hartford Courant, December 11, 1922]

And who could forget this all-time classic:
"Capture Giant Negro Moron at Gary..." [Chicago Tribune, November 21, 1926][19]

Washington State: At Least He Wasn't Lynched

In Seattle, Dixon's *Clansman* warnings and the New York newspapers' tales of Giant Negroes seem to have had an effect. Though the city had been welcoming to blacks of both modest accomplishment as well as those with impressive business savvy (while suppressing the rights of the Chinese), the tide of public opinion began to turn in the early 1900s.

---

[19] For more of Mills' work uncovering the antics of Giant Negroes, visit his blog at http://undercoverblackman.blogspot.com/

Historylink.org explains that in 1909, a group of white citizens in Seattle began to oppose the presence of black soldiers stationed at Fort Lawton. They began a public opinion campaign to lobby for their removal. Military officials declined to relocate the black soldiers, and over a nine-month period, the campaign lost steam.

Then, in mid-1910, an incident became a rallying point that revived the local anti-black bigots.

From *HistoryLink*:

> On the night of June 4, 1910, a middle-aged white woman living near the post accused a black soldier of assaulting her with intention to do sexual mischief. The woman, Mrs. J.W. Redding, testified that a soldier, "tall and slender, and quite black," came by her house in the early evening and asked for some food to eat.

> When Mrs. Redding turned him away, he shortly returned and sprang upon her, reeking of liquor and apparently intent on doing sexual and physical harm to her.

> When her young daughter was drawn to the scene because of the noise, the man fled and Mrs. Redding rushed to a friend's house for help. She had a gash on her lip received in the struggle.

The authorities brought her to a lineup but she couldn't make the identification. After regrouping three times, authorities helped her identify the man they had chosen as guilty. The issue in her trouble with identification was that the soldier they had railroaded was lighter-skinned, shorter, and more stout than she'd related in her initial testimony. She was looking for someone who actually fit the description she'd given: "tall and slender, and quite black."

During the trial, the all-white jury took ten minutes to reach a decision. The accused soldier (by historical accounts, innocent) was sentenced to four-to-ten years of hard labor in the state penitentiary in Walla Walla.

Justice certainly wasn't served, but at least he wasn't lynched.

1910 THROUGH 1919

Leah Tyler's White Ancestors in the 1910s

When we look at the 1910 census for the white side of our family, we see Ai and Eliza living in separate homes. Their separation wasn't borne out of marital woes. Instead, Ai and the two oldest sons were farming on the land around Pampa. Eliza and the younger children were living about ninety miles away in Walla Walla, Washington.

There were far greater educational opportunities in Walla Walla, so the family had purchased a second home there in order to give their children the benefit of extended schooling.

Figure 9: One of Otto's class pictures from his schooling in Walla Walla.

Leah Tyler's Black Ancestors in the 1910s

When we look at the 1910 census record for Tolliver and Jemima's children, we see that they were all listed as being able to read and write but they still had not been attending school.

Videlia was seventeen years old. Two years later, in 1912, she would give birth to her only child, Beatrice. She gave her child the last name of Johnson. I learned from a family member that Beatrice's father went by the name "Pearlie," but no one in the family knows if that was his given name or a nickname.

I decided to go through the Wilmot census ledger line by line, looking for a Johnson family with a teenage son. That was the only thing I could think of to do in my attempt to learn more about Beatrice's father.

In all of Wilmot there was only one Johnson. He was a single man, twenty-six years old, who lived a few doors down from Videlia's home in 1910. His name was Clarence Johnson and he rented a room in a nearby boarding house. Perhaps he was traveling and looking for work. He reported his occupation as "odd jobs."

The census shows that Tolliver continued to sharecrop, but his boys, General Sherman and William H. also listed their occupation as "odd jobs."

When I read these entries that say "odd jobs" a knot forms in my stomach because of what I know about the convict leasing system that existed at that time.

Convict Leasing

What I've learned from reading *Slavery by Another Name* by Douglas A. Blackmon is that black men who were unemployed for even a short time were at high risk for being channeled into the prison slavery system.

The practice was called convict leasing and it served as an important part of the *Not-Slavery*-Slavery system of that time. The convict leasing system had risen up to fill the need for cheap labor after slavery was outlawed, and the threat of "the lease" was a powerful source of intimidation. Just uttering the words "the lease" was often enough to remind blacks not to challenge the racial caste system in any way. Convict leasing was also referred to as "the chain gang" though the chain gangs were mild compared to the conditions blacks were subjected to in mining operations.

The constitutional amendment that outlawed slavery, Amendment 13, reads (emphasis mine):

> *Neither slavery nor involuntary servitude,* **except as a punishment for crime** *whereof the party shall have been duly convicted, shall exist within the United States, or any place subject to their jurisdiction.*

It seems obvious in retrospect that Southerners read the amendment and concluded that the easiest way to reinstate slavery would be to arrest as many former slaves as they could.

Blackmon details how black men were often arrested for "vagrancy." A white man would identify a black man who looked strong and fit. He would approach the man and ask if he had any money in his pockets. If he did not, the white man would have the black man arrested for vagrancy. He would then collect a fee for having identified the black man as a good worker for the convict leasing system.

As the practice became more widespread and more people began collecting fees, whites became more strident. They would now ask a strong, fit man if he had any money, and if he did, they would take the money, pocket it, and ask the man again. This time, having no money left, the black man would be arrested for vagrancy just the same.

Once arrested, there was a system in nearly every county of the Southern states by which, instead of going to prison, blacks would be leased out to a businessman as more or less free labor. The prisoners were usually men, but women could be arrested as well. When women were given "the lease," their bondage nearly always included unrelenting sexual exploitation and abuse. The prisoners, male and female, performed hard labor laying railroad lines, mining iron ore, cutting timber and all other hard labor tasks that whites didn't want to perform. Prisoners performed the work with shackles on their feet and sometimes around their wrists and neck as well.

Reports filed by federal officials from the North, and uncovered by

Blackmon during his research, show that many companies were repeatedly cited for improper clothing, housing, or feeding. Sometimes the reports forced changes, but more often, things continued as if the reports had not been written at all.

Blackmon writes in great detail of the injustices and horrible living conditions as does a man named J.C. Powell who, in 1891 published an account of his life overseeing lease labor in Florida. His book is titled, *The American Siberia: Or, Fourteen Years' Experience in a Southern Convict Camp* and includes the following:

> There were no restrictions whatever...The punishments consisted of stringing up by the thumbs, "sweating" and "watering." [S]weating was shutting up in a close box-cell without ventilation or light.

> In watering...the prisoner was strapped down, a funnel forced into his mouth and water poured in. The effect was to enormously distend the stomach, producing not only great agony but a sense of impending death, due to pressure on the heart, that unnerved the stoutest. When deaths occurred, as they did quite frequently, the remains were wrapped in a blanket and buried in a shallow trench that barely covered the remains from the air...graves [were] desecrated by domestic animals, and there was no record kept of the dead or those who escaped.

According to Blackmon, many prisoners working in the iron ore mines around Birmingham committed suicide because the working conditions were so horrible that even a painful death was preferred. They cut their own Achilles tendons and drank chemical seepage from mine shafts so that they would develop dysentery and die. If they dropped dead, they might not even be buried. They might be left to rot where they fell.

A man arrested for vagrancy could easily be sentenced to a number of months but end up serving years because the companies who took them were able to intentionally keep shoddy records. For example, a company's records could make it look like men with shorter sentences were no longer there, even as these men toiled away day after day. Company officials also found ways to extend sentences by charging the men with new crimes while they were there. Blackmon writes of an incident in which a man was released from a work community only to be re-arrested the moment he stepped off the grounds. His new offense was stealing the clothes on his back. Certainly, had he shed the clothes instead, he would have been charged with indecency.

In the more corrupt counties, officials were able to make sure a prisoner-worker stayed until he was worked to death. Death was no problem for these businessmen because as soon as a worker died, they could notify local officials and request that another be sent to them.

Blackmon shows how crime rates in some areas rose and fell according to the seasonal needs of local businesses.

He also notes that while our US history books have long reported that Freedpeople and their descendants were lawless during these decades, committing high numbers of crimes, the truth is quite different. His work uncovers the true reason the crime statistics were so high. It wasn't that the former slaves were recklessly criminal; it was that a new form of slavery had been invented, one that required charging former slaves with crimes in order to take full advantage of their labor.

Northerners who learned of the high incarceration rates shrugged the information off, reasoning that if a man committed a crime, he had forfeited his rights.

In Frank Bell's *Slave Narrative* he says:

> Then I gets locked up in jail. I didn't know what for, never did know. One the men says to me to come with him and takes me to the woods and gives me an ax. I cuts rails till I nearly falls, all with a chain locked round feet, so I couldn't run off. He turns me loose and I wanders again. Never had a home. Works for men long 'nough to get fifty, sixty cents, then starts roamin' again, like a stray dog.

Frank Bell was lucky his imprisonment was based on seasonal work because the men who mined ore in Alabama were routinely worked year-round until they died or committed suicide.

"The lease" didn't just hurt the men and women who were captured and held. It also hurt the families left behind. Wives and children were often unable to keep up their sharecrop without the husbands and sons.

Husbands could be similarly short-handed when wives or daughters were stolen and given the lease[20].

Additionally, if a leased man was a landowner, the family left behind would soon fall into arrears and lose the land.

Blackmon includes stories of white landowners who accused black landowners of stealing their mules or killing their pigs, knowing the black man would be arrested and put into a lease arrangement.

The white neighbor/accuser could then offer to buy the land from the family left behind or could wait until the land was confiscated by the county and then move to purchase the land from the county.

Where Did They Go?

William H. left his mother Jemima's home sometime between the 1910 and 1920 census. I cannot find any record of him in Arkansas or Louisiana after that time. Clarence Johnson (the man I identified as Beatrice's possible father), also disappears from the census records in Wilmot, Arkansas during this decade.

Three things happened during this decade that removed many black men from their families. They were the convict lease, the war, and migration to the North in search of jobs. Any of these three things could have removed these men from Wilmot. The convict lease would, of course, be the most horrifying of these three possibilities.

Jemima's other son, General Sherman Eugene stuck around. He registered for the draft in 1914, reporting a Wilmot address.

First World War: Draft Registration in the South

When the US entered the war, black men signed up to serve their country with great enthusiasm.

Jami Bryan, writing for the armed services journal, "On Point," provides a broad overview of the black experience in World War I.

In his article "Fighting for Respect," Bryan writes:

African American males from all over the country eagerly joined the war

---

[20] Of course, besides the economic loss, losing a loved one to The Lease would have been emotionally distressing, if not devastating.

effort. They viewed the conflict as an opportunity to prove their loyalty, patriotism, and worthiness for equal treatment in the United States.

Southern whites weren't particularly interested in fighting for the government they'd tried to separate from (and lost to) just forty to fifty years before. In order to supply the required number of men to the service,

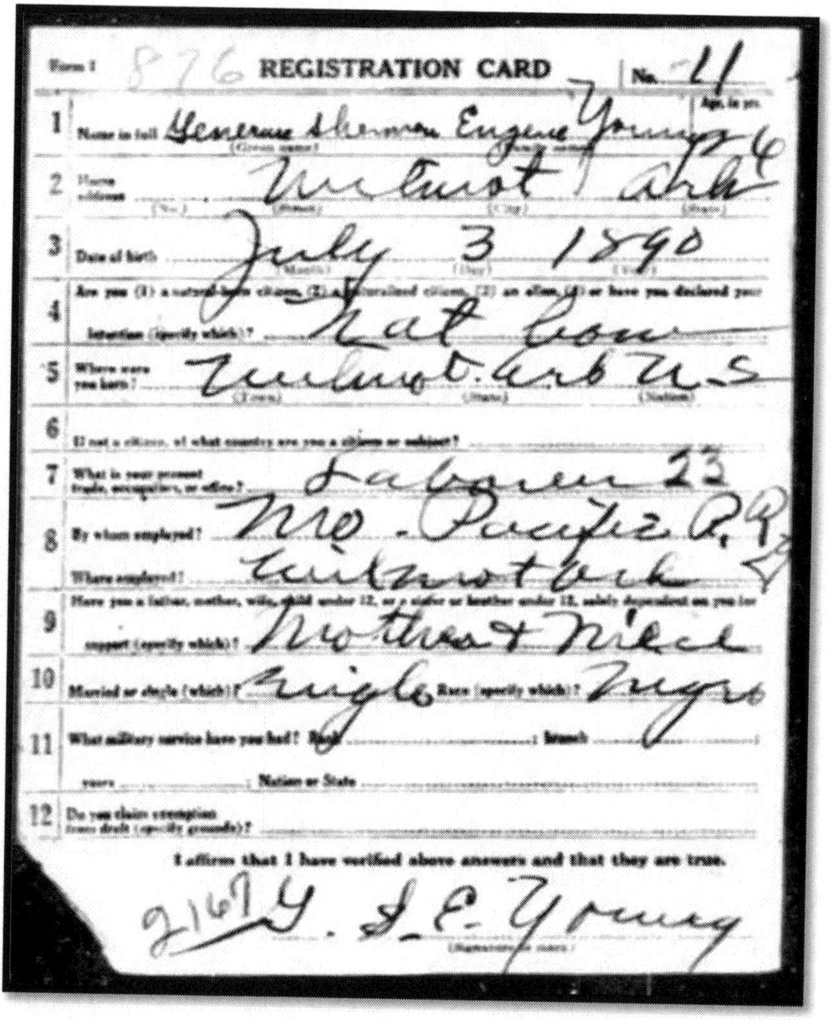

REGISTRATION CARD

1 Name in full: Generae Sherman Eugene Young — 24
2 Home address: Wilmot Ark
3 Date of birth: July 3 1890
4 Nat born
5 Where were you born? Wilmot. Ark U.S.
6
7 What is your present trade, occupation, or office? Laborer
8 By whom employed? Mo. Pacific R.R. Where employed? Wilmot Ark
9 Mother & Niece
10 Married or single (which)? Single Race (specify which)? Negro
11 What military service have you had? Nat
12 Do you claim exemption from draft (specify grounds)?

I affirm that I have verified above answers and that they are true.

G. S. E. Young

Figure 10: General Sherman Eugene Young's draft registration card. We see that he lived in Wilmot, Arkansas. He lists his birthday as July 3, 1890. He's a natural born citizen. He works as a laborer for the Missouri Pacific Railroad. He notes that he supports his mother and niece. The niece, we think, is Beatrice, my husband's grandmother.

most Southern draft boards were happy to continue sending black men until they met their quota.

In most communities farmers were given deferments because their crops were needed by citizens and soldiers alike. But this was the South, where black landowners would have been prime targets. Bryan notes that black landowners were often sent to war even as white wage laborers were given deferments.

Some white postmasters were known to target black men in a different way. They would pull the draft registrations of black men and destroy them, then report those men as draft dodgers. The targeted men would be arrested and given the lease. The postmasters could then collect a fee for each arrested "draft dodger."

In searching the WWI Draft Registration records, I can't find anything for William H. or Clarence Johnson. Could their cards have been pulled and destroyed intentionally? Or had they avoided filing in Arkansas by taking off for Chicago, or some other Northern destination, where their labor was prized in the factories and essential to the war effort in a different way?

The Black Servicemen's Plight

So we know that Sherman registered for the draft but we don't know if he was ever called up. If he *was* called up, his most likely assignment would have been hard labor in a service battalion.

I looked for Sherman's service records by searching the military records of the National Archives. I found nothing on Sherman but stumbled across a collection of papers called the Negro Subversion files[21].

This set of files documented a lot of disparate events and people. The only thing the people seem to have had in common was that they were all black. Curious about the subversive activities, I proceeded to go through almost a thousand pages of documentation. Rather than finding out about nefarious plots and machinations, I learned about how freaked out our

---

[21] The files belonged to the Military Intelligence Division (MID) of the War Department. These files are easily accessed using the web service Fold3.

country's white officials got over the smallest expressions of dissatisfaction from anyone black. Most of what I read had me shaking my head at their comically overwrought reactions.

There were some documents, however, that touched me. These were the letters black servicemen wrote to US Military officials describing how poorly they were being treated even as they were serving as members of our nation's armed services.

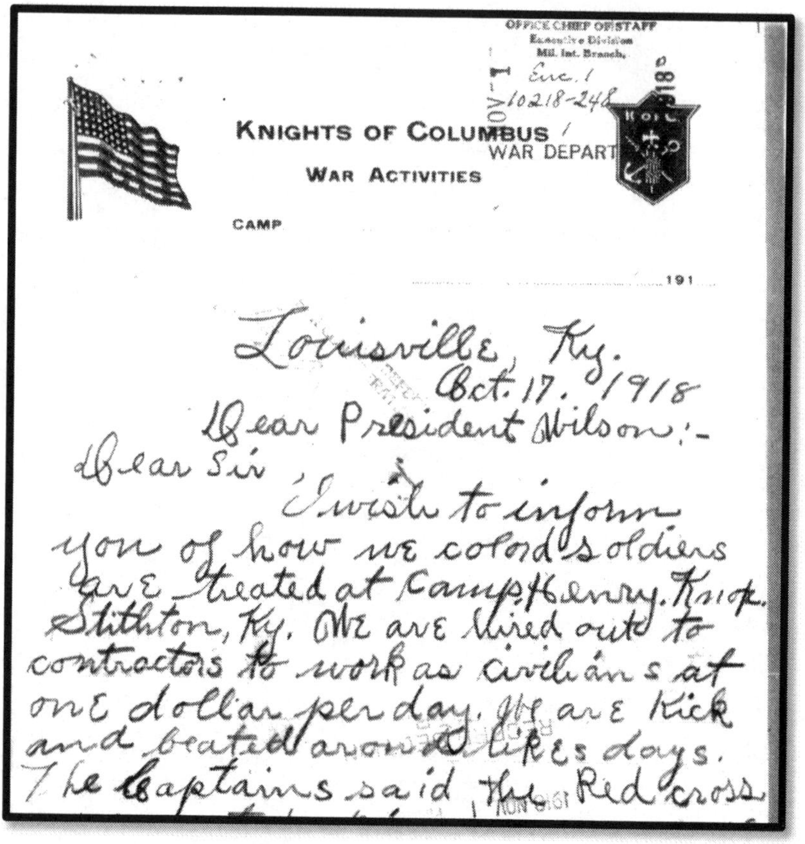

Figure 11: A letter from a black serviceman to President Woodrow Wilson.

A letter from Louisville, Kentucky arrived in the MID offices on November 1, 1918. The letter was dated as having been written on October 17, 1918.

The letter read:

Dear President Wilson;

Dear Sir,

I wish to inform you of how we colord soldiers are treated at Camp Henry Knox, Stithton, KY. We are hired out to contractors to work as civilians at one dollar per day. We are kick and beated around like dogs.

The Captains said the Red cross were not feeding us no more and the contractors would quit the last or first of next month and the U.S would not pay us no more so we want to know what we are to do. We are the boys what did not pass for oversea service. We have been at said camp for ten days and have not received no meat and working in coal, digging or any work they wants us to do.

Another letter from the same camp, sent on November 3rd, and signed by Private Charlie Long read:

Sir we are here without half enough to eat and no clothes for the winter and no fire at all and no hot water to take a bath with. [We are] handling the pick and shovel, in the ditch handling lumber and unloading gravel. [The work is harder] than the penitentiary.

We can't get home to see our people at all...Please we are in terrible need here if you only knew it. We are half naked and half-starved here and if you would come you would see it for yourself. We are treated worse than dogs here in this place.

Both of these letters were routed to the top Military Intelligence officer in the War Department. That office promptly flagged the letters as Negro Subversion material. In a letter dated November 22, 1918, the office of the director of Military Intelligence sent notice back to Camp Henry Knox that it had received the letters. They included copies of the letters and advised the staff at Camp Henry Knox that they should take "whatever action you think advisable."

That phrase, "whatever action you think advisable," alarmed me. In the modern era most people would see the black soldiers as whistleblowers and their communications and identity would not be revealed to the accused "culprits" of the misdeeds. In this case, the very staff that had created the problems were alerted and asked to investigate the claims. Why not dispatch an investigator from the MID instead? And why was the prescribed remedy "whatever action" instead of specific instructions or a list of actions?

I also noted that the paper mail system along with bureaucracy, had conspired to leave these black servicemen without remedy for almost a month after the first letter had been sent. The letter writers must have felt hopeless as the days grew even colder and nothing changed. Perhaps they had started to lose hope that the letters would ever reach someone who cared.

Staff at Fort Henry Knox wrote back on December 12, 1918 to state that blacks are "childlike in mentality" and once they were interviewed regarding their grievances, they began coming up with longer lists of mistreatment. The "longer lists" statement in the context of the memo implies that the servicemen were simply exaggerating their mistreatment in order to reap (undeserved?) benefits. The letter states that the officers in charge of the black servicemen have been asked to "educate their men."

While Fort Henry Knox higher-ups probably didn't intend to sound ominous, that's the way it sounds to me.

The staff member writing the memo back to the war department acknowledges that the camp has the funding and resources to make conditions better for the black servicemen. The white servicemen at Camp Henry Knox have warm barracks and much better rations. These facts lead me to conclude that the conditions imposed were not wartime exigencies, they were simply the same old Jim Crow system designed to make white servicemen feel special and to squeeze every possible ounce of effort from black men while awarding them as little compensation as possible.

Even modest speculation will lead us to infer that the black servicemen would have been incredibly easy to exploit. Since wartime service called for sacrifices from all service members, a piling on of the worst possible work details, and least desirable perks, would have been easy to arrange.

Once arranged, this *Armed Services Slavery* would have been slow to dismantle. After all, as these letters and the official reaction to them shows, the black servicemen's complaints were quickly and easily written off.

The Great Migration Begins

The Great Migration is the label given to the exodus of blacks from the Southern states to the Northern cities. In *The Warmth of Other Suns*, Isabel Wilkerson notes that as the nation ramped up to fight in the first World War, Northerners went South to recruit blacks as factory workers:

> [T]he masses didn't pour out of the South until they had something to go to. They got their chance when the North began courting them, hard and in secret, in the face of southern hostility, during the labor crisis of World War I. Word had spread like wildfire that the North was finally "opening up." The recruiters would stride through groupings of colored people and whisper without stopping, "Anybody want to go to Chicago, see me."

Needless to say, when Southerners recognized that blacks were leaving, they tried to intimidate them. From the *Jim Crow Narrative* of Willie Harrell:

> I had to slip off at night. When I left Mississippi, I left at night when they was in the bed asleep, around two and three o'clock at night. I got by their house. On a plantation, you can tell when they go to sleep, because the lights go out.

> When they put them lights out, you know they gone to bed then. They had a gate. I just stepped across there.

> I bet you I walked about five or six miles in the woods. Onliest way I could see [was] these little lightning bugs at night [that] light up. That's the onliest way I could see at night, and [my] clothes was tore off where I was going through the woods and trees and couldn't see, it was tearing my clothes off until I got from there where I could catch this train.

> Man, I was as raggedy as a pan of kraut when I got here in them. Didn't have nothing but what I had [on], and they was tore all off. Old pair of shoes. Bare, with no socks or nothing on.

When whites noticed that so many blacks were leaving to go North, they began making their appreciation of blacks known. Various outpourings of appreciation became public and frequent.

As noted in Wilkerson:

"It is the life of the South," a Georgia plantation owner once said. "It is the foundation of its prosperity. God pity the day when the negro leaves the South."

Writing in *Trouble in Mind*, Leon F. Litwack quotes a planter:

"I must have [blacks] to work for me," a Virginia planter conceded some years after emancipation. "I can't do nothin' on my place without 'em. If they send all the [blacks] to Africa, I'll have to go thar too."

Litwack also notes:

[A] Charleston man conceded, "We must have their labor... If I had to work my land with whites, I'd quit. I couldn't manage or depend on them."

Since black migrants were forced to go through all kinds of machinations to board a bus or train out of the South, they must have sighed with great relief as they neared their destinations. Most did not understand that racism would be there to meet them on the other end of their ride.

In Richard Wright's novel *Black Boy*, he describes his vision of the North:

I dreamed of going north and writing books, novels. The North symbolized to me all that I had not felt and seen; it had no relation whatever to what actually existed. Yet, by imagining a place where everything was possible, I kept hope alive in me.

Wright felt forced to steal so he could afford a train ticket to go north:

An hour later I was sitting in a Jim Crow coach, speeding northward, making the first lap of my journey to a land where I could live with a little less fear. Slowly the burden I had carried for many months lifted somewhat. My cheeks itched and when I scratched them I found tears. In that moment I understood the pain that accompanied crime and I hoped that I would never have to feel it again. I never did feel it again, for I never stole again; and what kept me from it was the knowledge that, for me, crime carried its own punishment.

With ever watchful eyes and bearing scars, visible and invisible, I headed North, full of a hazy notion that life could be lived with dignity, that the personalities of others should not be violated, that men should be able to confront other men without fear or shame, and that if men were lucky in their living on earth they might win some redeeming meaning for their having struggled and suffered here beneath the stars.

Wright was not alone in his idealistic notions about life in the North. For this reason, many blacks in the South referred to the North as "The Promised Land."

Price Davis, in his Jim Crow Narrative:

I got there at Washington, D.C., changed buses, and a black woman come up and she told me, she said, "This is good now, son. You can sit wherever you want to sit on the bus."

I said, "I can?"

She said, "Yeah." She said, "You get you a seat."

I did not move to the front, but I did not sit in the back. I moved middle ways. When I got to New York, got a cab and went to Harlem, I looked around. I saw a black policeman directing traffic.

I said, "Oh, my God, this is the Promised Land."

The sudden influx of so many blacks arriving in Northern cities caused alarm in these predominantly white communities. Whereas before the Great Migration, blacks had moved north in a slow trickle, they were now coming in droves.

Almost overnight, blacks didn't need to have middle-class values to make it in the North. A recruiter might buy a man a train ticket, and that man would be in Detroit, working, three days later. The new migrants often lived with people who had migrated just months before, and this made it even easier for single, carefree types to inundate the cities. Up until this great surge, black migrants had been sober, hard-working families who got by on very little for many of their earliest years in any area. Suddenly migrants were young and single, ready to enjoy the full social lives their wages could provide.

Many of the migrants, having come from a life of deprivation, must have felt positively unfettered, not only from the oppressive rules of Jim Crow but also from the watchful eyes of parents and grandparents.

Working-class Whites: Fighting for Survival

Whites in the lowest social and economic positions in the Northern cities had reason to fear the arrival of blacks: It was common practice and perfectly legal to pay blacks lower wages.

Lower wages for blacks would undermine their own wages. In short, the arrival of blacks was a bad thing for poor whites, as it was sure to either put them out of work or reduce their pay. For this reason, whites often threatened to strike if there was any attempt to hire black workers.

The elite businessmen who negotiated wages enjoyed these racial divisions in the workforce. They'd learned the racial bribe from Southern elites. They could have paid blacks equal wages or even raised the wages of whites as a bargaining chip for bringing in black coworkers. However, keeping these worker populations at odds with one another benefitted the business owners. Often, when white workers protested their working conditions, blacks were brought in as strikebreakers.

Leon Alexander related in his *Jim Crow Narrative*:

> *There was discrimination in the hiring practice, in the promotion practice, in all of these things, there was discrimination in it.*

> *The coal operators knew how to play the game of divide and conquer. See in Pennsylvania they had a lot of Polish that came into Pennsylvania working in the coal mines. So they played them off against the other races that was working. By promoting them and giving them favored status, it made the other races mad with them, and they could keep you from getting together.*

White Experiences in the First World War

With the first World War underway, Ai and Eliza were determined to keep their sons from going off to do battle. Ai had pulled all the right strings: One son was put in charge of the farm, another had a medical issue and Otto was enrolled in college. Whitman College had formed in Walla

Walla and Otto was taking classes there.

He was the youngest son and was always thought of as "the baby boy" by his parents and siblings. He fantasized that being a soldier would make him a man, and everyone would have to recognize him as such. Otto registered for the draft on September 12, 1918.

After registering, he didn't want to wait for his number to be called. He wanted to enlist right away, despite his parent's assurances that, as a member of the upper class, he had no obligation to serve.

Figure 12: Otto was able to go to school until he was 19 years old. Only the rich had the luxury of education at this age. Otto is joined in this picture by two of his sisters. Women receiving this much education was even more rare during that time period.

Ai was adamant that Otto would not enlist. Otto decided to do it anyway and hopped a train to Spokane.

Ai got wind of Otto's plans and sent one of his employees to intervene. The employee was successful and Otto returned sullen and restless. Weeks later, on October 31, 1918, Otto succeeded in sneaking off to enlist.

Not long after that, he was on a train bound for Texas where he was scheduled to complete his basic training.

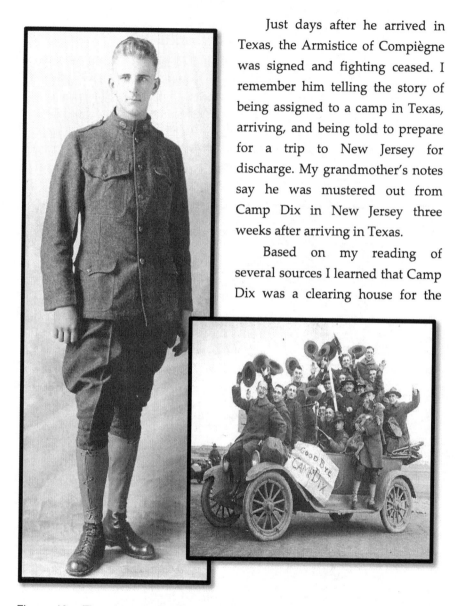

Just days after he arrived in Texas, the Armistice of Compiègne was signed and fighting ceased. I remember him telling the story of being assigned to a camp in Texas, arriving, and being told to prepare for a trip to New Jersey for discharge. My grandmother's notes say he was mustered out from Camp Dix in New Jersey three weeks after arriving in Texas.

Based on my reading of several sources I learned that Camp Dix was a clearing house for the

Figure 13: Though my grandfather's military career was comically short and uneventful, he did arrange to have a formal portrait taken in full uniform. Searching for some idea of what his service experience was like at Camp Dix, I came across a photo from the National Archives showing soldiers mustering out from there. White experiences in the first World War had a decidedly different tone than the experiences of black servicemen. Can we take this photo, "Good Bye Camp Dix," as indicative of Otto's experience during his few weeks of service?

discharging of soldiers. I imagine that the elation of soldiers returning from Europe and on their way to see family and friends would have made Camp Dix a pleasant environment to serve within. Did Otto's experience as a serviceman consist mainly of helping Fort Dix soldiers leave the service?

What a stark contrast that possibility provides when compared to the experiences of the black servicemen serving a Camp Henry Knox.

In any event, on December 8, 1918, just thirty-nine days after he'd enlisted, Otto was on a train back to Whitman County, Washington, with honorable discharge papers and a paycheck for $124.85.

He told everyone who asked that he'd served in the Tank Corps, after all, that *had* been his assignment.

The Clansman: Now A Three-Hour Motion Picture

Remember that when the book, *The Clansman*, first appeared in 1905 it had been positioned as a cautionary tale to Northerners. Dixon wanted Northerners to know just how much power blacks held during Reconstruction and how terribly the whites had been treated. Never mind that these things were untrue and his book was wildly fictional.

Also recall that as the story progressed, white Northerners were shown coming to the understanding that their enemy all along had been blacks, and the white Southerners were truly their brothers and sisters.

In 1915, the book was made into a motion picture called, "The Birth Of A Nation." Unlike modern times where most films open across the country on the same day, this film was carried from city to city for local screenings.

The film is revered by many, even today, not for its deplorable content but for being the first film that harnessed the power of film to evoke emotions. The film was well-crafted to terrify white audiences.

Writing in his book, *Red Summer: The Summer of 1919 and the Awakening of Black America*, Cameron McWhirter notes:

> *In 1919, [the] three-hour film* Birth of a Nation *was still packing theaters four years after its initial release. NAACP efforts to block showings had limited success, with bans in Chicago and some other cities.*

Controversy fueled the film's notoriety. Starring Lillian Gish, it was based on the best-selling 1905 novel The Clansman *by Thomas Dixon Jr., replete with black rapists, carpetbagger Svengalis, and heroic white southerners. In the penultimate scene of the film, blacks come out of their cabins on Election Day only to be met by armed Klansmen, who force them back into their hovels. It is presented as the triumph of virtue.*

President Wilson saw the movie in a private showing with [the film's director] in the White House. He should have liked it. His two-volume History of the American People *(1902), which extolled the Klan, was quoted in the film.*

Red Summer Riots of 1919

Thirty-eight riots took place between May and October of 1919. In all these cases, mobs of white people attacked blacks, destroying black homes and businesses and injuring or murdering black people.

The thirty eight riot locations and the date of their occurrence are listed below.

Date	Location
May 10, 1919	Charleston, South Carolina
May 10, 1919	Sylvester, Georgia
May 29, 1919	Putnam County, Georgia
May 31, 1919	Monticello, Mississippi
Jun 13, 1919	New London, Connecticut
Jun 13, 1919	Memphis, Tennessee
Jun 27, 1919	Annapolis, Maryland
June 27, 1919	Macon, Mississippi
July 3, 1919	Bisbee, Arizona
July 5, 1919	Scranton, Pennsylvania
July 6, 1919	Dublin, Georgia
July 7, 1919	Philadelphia, Pennsylvania
July 8, 1919	Coatesville, Pennsylvania
July 9, 1919	Tuscaloosa, Alabama
July 10, 1919	Longview, Texas
July 11, 1919	Baltimore, Maryland

Date	Location
July 15, 1919	Port Arthur, Texas
July 19, 1919	Washington, D.C.
July 21, 1919	Norfolk, Virginia
July 23, 1919	New Orleans, Louisiana
July 23, 1919	Darby, Pennsylvania
July 26, 1919	Hobson City, Alabama
July 27, 1919	Chicago, Illinois
July 28, 1919	Newberry, South Carolina
July 31, 1919	Bloomington, Illinois
July 31, 1919	Syracuse, New York
July 31, 1919	Philadelphia, Pennsylvania
August 4, 1919	Hattiesburg, Mississippi
August 6, 1919	Texarkana, Texas
August 21, 1919	New York City, New York
August 29, 1919	Ocmulgee, Georgia
August 30, 1919	Knoxville, Tennessee
September 28, 1919	Omaha, Nebraska
October 1, 1919	Elaine, Arkansas

In addition to the riots, between January 1 and September 14, 1919, there were at least 43 lynchings. Of these, 16 were hanged, 19 shot and eight were burned at the stake[22].

After the War: White and Black Experiences

After Otto's several weeks of service as a soldier he returned to Whitman County and took up where he'd left off, working for his father, Ai, and living at home with his parents.

He'd directly disobeyed his father by enlisting. I suspect he'd believed that going off to do battle would soften his father's rage. Unfortunately for him, the war had ended and Otto arrived back home never having faced

---

[22] The table and the numbers on lynchings come from The Haynes Report written by Dr. George E. Haynes. Haynes was working for the federal government as director of Negro Economics for the U.S. Department of Labor when he compiled the report.

any danger at all.

Ai's rage was still fresh.

Where Otto had been the sweet baby boy of the family, he was now the rebel son and would have to win his father's favor back through blind obedience for many years to come.

During the war, Ai had gone from being the unofficial banker of the town, to the official banker. He'd founded a bank and installed himself as president. He served that post in addition to his activities running his various farm operations and businesses. His bank presidency meant still more money and more power accrued to his and his sons' families.

As for black servicemen, the life of toil and mistreatment continued. Black servicemen at Camp Alexander, Virginia came to believe that they were being held almost as chain gangs while white servicemen were being sent home.

William C. Elkins, an Army song leader, wrote a letter dated December 20th, 1918 and he addressed it to

Figure 14: It's hard to imagine a picture that could better illustrate the relationship between Otto and his father, Ai, after the war.

Captain Paul B. Johnson, a morale officer in Newport News, Virginia. Elkins titled the letter, *Desires and Complaints*[23].

> *For the past three or four weeks men have been detailed...on the road work between Newport News and Richmond and some of them claim they work in water almost up to their waist.*

> *Men claim their dependents have not received allotments for periods*

---

[23] Elkins began his letter: As per request I am hereby submitting in writing what I might term "Desires and Complaints" of men in the Negro Reserve Labor Battalion in Camps Alexander and Stuart, Newport News, and the Army Base, Norfolk, Va.

ranging from three months to six months and some claim they have been in the service fourteen months and their dependents have never received an allotment.

Men who have farms or other business interests desire to return home to give personal attention to business.

Men claim there are many unoccupied barracks at Camp Alexander, while they are compelled to remain housed in tents.

Men claim they are detailed on private contract work.

Men now claiming there is a decided let down in supply rations.

There are men who claim to have signed their discharge papers as much as three weeks ago, but who are still detained in the Camps, simply being shifted from one place to another.

On December 22nd, 1918, A. Roberts, an Intelligence Officer wrote a memo to Captain Henry A. Taylor. Roberts had been sent to investigate the conditions for the black soldiers. His confidential report included the following:

When the discharging of the men began, one could be on the road between Newport News and Camp Alexander and see several truckloads of soldiers coming to town with their baggage and discharges, and as these men would go by they would wave their discharges, which had some effect on the colored men working along the roadway.

[It] has been thoroughly explained to them that they are working on government work, and that they are drafted as laborers and that while civilian government employees are over them in a way there is always a commissioned officer at hand.

Capt. McKinney informs me...that recently they have been discharging men who live within 350 miles of here, according to orders, and that he has seen a great many of the men that were not discharged sit right down and cry when those who were discharged were leaving camp.

It has been explained to these men that their turn was coming. Then again, they have seen a great many white soldiers being transported over the road to the depot, who have been discharged, and they all feel that they should be discharged also.

There were other incidents where black servicemen became suspicious that their discharges were being withheld so that they could be worked indefinitely. That would have definitely amounted to Armed Services Slavery. The objective observer can be asked which was more plausible: that the black workers were childlike in mentality and didn't understand what was going on, or that our federal government was being racist; squeezing out as much super cheap labor from the black workers as they could, before someone or something forced them to let the black workers go.

My husband's great-uncle General Sherman Eugene either returned to his hard labor working for the railroad or had never left it in the first place. Either way, his experiences and benefits would have remained roughly the same.

Otto had not worked nearly as hard as the black servicemen had and yet, he returned from the war to his comfortable place in a wealthy family.

NAACP leaders had encouraged blacks to participate in wartime service because they believed it would increase blacks' standing as loyal citizens. As it turned out, their loyalty and sacrifices did not lead to the improvement of their conditions. Most black men returned after war service to the same hard, unskilled labor positions they'd always held and their families remained in abject poverty.

How's That *Separate But Equal* Thing Working Out?

Twenty-five years prior to the 1910s the Supreme Court had ruled that separate accommodations for blacks and whites could be legal, as long as the two sets of accommodations were equal[24]. Whites in the Southern states regularly assured Northern whites that the program was a success and both races were satisfied with the separation.

An article in the November 1915 issue of the NAACP's Weekly newspaper, *The Crisis,* reveals that, in fact, accommodations were not equal

---

[24] Plessy v. Ferguson

and blacks were not satisfied:

> *The laws provide for equal accommodations for the passengers of both races, but the following conditions demonstrate that they are dead letters on the statute books:*
>
> *1. Accommodations are not equal. The colored coaches are antiquated wooden cars which are often discarded white coaches.*
>
> *2. Reservations for colored passengers are inadequate, the coaches often being dangerously overcrowded.*
>
> *3. Sanitary conditions on colored coaches are indecent. The coaches are generally filthy. In some cases there is but one toilet for both men and women and that often in a foul condition.*
>
> *4. White officials (conductors and brakemen) are often objectionable and insulting to colored passengers. They use the colored coach as dressing and lounging room and in some cases as a smoking' room.*
>
> *5. "Butchers" or venders use the Jim Crow coach as a storeroom for their cases of fruit, candy, cigars, soft drinks, and magazines. They are frequently familiar and insulting in their manner to colored passengers.*
>
> *6. White passengers have free access to the colored coach. They pass through it at will, lounge in it, and in many cases smoke in the presence of women and insult them.*
>
> *7. Accommodations for long-distance colored passengers are disgraceful. [Sleeping] Berths in Pullman cars cannot be secured except in rare cases so that the colored passenger must sit up all night in the unsanitary and uncomfortable Jim Crow coach. He may not even wash his face, for washing accommodations are rarely found.*
>
> *If he is hungry, he must starve for he cannot enter the diner or eat at the counters of railway restaurants. Often he cannot even purchase food there to take away and eat because there is no time to serve him as white folks must come first. These are the conditions that the colored man in this country is forced to meet daily while he pays the same fare as the white man.*
>
> *[T]here is no escape from the humiliation and discomfort of railway travel.*

The colored man and his family must, in traveling, submit to conditions that are galling to manhood and to decency, conditions that no decent, self-respecting people should endure.

THE 1920s

Leah Tyler's White Ancestors in the 1920s

By 1920, Otto was beginning to think about marriage. He started courting a woman he met at church named Leah Jones. Leah was close friends with two of his sisters. He wooed her by taking her out in one of his father's cars. They were young, and cars were fun. After a few months, Otto told his father he'd like to marry Leah. Ai and Eliza did not think Leah was worthy of their son but gave him permission anyway. My grandmother was bossy and my grandfather was accustomed to following orders. I've joked to my family that Ai probably allowed the marriage out of spite, thinking Leah

Figure 15: This is my grandparents' engagement portrait. My grandmother's feminist hairstyle and deconstructed dress show that she was a thoroughly modern woman.

would make Otto miserable for many years to come.

Leah wasn't very fond of Ai either. My grandmother told me, in a video-recorded interview I conducted in 1987, that she had always been scared of her father-in-law, Ai. When asked why, she turned to Otto, "Why *was* I scared of him?" to which Otto replied, "*I don't know.*" That caused my grandmother to joke, "Well, *you* were scared of him, too!" They exchanged a glance and began giggling together.

Otto and Leah married in 1921.

Thanks to Otto's parents' wealth, the newlyweds had a ready-made life. "Well, we didn't have any money or anything, and Otto's dad give us every cent we had. That's the only way we lived," my grandmother said.

Ai and Eliza had begun spending winters in Pasadena, California, with Ai returning to Whitman County during planting and harvest seasons. Ai was investing in businesses in the Pasadena area by that time. Otto and Leah had expected to be given a farm but, instead, Ai assigned them to a post in Pasadena running a gas station Ai had purchased.

Otto and Leah ran the station, begrudgingly, for a period of time. Leah began to nag Otto, begging him to approach Ai and ask for a farm they could run back in Whitman county. Once Leah became pregnant, Otto was able to make the request on the grounds that his wife needed to be near her mother when the baby arrived.

After repeated requests, Ai reluctantly arranged a plot of land for Otto to farm on his behalf, and back to Whitman County my grandparents went.

Leah gave birth to two sons. The first was born in 1922 and the second in 1923.

Leah Tyler's Black Ancestors in the 1920s

In the 1920 census we see that Jemima, her son General Sherman and her grand-daughter Beatrice were living together in Wilmot, Arkansas. Tolliver had died sometime between the 1910 census the 1920 census because Jemima is listed as a widow.

What can be said of Tolliver's life? Did he get what he deserved? Should we consider his life in terms of the vaunted American ideals of *personal responsibility* and *bootstraps*? We know he worked hard, and we know he did so for his entire life. He married and created a family and he never stopped providing for that family. Still, he died penniless. How could this have happened in America? The country where working hard was supposed to result in achieving the American dream?

And what can be said of Jemima? She was now a widow who had to depend on her son. Why hadn't all those decades of toil resulted in a comfortable retirement? Finally there was eight-year old Beatrice, my husband's grandmother. Beatrice was living with her grandmother and uncle. Where was Beatrice's mother?

I searched the 1920 Census records in pursuit of Videlia. Could she have gone North as so many others did during the war? When I couldn't find Videlia, I looked for her other brother William H.

Sure enough, I found a William H. Young living in Chicago. The census record shows Chicago's William H. Young as having been born in Arkansas and the birth year is a perfect match to that of Videlia's brother.

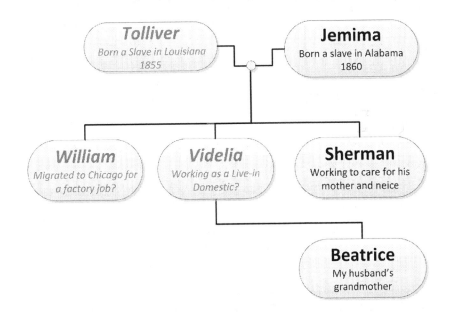

Figure 16: By the time the 1920 census was taken, Tolliver had passed on and William and Videlia were MIA. This left the core household of Jemima, Sherman and Beatrice.

Of course I can't be absolutely certain he's the right guy, because both "William" and "Young" are common names, but finding that census record gave me a tiny bit of peace.

Videlia's absence from her mother and daughter's home is more disturbing. Had she married and left her daughter behind? Had she gone North like her brother, promising to send money back so Beatrice could join her later? Or was she simply across town, living, against her own wishes, with a white family as their maid, perhaps so that she could provide money to help Sherman in the support of her daughter and mother? The most common job for black women, in the South, at that time, was as a live-in domestic worker for a white family.

The Live-In Domestic

In looking at the census records of the 1920s, it is easy to find black households listing fathers and children, but no mother, while the white households list a married black woman as residing there.

In 1912, a New York newspaper called *The Independent*[25] ran a feature article about the life of a black woman in the South who worked for a white family, caring for their children.

The article was presented as if a black woman had been interviewed, and her exact words transcribed. While the article doesn't sound to me like an authentic voice, I do believe the details presented are an accurate amalgamation of the lives of black women living and working as domestics during that time. Because of this, I consider the article at least somewhat informative of the life that Videlia might have had as a live-in domestic worker in Jim Crow Arkansas.

I have excerpted several passages from the article here:

[M]ore than two-thirds of the negroes of the town where I live are menial servants of one kind or another, and besides that more than two-thirds of the negro women

---

[25] Archives of the paper are available from Old Dominion University. According to Old Dominion University librarians, *The Independent* was a New York weekly newspaper founded in 1848 and published until 1921. It included social topics, primarily opposition to slavery and religious articles.

here, whether married or single, are compelled to work for a living--as nurses, cooks, washerwomen, chambermaids, seamstresses, hucksters, janitresses, and the like.

I will say, also, that the condition of this vast host of poor colored people is just as bad as, if not worse than, it was during the days of slavery. Though today we are enjoying a nominal freedom, we are literally slaves. And, not to generalize, I will give you a sketch of the work I have to do--and I'm only one of many.

I frequently work from fourteen to sixteen hours a day. I am compelled to by my contract, which is oral only, to sleep in the house. I am allowed to go home to my own children... only once in two weeks, every other Sunday afternoon--even then I'm not permitted to stay all night.

If the baby falls to sleep during the day, as it has been trained to do ...I am not permitted to rest. It's "Mammy, do this," or "Mammy, do that," or "Mammy, do the other," from my mistress, all the time. So it is not strange to see "Mammy" watering the lawn with the garden hose, sweeping the sidewalk, mopping the porch and halls, helping the cook, or darning stockings.

I live a treadmill life; and I see my own children only when they happen to see me on the streets when I am out with the [white] children, or when my children come to the "yard" to see me, which isn't often, because my white folks don't like to see their servants' children hanging around their premises.

I am the slave, body and soul, of this family. And what do I get for this work--this lifetime bondage? The pitiful sum of ten dollars a month! And what am I expected to do with these ten dollars? With this money I'm expected to pay my house rent, which is four dollars per month, for a little house of two rooms, just big enough to turn around in; and I'm expected, also, to feed and clothe myself and three children.

I think of the low rate of wages we poor colored people receive, and... I hear so much said about our unreliability, our untrustworthiness, and even our vices.

[W]e have to work for little or nothing, or become vagrants! And that, of course, in this State would mean that we would be arrested, tried, and dispatched to the "State Farm," where we would surely have to work for nothing or be beaten with many stripes!

I remember very well the first and last place from which I was dismissed. I lost my place because I refused to let the madam's husband kiss me. He must have been accustomed to undue familiarity with his servants, or else he took it as a matter of course, because...soon after I was installed as cook, he walked up to me, threw his arms around me, and was in the act of kissing me, when I demanded to know what he meant, and shoved him away.

I was young then, and newly married, and didn't know then that what has been a burden to my mind and heart ever since: that a colored woman's virtue in this part of the country has no protection. I at once went home, and told my husband about it. When my husband went to the man who had insulted me, the man cursed him, and slapped him, and--had him arrested!

The police judge fined my husband $25. I was present at the hearing, and testified on oath to the insult offered me. The white man, of course, denied the charge. The old judge looked up and said: "This court will never take the word of a [black person] against the word of a white man."

Many and many a time since I have heard similar stories repeated again and again by my friends. I believe nearly all white men take, and expect to take, undue liberties with their colored female servants--not only the fathers, but in many cases the sons also. Those servants who rebel against such familiarity must either leave or expect a mighty hard time, if they stay.

I know of more than one colored woman who was openly importuned by white women to become the mistresses of their white husbands, on the ground that they, the white wives, were afraid that, if their husbands did not associate with colored women, they would certainly do so with outside white women, and the white wives, for reasons which ought to be perfectly obvious, preferred to have their husbands do wrong with colored women in order to keep their husbands straight!

And again, I know at least fifty places where white men are positively raising two families--a white family in the "Big House" in front, and a colored family in a "Little House" in the backyard. In most cases, to be sure, the colored women involved are the cooks or chambermaids or seamstresses, but it cannot be true that their real connection with the white men of the families is unknown to the white women of the families.

No matter what they call us--no matter what we teach our children to call us--we must tamely submit, and answer when we are called; we must enter no protest; if we did object, we should be driven out without the least ceremony, and, in applying for work at other places, we should find it very hard to procure another situation. In almost every case, when our intending employers would be looking up our record, the information would be given by telephone or otherwise that we were "impudent," "saucy," "dishonest," and "generally unreliable."

[C]olored girls who are nurses... can be seen almost any afternoon, when the weather is fair, rolling the baby carriage or lolling about on some one of the chief boulevards of our town.

It is a favorite practice of young white sports about town--and they are not always young, either--to stop some colored nurse, inquire the name of the "sweet little baby," talk baby talk to the child...and in nine of ten cases every such white man will wind up by [flirting with] the colored nurse and seeking an appointment with her.

Ah, we poor colored women wage-earners in the South are fighting a terrible battle, and because of our weakness, our ignorance, our poverty, and our temptations we deserve the sympathies of mankind.

Jemima's Plight as a Poor, Black Widow

In the days before a federal social security program existed, widows should have been able to appeal to local charities and community chests if they were destitute. Of course, in the South, charitable organizations would likely have been extra-careful about providing financial support to elderly blacks. Whites believed that when a black family had even a trickle of money coming into the home, they would choose to meet their own needs through hunting, fishing, and farming their own vegetables. In other words, blacks would far prefer to scrape by than to work for whites. Therefore, even a paltry widow's pension could be seen as destabilizing the Southern economy.

Some states were just beginning to organize relief systems for widows and the elderly but most did not include blacks in their plans. Whites found it preferable that some elderly black people might starve to death than to take the chance that by giving them a bit of money for food and medicine, those elderly people might share what they received with someone healthy enough to work.

Segregation in the Northern Cities

If Beatrice's Uncle William was living up in Chicago he would have known first-hand that life in the North was not as bad as the Jim Crow South, but it certainly wasn't the promised land.

In *American Apartheid: Segregation and the Making of the Underclass,* Douglas S. Massey and Nancy A. Denton note:

> As the size of the urban black population rose steadily... white racial views hardened, and the relatively fluid and open period of race relations in the north drew to a close. Doors that had permitted extensive interracial contact among the elite suddenly slammed shut as black professionals lost white clients, associates and friends.

Massey and Denton go on to detail how, in the aftermath of the Red Summer riots, middle-class blacks who had been living peacefully for decades in predominantly white neighborhoods were threatened with violent expulsion if they didn't voluntarily remove themselves to "black" neighborhoods.

Whites had decided, somewhat suddenly, to push all blacks back into newly designated black neighborhoods.

When white neighborhoods tried to force black families out by using violence they often destroyed homes unintentionally. Out-of-control protests resulted in dwellings set on fire or bombed. These mob actions left the disputed residences in shambles. Whites pretty quickly realized that they needed to find better ways to drive out blacks. It didn't make much sense to destroy perfectly good structures just so blacks would leave. They changed their strategy and began creating quiet, but effective, coalitions.

From Massey and Denton:

> A typical organizational solution to the threat of black residential expansion was the formation of neighborhood "improvement associations." Although ostensibly charted for the purpose of promoting neighborhood

security and property values, their principle raison d'etre was the prevention of black entry and the enforcement of the color line.

These voluntary associations employed a variety of tools in their efforts to preserve the racial homogeneity of threatened neighborhoods. They lobbied city councils for zoning restrictions and for the closing of hotels and rooming houses that attracted blacks; they threatened boycotts of real estate agents who sold homes to blacks; they withdrew their patronage from white businesses that catered to black clients; they agitated for public investments in the neighborhood in order to increase property values and keep blacks out by economic means; they collected money to create funds to buy property back from black settlers or to purchase homes that remained vacant too long; they offered cash bonuses to black renters who agreed to leave the neighborhood.

These organizations also developed contracts called restrictive covenants. These were legal contracts wherein all the residents of a neighborhood signed an agreement stating they would not sell their homes to black people for a set period of time. The time period was usually around twenty years.

The use of restrictive covenants became popular quickly. As soon as one neighborhood had put one in place, contiguous neighborhoods decided that they, too, needed a similar covenant in place. The motivating factor, of course, was economic[26]. Whites felt that if blacks moved into their neighborhoods, the value of their homes would decrease. In order to protect their economic investments in their homes, they felt the restrictive covenants were necessary.

Childrearing in the 1920s

As noted in an earlier chapter, rich women like my great-grandmother Eliza and my grandmother Leah relied heavily on childcare books and discussions with other mothers. Their personal discussions

---

[26] This is not to say that the white homeowners were not also racist, they very well might have been, but the economic factors that sustained and encouraged bigotry and racism are important to note.

focused on putting into practice the latest research that had been announced in books and pamphlets published expressly for them.

When Otto and Leah began raising their two sons, the science of behaviorism, a subset of psychology, was extremely influential.

In *Raising Baby by the Book*, Grant explains:

> [P]rofessionals and parents alike during the 1910s and 1920s viewed the infant as being endowed with "strong and dangerous impulses" that must be eradicated...Thus mothers should beware of overly indulging their young ones, lest they mature into little tyrants.
>
> Mothers of the 1920s were enjoined to allow their infants to "cry it out," to avert "spoiling" and unruly behavior that might follow if babies were picked up whenever they cried. Informed parents were to approach problems of eating, sleeping, and elimination with impersonal objectivity. [There were] warnings against excessive displays of affection toward children.

My grandmother, Leah, fell in line with the modern mother's marching orders. She was very strict when raising her sons; almost abusive by today's standards. She thought what she was doing was right for her sons because she was following the instructions she read in books and pamphlets, often authored by doctors.

On the black side of the family, Jemima was raising her granddaughter Beatrice. She'd raised her three children, and was now raising another. She would not have been fretting over what the latest books had to say. She was far too tired to wring her hands over such esoteric concepts.

The Klan in Whitman County

The movie, *Birth of A Nation*, triggered the formation of Klan chapters all over the country. The Klan was larger and more diverse in the 1920s than it had been before, or has been since.

Whereas night riders and secret societies had always been popular in all the Southern states, there were suddenly Klan chapters in places like Topeka, Kansas; Stockton, California; Larimer, Wyoming; Portland,

Oregon and countless other cities as well as the sleepiest little towns.

There was also a Klan chapter in Whitman County, Washington.

It's hard for me to convey just how startling it was to learn this. My siblings and I had spent a lifetime believing that Lacrosse, Washington was a little slice of perfect human harmony. As children we'd been told the area was wholly white because black people didn't like living in cold climates. I believed that no one in the area could be a racist because becoming a racist, I thought, required contact. I believed all bigoted beliefs came from unfortunate personal interactions that resulted in misunderstandings.

Further, racist attitudes didn't seem like something people who lived in all-white areas would bother to pass on to their children. I guess I just thought it would be a stupid use of their time; like teaching scuba diving to a kid who would never visit the ocean.

An article in the *The Bunchgrass Historian,* written by Craig Holstine, called "The Ku Klux Klan in Whitman County in the 1920s" disabused me of my fanciful notions about Whitman County.

According to Holstine, Klan activity in Whitman County centered on disenfranchising Catholic voters, driving out a trade union thought to be communist in nature, and threatening people who were brewing alcohol, selling it, or drinking it.

A white man known to get drunk and beat his wife was much more likely to get a night visit from the Klan in Whitman County than was a black or Chinese family that worked hard and kept to themselves.

The article states that a Jewish businessman in the nearby town of Colfax was also left unmolested.

In 1920 there were fourteen blacks in Whitman County living among 31,323 whites. There were forty-one people classified into a group named "others"—that group included Chinese and American Indians. These low numbers may be the reason blacks were not a focus for Klan activity; they simply didn't pose any kind of threat to white power in the region.

The Washington State government seems to have been trying to dismantle the Klan or at least keep it from growing larger. They passed a law in the early 1920s making it illegal for people to gather in groups of three or more, with their faces disguised, unless it was for a masquerade ball.

Holstine notes that by the end of the 1920s, the Klan in Whitman County had dissolved. He theorizes that in these small towns, hooded men could easily be identified by their voices or the way they walked, thus making the secrecy of the Klan hard to maintain.

It is also stands to reason that with so many secret societies available to help manipulate the operations of their communities, a group that required dressing up in robes and carrying out cross-burning rituals in the middle of the night was probably not attractive to many people. Of all the secret societies, it could be said that the Klan, with its silly costumes, was far and away the least dignified.

Most secret societies aimed to keep a sophisticated aura and therefore avoided sloppy shows of violence. They would not have gone out in angry mobs; instead they would have looked for ways to be more like genteel puppeteers, delicately pulling just the right strings to get the outcomes they, as a group, desired for their communities.

Freemasons and Daughters of the Eastern Star

My grandparents were intensely involved in the Freemasons and its sister group, the Daughters of the Eastern Star. My grandmother had scrapbooks full of local news articles about the various events she and my grandfather participated in. Her jewelry boxes were filled with items bearing Freemason and Eastern Star emblems. There were cufflinks, amulets, lapel pins, and rings.

My grandmother told me that both of their organizations were very exclusive and the only way a person could join was to be invited by a member. They did not invite women to join unless they had money or their husband had a position of power. The members needed to have money, she explained, because the group had work to carry out, and they needed money to do their work. People who had power were also needed because they were able to help get things done. She likened their work to that of an informal city council. Their job, as they saw it, was to guide the women of the community toward behaving in accordance with community norms and values. I was too young at the time to realize that I would later want to know the details of the techniques by which they performed their "guidance."

The same was true, she said, of the Freemasons that my grandfather participated in; those men saw their job as that of guiding the male community members toward behaviors consistent with community norms and values.

Many people have developed theories about the secrets held and the activities engaged in by the Freemasons. A web search of phrases like "masons racist" or "masons illuminati" will bring up countless conspiracy theories about the shady practices of the various secret societies.

Taking what I hope is a less sensationalist perspective, I suspect that the rituals and symbols were consistent across the various chapters, and that those consistent tenets and practices were based on goodwill and high moral values. If particular chapters engaged in more sinister plots or more questionable rituals I'm thinking those would derive from the choices of that particular chapter's members.

Loewen, writing in *Sundown Towns*, notes two examples where more or less secret societies took action and spearheaded the racist banishments of families. In 1885, the Knights of Labor in Rock Springs, Wyoming led a mob of whites who massacred the town's 900 Chinese residents. Some were shot, some were burned alive in their homes and still others were driven into the countryside and left to freeze to death.

The other secret-society driven incident related in Loewen's book involved the banishment of blacks from Washington County, Indiana. The county had around 187 black residents just before the Civil War, yet, by 1870, only eighteen black residents remained. According to a local Washington County historian who spoke with Loewen, the expulsion was led by a society named the Knights of the Golden Circle.

Social psychology research predicts that these secret societies would be rich breeding grounds for embarrassingly evil plots that might arise for use against "undesirable" residents. The same research indicates that someone mild mannered, kind, charitable and honest by the light of day could easily have participated in the planning and carrying out of uncharacteristically sadistic plots when they operated under the perceived anonymity of roles outlined by these societies.

De-Individuation, Foot-In-The-Door, Self-Labeling and The Big Lie

Philip Zimbardo, in his book, *The Lucifer Effect: Understanding How Good People Turn Evil*, writes about techniques that social psychology researchers have proven, time and again, encourage good people to do evil things. Zimbardo:

Deindividuation makes the perpetrator anonymous, thereby reducing personal accountability, responsibility and self-monitoring. This allows perpetrators to act without conscience-inhibiting limits.

In other words, under the influences of deindividuation people begin to perceive of themselves less as individuals, with personalities, values, morals, and free will and more as cogs in a human machine of larger purpose.

Many studies have shown that masks, mirrored sunglasses, uniforms, costumes such as the hoods of Ku Klux Klan, and one-way glass can instantly change people's behavior, making them much more antisocial and cruel.

To encourage the deindividuation of individuals over time, organizations use techniques like the foot-in-the-door tactic. This tactic starts when a member is asked to do something small, and often harmless, because it serves the group. Once a member has completed their first task, they are encouraged to label themselves as someone who puts the needs of the group above their own needs. When the leadership of the group asks the individual to carry out the next task, usually involving a larger sacrifice of time and a greater suppression of individual needs or ethics, the member will go on to comply with that next act as well. So it goes, with each task requiring greater and greater suppression of one's own moral code in favor of something that will benefit the group.

Those who fall prey to the technique are not more evil, sadistic, or socially deviant than those who don't. In fact, throughout Zimbardo's book he provides numerous examples of how people who have participated in historical atrocities like The Rape of Nanking in the 1937, Hitler's Holocaust during the 1940s, and the Rwandan genocide of 1994 turn out to be very sane, moral people who believed that they had to do what they did in order to protect their loved ones and/or achieve a greater good.

Very often, that greater good is something social psychologists call *The Big Lie*. The name of the technique comes from Adolf Hitler's famous book, *Mein Kampf*. Hitler (in an English translation by James Murphy) explained:

> *In the big lie there is always a certain force of credibility; because the broad masses of a nation are always more easily corrupted in the deeper strata of their emotional nature than consciously or voluntarily; and thus in the primitive simplicity of their minds they more readily fall victims to the big lie than the small lie, since they themselves often tell small lies in little matters but would be ashamed to resort to large-scale falsehoods. It would never come into their heads to fabricate colossal untruths, and they would not believe that others could have the impudence to distort the truth so infamously. Even though the facts which prove this to be so may be brought clearly to their minds, they will still doubt and waver and will continue to think that there may be some other explanation. For the grossly impudent lie always leaves traces behind it, even after it has been nailed down, a fact which is known to all expert liars in this world and to all who conspire together in the art of lying.*

Wars, genocides, and mass killings of all kinds are founded on Big Lies. To take any group of people to battle it's critical to convince the group's members that they have come to a point where there is no longer any other choice: they have reached a point of "kill or be killed." In the United States we are taught that jihadists want to destroy our way of life because they hate our freedom. Those same jihadists are told that the US wants to destroy their way of life by corrupting them with porn, alcohol, drugs, divorce, gay marriage and who knows what else. Neither group is more moral than the other. Both believe that the killing is no longer avoidable. The Big Lie in this case is the inevitability of it all.

The Big Lies of slavery and Jim Crow were that 1) blacks were subhuman, 2) God gave white people the job of caring for blacks because they weren't capable of doing it themselves, and 3) that if whites didn't ensure that the white race remained pure, America would backslide into the mediocrity of a muddy brown race that would be have to be taken over by a new influx of pure whites from Europe.

White children during the Jim Crow era (and even within white supremacist organizations today) are taught from an early age to put the "good" of the all civilization ahead of fleeting "favors" for blacks.

It's easy to imagine a white child in the South who might observe the pleading eyes of a black child, learn that the "colored" water fountain was out of service, and wonder aloud why that thirsty black child shouldn't be allowed to sip from a "white" water fountain, *just this once.*

Yes, the child might be told, *that would be the easiest thing to do in the short term, but it would become a slippery slope and before long blacks would begin running wild.*

Chaos would ensue and soon enough civilized society would cease to exist. Wouldn't that be a far worse outcome for that black child than just being thirsty for an extra half hour? That child will find water soon enough – either at home or at another designated "colored" fountain.

See, God put us in charge of things because we are strong enough to do the right thing, even when it's hard. We would not be fulfilling God's wishes if we did not oversee their lives and keep them in line.

The *White Man's Burden* was one of several complimentary *Big Lies* that allowed whites to drift off to sleep with a clean conscience every night.

THE 1930s

The Great Depression

When the Great Depression hit, my white grandparents were not significantly affected. Otto and Leah's home, their cars, and their farm equipment were paid for. Their farmland had never required loan payments and had not been used as collateral for other debts. The years were lean for them, but they did not suffer to the degree that many others did.

It was during this time that Ai's authoritarian style and Otto's lack of ambition really paid off. Otto didn't actually own the land he was farming. The land still belonged to Ai, and Ai had always paid cash for everything.

Economic hard times are known to compound on those who are the poorest, causing them the most suffering of all. Our black family members would have been deeply affected by the depression because they were at the bottom of the economic system.

As the rest of the country plunged into desperate times, President Franklin D. Roosevelt responded with a series of programs that were designed to keep people from starving to death. The series of programs and policies were known as The New Deal.

A book by Ira Katznelson called *When Affirmative Action Was White* details how New Deal programs were designed to exclude blacks and offer the "hand up" to whites only.

Senators and congressmen from the South were happy to get the federal money for their states' residents, but they essentially said *not so fast* to Roosevelt's proposal of federal oversight. They wouldn't vote to pass his programs unless the wording included a promise that they would be able to decide, on a local level, which families would get the benefits. The

111

lawmakers of the Southern states didn't want that money to "spoil" black workers. They made sure the law allowed them to rig their systems to deny benefits to blacks. Once they had the promises they wanted, they voted to pass the legislation.

This strategy would work for Southern States over and over and it came to be known as the "states' rights" argument. Elected officials from the South used a particular phrase from our constitution[27] anytime they wanted federal money, but not federal oversight, which they considered "meddling." Because of this, the phrase "states' rights" came to be associated with Southern oppression of blacks.

Katznelson details how blacks were systematically denied access to the funds supplied by these Depression-era programs.

He writes:

> In some Georgia counties...federal relief monies excluded all blacks; in Mississippi, relief was limited to under 1 percent. Where landlords customarily had a paternalistic relationship with their tenants, particularly with sharecroppers, they possessed a strong impulse to prevent "their" black farmers from forging a direct relationship with federal relief.

In 1935, the Social Security Act (SSA) was making its way toward passage. The SSA would provide care for older citizens once they could no longer work. It also provided payments for women and their children if the husband/father died. The SSA, when it finally passed, excluded farm workers and domestic workers. Keep in mind, this was during a time when nearly every black man in the South was a farm worker and every black woman in the South was a domestic worker.

Many historians point out the fact that the exclusion of farm workers and domestics also hurt poor whites. They claim that this proves the policy could not have been racially motivated, yet we know from history that rich whites have been more than willing to betray poor whites when a policy serves their economic interests as elites. Elites could be confident that if poor whites realized the policy would hurt them financially, they could be

---

[27] It's called the enumerated powers clause and it's a list of things the Federal Government is allowed to govern. Everything not on the list is, by default, left for the states to run.

easily manipulated into blaming poor blacks for their problems.

How could they afford to feel so confident? Because it had been working for so long. Remember back in 1866, a year after slavery was overturned? Black people who had spent their lives carrying freeloading whites on their backs were painted as freeloaders almost overnight.

The propaganda peddled by rich whites has worked pretty much every time.

In any event, farm and domestic workers were excluded from Social Security benefits and Katznelson details the arguments leading up to the bill's passage. These details make it clear that white Southerners insisted on these workers' exclusion expressly because they didn't want blacks to be able to get the benefits.

These special categories (among others) are still in effect today. A nanny will not qualify for Social Security unless they report at least $1,900 a year in wages. That's just $150 a month. Most domestics are paid higher wages than that, so they should easily qualify.

But often, this "easy" qualification never happens.

Here's why:

Imagine a rich family, we'll call them the Ritzes. Then imagine a worker, we'll call her Linh, and we'll imagine her as a first-generation Vietnamese immigrant. The Ritzes want to hire Linh as a full-time domestic worker. They offer her the job and offer also to pay her "off the books."

Linh doesn't understand the term. The Ritzes explain that by not reporting to the government that they have hired her, she will not have to pay taxes on her earnings. They describe government paperwork and deductions that don't sound good to Linh.

Linh agrees to be paid cash each week. Linh is negotiating salary based on the cash she needs to pay her bills and feed her children. The amount they offer to pay her is enough to cover those needs so she accepts it. When the Ritz's offer her this "deal" they are actually creating a much better deal for themselves. By not reporting their employment of Linh, they get out of paying the employer part of Linh's taxes.

Linh doesn't understand the benefits for the Ritzes and the Ritzes aren't motivated to help her understand. The money that the Ritzes would be paying as Linh's employer would set up Social Security, Medicare and Unemployment benefits for Linh. If Linh needs to make $320 a week in take-home pay to cover her bills, the Ritz's can shell out $320 cash off the books or they can shell out $380 a week and cover her for Social Security and Medicare as well. For close to $500 extra a year Linh would also be covered for unemployment benefits.

Linh ends up working for the Ritzes for twenty years and during that time no one ever reports her income as the Ritzes' employee. When she injures her hip and can't work as effectively as before, the Ritzes "let her go."

They don't have to pay her severance and she doesn't qualify for unemployment because no one has ever paid into the system for her.

Now she has no choice but to apply for welfare. This subjects her to much more bureaucracy and humiliation than she would have to go through if she were a recipient of unemployment and Social Security benefits. In her old age, she will not get Social Security even though she has worked very hard her entire life.

When I lost my job in 2011, I qualified for unemployment benefits. I was what the rich call a "maker" and I benefitted from a fund I had deposited money into with each paycheck I received. I could hold my head high and claim that I wasn't on the dole because I was simply spending my own emergency fund.

When Linh has to go on welfare because the Ritzes tricked her out of qualifying, it looks like she's a "taker."

But who are the real takers in this scenario? Linh, who worked so hard for twenty years? Or the Ritzes who tricked her out of the dignity of receiving Social Security like other hard workers?

When a person agrees to be paid cash and has no other job that qualifies them for Social Security and unemployment benefits, they're being taken advantage of by their employers. If the work is very short term perhaps that's not a big deal, but if the work is full-on employment, the employers are exploiters.

Leah Tyler's Black Ancestors in the 1930s

The 1930 Census record for the black side of our family is somewhat disheartening. Remember that in 1920, Jemima, her son General Sherman and her granddaughter Beatrice were living together. Tolliver had died and Jemima's other children William H. and Videlia were not listed as living in her home. I theorized that Videlia was working as a live-in maid for a white family and I crossed my fingers that William had gone to Chicago as part of the first wave in the Great Migration.

In 1930, we see even further splintering of the family. Jemima died between 1920 and 1930. Sherman left Wilmot, Arkansas and moved to nearby Monroe, Louisiana. He was working in a paper mill and living in a boardinghouse.

Beatrice had been sent to live with an older black woman in nearby Gould, Arkansas. The older woman was a sharecropper, and Beatrice was listed in the census as her adopted daughter. The adoptive mother, Belle McTory, was listed with an occupation of farmer, and Beatrice's occupation was listed as a farm laborer.

Poor Beatrice had lost her grandmother, Jemima, whom she may have come to see as her mother. The closest thing to a father figure she'd ever known was her Uncle Sherman, yet economic conditions seem to have forced them apart as well.

She had been farmed out to a friend or acquaintance either in an adoption capacity (at best) or in an indentured servitude arrangement (at worst). Beatrice might have counted herself as all alone in the world.

The bright spot on the 1930 census record though, is the checkbox that indicates Beatrice was attending school. Gould, Arkansas, was larger than Wilmot and the move seemed to have enabled Beatrice, my husband's grandmother, to finally attend school. Beatrice was already seventeen or eighteen years old, though, and it wouldn't be long before she'd want to start a family of her own.

Leah Tyler's White Ancestors in the 1930s

According to the 1930 census, Otto and his wife Leah were living in

Whitman County, Washington, still farming the parcel of land Ai had set up for them. Their sons were, of course, in school.

As previously noted, they spent a lot of their social time involved in Freemason and Eastern Star activities. They also socialized with Otto's many siblings' families.

People like Otto and Leah (neither of whom had ever met a black person), were afraid of black people. Their fear was based entirely on stories they'd heard or newspaper articles and books they'd read.

Perhaps they'd even seen the film *Birth of a Nation* or read *The Clansman*. Their exposure to propaganda about the lawlessness of blacks would have convinced them that Giant Negroes were constantly plotting to bring crime and danger to their communities.

In addition to their naiveté

Figure 17: Otto's mother-in-law, Otto and his two sons. The structures in the background are barns that were being refurbished.

with regard to those who did not look like them, they were also fairly ignorant about how the world worked. That ignorance allowed them to indulge in an extremely simplified world view. From what they'd been taught and seen around them those who worked hard benefitted from that work. Those who don't want to work, or who choose to work as little as possible, ended up poor.

Birth Control in the 1930s

Otto and Leah's sons were aged seven and eight in 1930. Their last child, my mother, would come thirteen years later, in 1943. This put twenty years between my mother and her brothers. Decades later, on videotape, my grandparents were asked why there had been so many years in between their first two boys and their baby girl.

I held the camera on my grandparents as my mother asked, "What was going on in those twenty years in between?"

My feisty grandmother replied, "Well, we were busy working for the Red Cross." Her answer brought a round of laughter from everyone in the family and a quiet chortle from Otto.

We did not pressure her further, even though we were all curious. How had they avoided having another child all those years?

According to a white paper on the history of contraception published by Planned Parenthood in November of 2006, middle-class white women of that time period tended to favor abstinence.

While condoms had existed for centuries, speaking of them was considered obscene and doctors would only prescribe them for men who reported plans to have extramarital sex. They were not allowed for men hoping to avoid having more children with their wife.

President Teddy Roosevelt had warned white citizens in 1903 that they should have as many children as they could because limiting white children would create a numeric disadvantage. Roosevelt called birth control "race suicide."

Three decades later, birth control was still a taboo subject. It wasn't until 1938 that a federal judge would lift a federal ban on the discussion of birth control. Prior to the lifting of the ban, discussions about birth control were against the law.

But it wasn't just the discussions that were looked down on, my grandmother would have been thought unpatriotic if she'd admitted she was acting to avoid additional pregnancies.

It's easy to imagine my timid grandfather working up the nerve to make a move on my grandmother as rarely as once every few months, only to have his advances shut down by my strong-willed grandmother.

As for the birth control methods Beatrice might have used, several *Slave Narratives* mentioned cotton root bark as an abortive elixir. If herbal methods were known by Jemima, she would most likely have taught them to both Videlia and Beatrice.

Abstinence as birth control, especially as a white strategy and specifically in the South, would have put Videlia and Beatrice even more at risk of being raped by white men.

Black women were routinely exploited[28] by white male employers (or even any white man they happened to cross paths with), but this exploitation would surely have increased during periods when a white man's wife was refusing to participate in her "wifely duties."

If a black woman was working as a domestic, she was expected to indulge her employers' advances as well as those of any sons he had living at home. If these women did not submit, they would often be forced. Anything other than willing participation might end in their being fired, and word would be passed around town that they should not be offered employment by any other family.

In short, the lack of birth control for black women was far more damaging for them than it was for white women.

From the *Jim Crow Narrative* of Ann Pointer:

> *Everywhere the [white] man has got, maybe from eight to fifteen tenants, on his place, there is a woman there that he is messing with. Then you going to see the flowers start to blooming, the children start to popping.*

> *You don't know what he's doing until the flowers start to blooming, that's what they say. When you see these mixed-up children come out {snap} from there, you know that he's stirring about.*

> *He does it undercover, but everybody know what's going on. But they ain't going to say nothing. They talk about it, but they can't do nothing about it because the man own them. It's like I say, what is slavery? Yes, they abolished the chains, they abolished this here, abolished that, but you still a slave—you understand me?*

> *You don't have to wonder about these flowers blooming. You can just look*

---

[28] For more on this topic see: Danielle L. McGuire, *At the Dark End of the Street: Black Women, Rape, and Resistance—A New History of the Civil Rights Movement from Rosa Parks to the Rise of Black Power*

at the population and tell. Haven't you paid attention to that? Different people mixed up. You don't know what they are.

They got some everything in them, and you can see that there's been visitation by someone just [by] looking at the group, this bouquet. That's what I'm saying. And the Klan [is] talking about they want a pure race. Now who mixed up this race, you understand me?

The bouquets have been made now. In the classroom, if you look at a class of 32 children, you see some of everything. You know what I'm saying. It's been like that all of the time, and it brought about a lot of dissension among the blacks as well as whites.

If a [black] man's got a wife, and she have a white baby, he on the man's place [and] he can't say nothing. You see what I'm talking about? Do you see the injustice in that?

Even though he doesn't like it. Now you know what he's going to do? He's going to mistreat his wife under the cover and give her a very, very bad time, and this child will be knocked about, which is wrong.

Going back to the [white] man, he done stood it all up and he gone on about his business, left it like that.

As if the lives of black men weren't emasculating enough under the rules of Jim Crow, many black men were also forced to care for a white man's child, the result of his wife having been raped, and he had to feed that child from the same pitiful earnings he was using to raise his own children.

Continued Disparities in Health Care

My white great-grandparents, Ai and Eliza, had moved to Pasadena, California, in part because one of their daughters contracted tuberculosis. During that time period, people with tuberculosis had few options. Many were put in sanitariums in an attempt to keep the disease from spreading. Ai and Eliza would have spent any amount necessary on a cure, if only one had been available. Instead, they could only hope the sunny weather of Southern California might keep her alive a little longer. Like most of those infected, she died within five years of her infection.

Meanwhile, Jemima, Tolliver, their children and grandchildren had little health care available to them over the years. We cannot know whether Tolliver and Jemima's deaths might have been delayed if Medicare had existed, or they'd had access to better health care by some other means.

Ira Katznelson explains:

> Black health, not surprisingly, reflected a dire state of poverty. The cost of a doctor's visit, usually $3 in the early 1930s, was out of reach for most maids and farmworkers. So, too, was medicine. Most southern hospitals refused to admit African American patients.

Blacks were educated and licensed as physicians, but hospitals often did not allow them to use their facilities so they were unable to perform surgery and other advanced medical procedures. They were left to practice independently, and often their only potential patients couldn't afford to pay them.

Sherman, William, Videlia and Beatrice probably relied on herbal remedies most of the time. It would have been rare for them to seek and receive medical care from doctors and nurses because it was far too expensive.

Imagine if Sherman had attempted to get medical treatment at the Tuskegee Institute, the venerated home-base of Booker T. Washington, and an institution that many blacks revered, but few could afford.

Let's say that he goes there seeking medical care only because the economic depression has rendered him desperate, and it is his last hope. Not only do they accept him in for a doctor's visit that day, at the end of the visit, they offer him an amazing deal.

It's sounds almost too good to be true. Tuskegee has offered him totally free health benefits including burial insurance and regularly scheduled examinations. All prescribed medications, all procedures, any surgeries needed: all of it will be covered.

Sherman would simply have to agree to return regularly for examinations. On examination days he would receive free meals and sometimes a little bit of cash.

Free food was certainly no pittance during the Great Depression. What a blessing that would have been for a man like Sherman who was otherwise unable to afford healthcare.

The program I'm describing began in 1932 and operated for forty years. The program treated around 600 of black men, free of charge.

Then, in 1972, details of the medical program were leaked to the media, exposing the truth.

Harriet A. Washington covers the Tuskegee Syphilis Experiment in her book *Medical Apartheid: The Dark History of Medical Experimentation on Black Americans from Colonial Times to the Present.*

White officials from the Public Health Service of the federal government partnered with the famed Tuskegee Institute for an experiment studying the long-term effects of syphilis.

Black men who had contracted syphilis were offered membership in the program but were not told they had the disease. Eight years after the study began, a cure for syphilis was discovered.

The experiment continued as planned. Rather than curing these men of their disease using penicillin, the study overseers opted to continue studying the natural progression of the untreated disease. Their only interest was in performing autopsies on these men's dead bodies.

Washington writes:

> O. C. Wenger, the PHS senior officer for its syphilis programs, swept them aside that year: "As I see it, we have no further interest in these patients until they die."

Those who died before 1972, when the whistleblowers revealed the truth, were never made aware they carried the disease. Many of the study participants infected their wives. Babies born to those infected wives contracted congenital syphilis, a horrifying disease with numerous symptoms that these families would have struggled to have treated, given that they were too poor to afford healthcare in the first place.

Laborers in Wheat Harvesting Communities

My grandparents lived in a small house built on their land in Whitman County. They received their mail at the Lacrosse, Washington post office.

Lacrosse's population was exclusively white. During the era of banishments and sundown towns Lacrosse would have had a choice of either remaining all white or becoming a sundown town.

Why hadn't Lacrosse become a sundown town instead? After all, sundown towns were efficient at exploiting black labor and creating luxury for whites by doing so. To deny blacks residence nearby was to give up the chance for farmers to have super-cheap field hands, and for farmers' wives to have the luxury of maids and cooks.

To become a Sundown Town. Lacrosse would have needed:

1) Open land surrounding the city proper, such that it could be declared a separate "black" town.

2) Relatively steady work that blacks would be interested in performing, and that they could perform strictly during daylight hours.

There was plenty of open land that could have been assigned as the "black" town. That would have been easy to accomplish.

It was the steady work that didn't really exist. It's feasible that blacks could have been hired as harvest workers, but they weren't.

To understand why blacks were not hired for harvest work, it's important to understand how harvest work was carried out by my grandparents.

Each year in the last weeks before harvest, a farmer like my grandfather (and later, my uncle) would employ several men to help out. My mother recalls that the harvest workers often lived together in a sort of barracks setup in the barn. This enabled the harvest team to get started very early each morning and work until sundown each evening.

The days would start early with my grandmother or aunt serving a large breakfast to the men. The men would go out and work all morning then, my grandmother or aunt would deliver the lunch meal to them. My uncle might use a CB-radio to let my aunt know where they'd be taking the meal.

The workers might congregate close to wherever the harvester combine was cutting. Other times, the workers might *not* congregate (my grandfather or uncle would make that decision) and my grandmother or aunt would drive to each truck separately, to drop off that day's lunch.

Throughout each day of the harvest, once a truck bed was filled with grain, the driver would catch the road into Lacrosse where they'd empty the grain at the grain elevator. After emptying their load, they would return to the field for another.

Whitman County, Washington farmers could have hired American Indians, Chinese Americans or blacks as the truck drivers. They could have paid much lower wages to those workers than they paid to white workers, and therefore increased their profits.

But perhaps the farmers believed that members of those ethnic groups would take off in the trucks, never to return. Each driver operated independently so it would have been fairly easy for a worker to drop off his grain and head out of town in any direction that pleased him. This, obviously, would have created a great hardship on these farms at exactly the moment when efficiency was so critical.

Also, if they had hired "undesirables," the entire harvest system of meals would've had to change radically. It would probably have been considered improper for my grandmother or aunt to serve meals to those workers directly. Therefore, another worker, likely a woman of color, would need to be hired to serve the workers' meals.

My grandfather and uncle would have had to take meals separately from their workers in order to establish the separateness needed to justify the lower wages. The ability to put in long hours on consecutive days would have been hobbled by the need to get workers to and from whatever Darktown the workers were quarantined into for off work hours.

Simply put, the logistics would have been an absolute nightmare and the savings in labor costs would most certainly have been offset by other costs for lodging and meals and other inconveniences brought on by the need for racial separation.

Wheat farming simply didn't lend itself to the exploitation of black (or other oppressed groups') labor. Most harvest workers came to the area strictly for the harvest season.

Those whites who did stay year-round worked stocking shelves in the grocery store or as mechanics at the gas station. These non-land-owning whites lived north of the railroad tracks. While southern Lacrosse had paved streets, the north side had only dirt roads. It wasn't that Lacrosse officials didn't have money to pave the roads, the dirt roads were an important symbol. It reminded poor whites of their place in the pecking order. If poor whites had agitated for better conditions, it's likely that Indians or Chinese would have been used to threaten them with replacement.

Seasonal workers came from nearby cities to work the harvest and were paid much better for those days of labor than they were paid for city jobs. In all the years my grandfather and uncle farmed, they were never approached by a harvest worker demanding more pay or better conditions. So without labor disputes to settle, ethnic laborers were never needed as a wedge.

My thought experiment and my conclusion serve a purpose. I've been able to live most of my life with the knowledge that my mother's parents did not express open hatred of blacks and they did not exploit them economically, but of course, I've spent too many years feeling smug about it.

Understanding American history as I now do, I have to admit (to myself especially) that if the farmers in Whitman County could have found a way to exploit black, Indian, or Chinese labor, they would have. And if they'd been exploiting that labor they would have needed to convince themselves, and teach their children, that those exploited laborers were less than human.

I can fantasize that my ancestors would have turned out to be the local *Good White People* who objected to the ill treatment of laborers, but to do so is ridiculously self-serving. What passed for *Good White People* back then were often people who had no issue with the pitiful wages being paid, they only wanted the *Evil White People* to smile more and make small talk as they handed over the measly wages.

Otto Inherits Some Wheat Land

Ai died in 1939. Half the land was retained by his wife, Eliza. The other half was distributed to Ai's children, including my grandfather, Otto.

Otto was forty years old when he got that first half of his inheritance. Until that time, he'd been operating directly under his father's formidable thumb. Once his father had passed, he finally had a measure of freedom. It wasn't clear to me that his mother might have been just as domineering a force in his life as his father had been – that realization came later, when I learned more about Otto's surprising decisions shortly after her death in the 1950s.

The Othering Process

As we've already discussed, to set the stage for systematic violence, certain psychological shifts need to be encouraged. Perpetrators need to undergo deindividuation so they can eschew responsibility for the actions they will take. Those targeted for violence need be dehumanized so that perpetrators can further avoid crises of conscience. Systematic dehumanization is called "othering."

Long-term *othering* propaganda, deftly orchestrated, lays a foundation that can be used on short notice to call the masses to violent action. Zimbardo explains the *othering* process:

> *The process begins with creating stereotyped conceptions of the other, dehumanized perceptions of the other, the other as worthless, the other as all-powerful, the other as demonic, the other as an abstract monster, the other as a fundamental threat to our cherished values and beliefs.*

> *With public fear notched up and the enemy threat imminent, reasonable people act irrationally, independent people act in mindless conformity, and peaceful people act as warriors. Dramatic visual images of the enemy on posters, television, magazine covers, movies and the Internet imprint on the recesses of the limbic system, the primitive brain, with the powerful emotions of fear and hate.*

THE 1940s

When the 1940s began, World War II was already underway for other nations. The United States had not yet become involved, but the Japanese would bomb Pearl Harbor on December 7, 1941 and shortly after that attack President Roosevelt would announce that we were declaring war on Japan. The close of the war came four years later, in 1945. The US dropped bombs on Hiroshima and Nagasaki and those bombings resulted in Japan's surrender.

The 1940s are thought of, in retrospect, as synonymous with World War II. Nearly everything about the lives of US citizens during that decade was tempered by, or in reaction to, the war that was raging in Europe and Asia. Once the war was over, from 1945 onward, Americans were focused on rebuilding their lives. For some families, the latter half of the 40s required accepting the loss of sons, brothers, boyfriends and husbands. For all families, the latter half of the 1940s involved a new sense of solidarity and pride in being "American," though it was still a little unclear what that label really meant because we were still a nation of immigrants.

Three years after my mother was born in Washington (1943), my husband's father, Bill, was born in Monroe, Louisiana (1946). My mother's birth after Otto and Leah's fortieth birthdays closed the generational mismatch in my husband's and my family's timelines.

Leah Tyler's White Ancestors in the 1940s

Looking in the census records from 1940, I find my grandparents, Otto and Leah, just where I expected they'd be; farming in Whitman County, Washington. My uncles were eighteen and seventeen years old. The Great Depression had finally lifted and most US citizens had started

Figure 18: My mother's brother (center) went to war. Leland died fighting in Italy and was buried in Salerno.

feeling optimistic about the future.

Otto's widowed mother was still alive and had moved to the city of Spokane.

The following year, 1941, when the US declared war on Japan, worries about harvest yields would take a back seat to worries about Whitman County's soldier sons. This time it was Otto's turn to try to keep his own sons out of soldiers' uniforms.

Otto's youthful enthusiasm for war, now aged by twenty years, had morphed into a mature realization that people who went away as soldiers, often didn't return.

He put his eldest son, Lester, in charge of farming the family land. Anyone farming the land was considered vital to the war effort so Lester was given an exemption. The second son, Leland, was enrolled in Washington State College and the family hoped that he would be passed over based on something like a student deferment, but that didn't happen.

When my uncle went away in early 1943, his forty year-old mother was pregnant with his sister, my mother, who would be named Kay Joy. My mother had never met her brother Leland but he'd received the news of her birth and knew what she'd been named. Other than that, there wasn't much more my mother could tell us about him.

When I was around eight years old, we were visiting my grandparents in Whitman County and I asked my grandmother about my

Uncle Leland. She left for a moment and returned to the table carrying two big boxes. She opened them, pulling out scrapbooks and smaller boxes and she arrayed them across the table.

She picked up a small jewelry-type box and opened it to show me his purple heart. She then picked up some fabric rolled around two dowel rods. As she unrolled, I saw that the fabric had been fashioned into two small flags.

"This is the first one and it has a blue star. I hung it up just after he left," she said, her voice beginning to shake.

She pulled the top flag aside, revealing the second and placing her finger on the gold star in the center. "This one—"

I looked up to see tears streaming down her face. She stood up from the table and her housecoat became a blur of pastel flowers. The snap of her slippers against her heels became a frantic rhythm as she disappeared behind her bedroom door.

My grandfather came over to where I sat, bewildered. He began placing all the smaller boxes and books back into the larger boxes. He grumbled as he did it, but I couldn't make out what he was saying. I sat still and silent as he packed everything away and took it from the table. Now, there were tears on my cheeks. Not for the loss of my uncle, but for the pain my grandfather was accusing me of having caused my grandmother.

A few years later, I asked again and this time my grandmother put them in the guest room for me and told me to look through them on my own. I spent several hours reading through diaries, letters and Western Union telegrams. I came to know my Uncle Leland just as I might a famous historical figure or a fictional character in a novel.

The war had been underway for a little over a year when Leland was called up in February of 1943. He started out at Camp Wolters in Texas.

On June 9, 1943 his company was shipped out of Texas on their way to Camp Shenango, Pennsylvania. As his train rattled northward, his mother was being driven to the hospital in the nearby town of Colfax where she'd give birth to his sister.

From the time Leland had been drafted, his parents had been

scheming to get him released. They'd written letters to everyone they could imagine might help. The replies came back with "furlough," "deferment," "discharge," and "release" conjectures but no hard results.

Otto and Leah had concocted a story about a dire situation on their farmland. Their US Congressman, Hal Holmes, advised them to gather affidavits from neighboring farmers who could back up their claim of the emergency requiring Leland's return.

The problem was, their neighbors had sons conscripted as well and there was no actual emergency. Their claim was simply fraudulent, an act of desperation aimed at forcing the return of their son lest he die in battle.

Fearing that Leland's movement from Texas to Pennsylvania meant their time was short, my grandfather got in one of his cars and drove 2,275 miles to Greenville, Pennsylvania.

Months before, a nationwide speed limit of 35 miles per hour had been instituted as a way to save tire wear because rubber was under ration. Obeying this speed limit, it would have taken Otto 67 hours of driving at the maximum allowed speed in order to reach Pennsylvania.

Gasoline was also being rationed. Luckily for him, as a farmer, Otto had a right to purchase additional ration stamps. He almost certainly committed some kind of fraud in order to get enough gas ration stamps to make it all the way to Pennsylvania.

Otto sent a telegram back to his wife, my grandmother, Leah, on June 24th, 1943. In that

Figure 19: Baby Kay Joy (my mother) on her father, Otto's knee. She was born in 1943.

telegram he stated:

"Arrived six this morning. Talked to Leland till 1130. See him at 7. Don't know when [I] will start home."

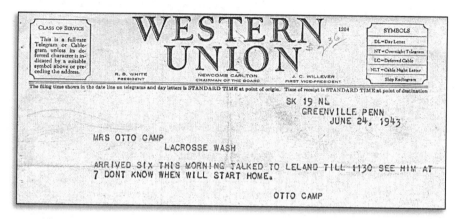

Figure 20: Otto sent word back to Whitman County, Washington that he'd arrived in Pennsylvania.

There are no further records of Otto's activities in Pennsylvania after that first telegram announcing he'd arrived. Before leaving, he'd promised my grandmother he would make face-to-face appeals to every man in Leland's chain of command, as high as he needed to go, until one of them finally granted Leland's release into his custody.

But the big scrapbook shows the next correspondence between Leland and his parents came when he sent them notice that he was shipping out.

According to Leland's diary, on July 25th he boarded a ship bound for what he called Oran, North Africa, a city in present-day Algeria. He noted that he was on a ship that was part of a 91 ship convoy.

On August 13th, he still hadn't reached Oran, but he was getting close. In his diary, writing just a few days after my mother's two-month-old celebration, he noted:

Today is Friday the 13th and nothing has happened as yet. It is now 7 o'clock and the Mediterranean Sea is calm. We passed the Rock of Gibraltar last night and no one saw it. I gave gun watch from 12 midnight to 4 am. [It gets] pretty cold and wet. The waves roll over the top and get you all wet. We expect to reach Oran tomorrow sometime. I am about 3,500 miles out at sea today and that's a mighty long way from home.

August 19th he wrote:

Joined the 36 Division and 141st Regiment. Have slept on the ground for three nights and expect to move out any time. Go swimming all day in the Med Sea.

When he referred to "swimming" he was most likely joking. After all, he was actually being trained for an amphibious assault.

In a letter written on September 1st, he seemed scared. His unit was preparing to invade Italy at Salerno as part of Operation Avalanche. He probably didn't know any of the specifics, but even if he had, he couldn't have written about them. That sort of information would have been censored from his mail.

Instead, he wrote:

Dear Folks, Kay + Les,

Well I finally got with my division and am with them for good now I guess. They are a bunch of nice fellows in the 36th Division. Our bunch I started with from the states got all split up over here...How is sister Kay? I'll bet she's growing already. Tell Les hello from me + I'm sure glad he's not in my place. Nobody wants to be where I am now or where I am going to be. Don't be worried if you don't receive a letter for a while because I'll write if I can + when I can. Don't forget, I've always thought the world of you + Daddy, Les and Kay + I still am thinking the same. Hope this is over soon.

Your loving Son,

Leland.

A telegram arrived in Lacrosse, Washington, on October 6, 1943. It announced that Leland was dead. There were a high number of casualties for the Allies during that landing at Salerno. My grandmother wrote letters and placed phone calls trying to discover more information but military officials had nothing to share – the casualties were too numerous and the operation had been too chaotic.

Later, a soldier who'd been on the same LCM3 landing craft would explain to my grandmother that Leland had been hit by bullets before he could even disembark. His corpse lay in the LCM3 for almost a week before the Allies secured the beach enough that officials could safely take inventory and get an official count of those lost.

Leland's death eviscerated my grandparents. Rendered gutless when my mother was less than a year old, they had nothing to prop them up or fortify them in the face of her whims and wishes. From an early age, five or six years old even, she recognized their intemperance and it shamed her. She began to calibrate her requests to avoid being lavished. In that way, my mother's brother's death cast a long shadow over her life.

Leah Tyler's Black Ancestors in the 1940s

Bill's parents, Beatrice and Sampson Tyler, had settled in Monroe, Louisiana. Sampson was fifteen years older than Beatrice. He'd served in World War I and in doing so, had qualified for veteran's benefits. Most black men had been diverted into labor units during World War I and given duties that cut them off from receiving soldier's benefits but it seemed Sampson had been among the lucky few.

On his draft registration card two decades prior, he'd listed his employer as a Carl McHenry. I found two Carl McHenrys living in Monroe in the 1910 census. One was a doctor, and the other was a lawyer. Being employed by a doctor or lawyer might have meant different duties for Sampson compared to other blacks of the area and era. His skills may have helped him get drafted into the service as a soldier and not a laborer.

According to family recollections, Sampson had access to health care for himself, Beatrice, and their children. In that respect, while he was significantly older than Beatrice, he would have been a good catch. Also, had she been looking to get out from under the life of sharecropping with her adoptive mother, Belle McTory, a marriage and a move to a big city like Monroe would have been an incredible opportunity.

I'm told by family that during the war Beatrice was a tap dancer on a radio show in Monroe. Learning of her tap-dancing career encouraged me to imagine her as someone with an open heart and an easy laugh. Maybe she was nothing like that, but once I learned she was a well-known radio figure around Monroe, that's how I began imagining her.

Childrearing in the 1940s

In 1946, a doctor named Benjamin Spock published a book on raising children that advocated a reversal of the harsh methods that had dominated since the 1910s.

In *Raising Baby by the Book*, Grant notes that Spock's book was priced very low and sold three-quarters of a million copies in its first year of publication.

What my grandmother read in Spock's book would give her permission to raise my mother in ways that were a complete about-face from the methods she'd used with her sons.

In the first edition of *The Commonsense Book of Baby and Child Care*, Spock espoused ideas like:

> *Your baby is born to be a reasonable, friendly human being. If you treat him nicely, he won't take advantage of you.*

And:

> *[E]ach child wants, himself, to eat at sensible hours and later learn table manners...In all these habits he will fit into the family's way of doing things sooner or later without much effort on your part.*

Spock's book was republished many times and in each new edition, Spock took into account feedback he'd received from mothers who'd come to see him or who had written him letters.

Spock later explained[29] that his first edition had been focused on shifting parents' techniques to fit the, then modern, understanding of a developing child's needs:

> *[W]hen I was writing the first edition, between 1943 and 1946, the attitude of the majority of people toward infant feeding, toilet training, and general child management was still fairly strict and inflexible. However, the need for greater understanding of children and for flexibility in their care had been made clear by educators, psychoanalysts, and pediatricians and I was trying to encourage this.*

Dr. Spock's philosophy in the late 1940s was a blessing for my

---

[29] In the forward to the 1957 version of the book.

grandmother. The hole left in her heart by Leland's death meant she had a deep need to cuddle, coddle, pamper, and indulge her young daughter, Kay Joy, without having to worry that the baby would be ruined by that affection. Rather than following Dr. Spock to the letter, Leah would have his book to back her up in the event that someone challenged her choices as a mother.

Most people would predict that a child raised the way my mother was would grow up to be an intolerably selfish and self-centered person. For some reason, my mother turned out just the opposite. She was kind, and generous and she relegated her needs and wants to almost everyone who crossed her path.

When my father held up her kindness as one of his favorite things about her, she explained that she'd developed that giving nature because, as a child, whenever she had friends over to play, she'd feared they would get jealous or angry and choose to leave. She made the choice to ensure that those around her always felt included in her good fortune, not cut off from it.

My mother was living proof that so-called "spoiled" children don't necessarily become sociopathically self-absorbed.

Spock's encouragement in the early 1940s ushered in a more gentle period in childrearing for many American families. It wasn't only whites who were reading Spock's book, within the homes of middle-class black families, Spock was similarly popular.

Still, Sampson and Beatrice weren't among those extraordinary blacks who'd succeeded in attaining a middle-class lifestyle. They were still poor and were still living in the Jim Crow South. That meant they had to parent Bill and their other children in ways that would prepare them to survive under those conditions.

Bill had to learn to follow even capricious orders without question. The rule among many poor, black, Southern families was that willful children needed to be broken by their parents because if they weren't, they would be killed by whites[30].

---

[30] The autobiography of Ta-Nehisi Coates, *The Beautiful Struggle: A Father, Two Sons, and an Unlikely Road to Manhood* contains a scene in which his father tells his mother as much.

The training for Bill would be just as it had been for his mother: follow orders, don't try to negotiate, don't question authority, don't expect fair treatment, and don't expect praise.

Internment Camps for American Citizens of Japanese Descent

Less than two months after the Japanese surprise attack on Pearl Harbor, a presidential order was signed proscribing the building of detention camps for Americans of Japanese descent.

As with any oppression of a people, those not oppressed often stand by, hoping for an opportunity to take advantage of the situation. When Japanese-Americans became aware that they'd been ordered to report to the camps, many arranged to quickly sell their land and businesses. Selling under such conditions meant they did not have the leverage to secure a fair deal for themselves. In these transactions, the sellers got far less money than what their land was worth and the buyers got land at severely discounted prices.

As we've seen, California, Oregon, and Washington already had a long history of anti-Chinese and anti-Japanese sentiment so it shouldn't have been surprising that racists along the West Coast saw the war as an opportunity to undermine Japanese people who had worked to build businesses or who owned farms.

The internment laws were popular among white farmers. Many resented Japanese land ownership and looked forward to the prospect of those families being uprooted in a way that might cause them to lose their livelihoods.

In a 1942 issue of the Saturday Evening Post, Austin E. Anson, managing secretary of the Salinas Vegetable Grower-Shipper Association, told an interviewer:

> We're charged with wanting to get rid of the [Japanese] for selfish reasons. We do. It's a question of whether the white man lives on the Pacific Coast or the brown men. They came into this valley to work, and they stayed to take over. If all the [Japanese] were removed tomorrow, we'd never miss them in two weeks, because the white farmers can take over and produce

everything the [Japanese farmer] grows. And we do not want them back when the war ends, either.

Some of those who were children at the time of internment are still alive today[31].

Blockbusting in Northern Cities

Just as they had during World War I, blacks flocked to the Northern cities during the second world war. They aimed to take advantage of the employment openings in factories there. Blacks arriving from the South faced a similar housing crisis to the one that migrants had faced during the first world war. In looking for shelter, blacks were not free to spill over into adjacent white neighborhoods because most northern cities still practiced strict segregation. The segregation was maintained through the collusion of real estate agents, homeowners, and apartment landlords.

Whites believed the restrictive covenants they'd developed in the 1920s and 30s were legal because they were private contracts between individuals. Then, in 1948, a case called *Shelley v. Kraemer*, made its way to the Supreme Court. The Court ruled that these covenants were, in fact, a violation of civil rights.

With restrictive covenants now illegal (and therefore non-binding) real estate agents saw an opening. They created and carried out a money-making scheme that would later come to be called *blockbusting*.

The first step in blockbusting was to arrange to help a black family purchase a home in an otherwise all-white neighborhood. If an actual sale was too costly, just the rumor of a new black resident would often suffice. In a relatively famous scheme agents hired a well-dressed black woman to walk through a white neighborhood pushing a baby carriage. Since she wasn't wearing a maid's uniform, people drew the intended conclusion that the woman had purchased a home in the neighborhood.

In many ways, the value of a home is based on the price at which the

---

[31] Two famous examples of people who were imprisoned in the camps as children are George Takei, who played Sulu on *Star Trek* and who enjoys a huge following on Facebook today; and Pat Morita (deceased), who played Mr. Miyagi in *The Karate Kid* trilogy of the 1980s.

owner is willing to sell it. When blacks moved into a neighborhood, whites believed houses would be worth less; so they were.

After starting a rumor in a white neighborhood, the agents would quickly follow up by going door to door handing out flyers and encouraging white home owners to get out before their property values dropped any further.

When a block was in the process of being busted, each white family that left was replaced by a black family. With each sale, the real estate agent was able to offer an even lower price to the next departing white family. A progressive white family that was sympathetic to blacks might not plan to move initially, but as more and more whites left and the selling prices got lower and lower, even *they* would feel that moving was an economic necessity.

Both the black and white homeowners were harmed. Whites sold for far less than the actual value of their homes, thinking they were lucky to get whatever amount they managed. They were always reassured by their real estate broker that they'd gotten a great price, *given the circumstances*. Whites also lost the connections and relationships they had created in their old neighborhoods.

Black homeowners were harmed, too, of course. In the 1940s, nearly all black families were denied conventional home loans so blockbusters would arrange financing on their behalf by using something called a land contract or a land installment contract. These loans had much higher interest rates.

Because their interest rates were so much higher, their monthly payments were much higher than they had been for the previous owner. Under those circumstances, the new homeowners were unlikely to keep the house's curb appeal at the previous owner's level.

Peeling paint, browning lawns full of dandelions, a weather worn roof: all these things could now take hold much more quickly than before. Also, blacks were still suffering job discrimination so many of the black buyers would eventually end up losing the house and all the money they'd put into it.

Finally, even those black families that were economically strong and stable, were ultimately harmed. Their goals in moving out of the segregated neighborhoods were undermined, as they didn't leave the segregated neighborhoods behind after all. Instead, they simply pushed the boundaries of the "ghetto" forward a few streets in each direction.

Writing in *American Apartheid*, Massey and Denton note:

> *In neighborhoods of single-family homes, the initial black entrants tended to be middle- and upper-class families seeking to escape the deplorable conditions of the ghetto. Like other middle-class people, they sought more agreeable surroundings, higher-quality schools, lower crime rates, bigger houses, larger properties...*

> *[T]hese quick-profit schemes meant that the ghetto constantly followed the black middle-class as it sought to escape from the poverty, blight, and the misery of the black slum.*

World War II Service for Black Men

The black side of our family didn't have any members serving in World War II. Beatrice's new husband Sampson, having served in WWI, was too old to be drafted. Together, he and Beatrice had several young children. Certainly none of them were old enough to be drafted. Beatrice's uncles, Sherman and William H. were also too old for the draft and she didn't have any brothers.

Those blacks who did go into the service were not treated well. In the early days of World War II, conditions were much the same as they had been during World War I.

Blacks were in segregated units and the majority were assigned to labor battalions. On May 26, 2004, *Washington Post* writer Nurith C. Aizenman authored a war retrospective that included interviews with several black men who'd served in World War II. In the article, entitled, "Black Soldiers Battled Fascism and Racism," she explains that:

> *Combat was not an option. Before the war, the Marines and the Army Air Corps barred blacks outright. The Navy accepted them only as cooks, stewards or longshoremen. The Army had only a handful of black combat units, mostly led by white officers.*

Aizenman writes that black leaders petitioned FDR to deploy blacks as combat soldiers. FDR was not able to overcome the objections of the military leaders at first, but as casualties mounted, their resistance softened:

> The Navy began commissioning a few black officers -- about 60 by the war's end -- and allowing blacks to fill skilled positions such as signalman and electrician on support ships.

> The Army Air Forces, precursor to today's Air Force, began training nearly 1,000 black pilots. Dubbed the Tuskegee Airmen after their base in Alabama.

> The Marines trained several hundred blacks for two combat battalions.

> Meanwhile, the Army began deploying black combat troops, including such storied units as the 92nd Infantry Division and the 761st "Black Panther" Tank Battalion.

Still, these black men were the exceptions. Most blacks were still toiling in the service units and being treated as second-class citizens.

Some whites tried to claim that blacks were better off (just as they had claimed during the first world war), saying that blacks had the better assignments because they *weren't* on the battlefields risking their lives. For the black community[32] the issue was that of serving with or without dignity. To suffer digging a latrine while being endlessly derided and insulted by your white commanding officers was not preferable to bravely defending one's country as a combat soldier, even if the latter resulted in one's death.

For their toil and suffering black servicemen did not earn the respect of grateful white citizens. In fact, after the war, when Congress moved to provide a benefit package for veterans, these all-black service units were easy to carve away from fighting units so that the benefits could be apportioned in conveniently racist ways.

---

[32] According to the statements of black leaders like W.E.B. Dubois made at that time.

The GI Bill

Had my mother's soldier brother, Leland, survived the war, he might have felt unsure about his career path. He wouldn't have had the farming experience that his older brother, Lester, had gained while he'd been away fighting.

He'd been attending college before the war so it would have made sense for him to return to college and finish his degree.

His parents, Otto and Leah, were in a financial position to have helped him pay for college, but there was also something called the GI Bill that could have provided him help as well. The bill was actually called *The Servicemen's Readjustment Act of 1944*, but since servicemen were referred to as GIs, the act was colloquially referred to as the GI Bill.

The GI Bill's benefits included money for education. GI's could choose to pursue a college degree, vocational schooling, or other training. There were also loan guarantees available for servicemen who wanted to start businesses or buy farms. There were also loan guarantees for mortgages to help GIs purchase homes.

The bill even included a provision for unemployment benefits. Veterans who had trouble finding jobs when they returned, could collect a year's worth of support while they looked for a job.

In retrospect, we understand that the GI Bill absolutely transformed the United States, creating the strong, broad, stable, (white) middle-class that made growth and innovation the mainstay of US society for the latter half of the 20th century.

Not surprisingly, whites in the South found ways to deny black servicemen all of these benefits. Once again, they believed that black men with advanced education, businesses, farms, homes, or unemployment checks would destabilize the Southern economy.

In the book *Uprooting Racism: How White People Can Work for Racial Justice*, Paul Kivel writes:

> During most of World War II, the armed services had been strictly segregated. After the war, many people of color were denied veterans' benefits because they had served in jobs that were not considered eligible for such benefits. Many more were deliberately not informed about the benefits,

were discouraged from applying when they inquired about them or simply had their applications for benefits denied.

Ira Katznelson writes even more extensively about the denial of GI Bill benefits to black soldiers in his book, *When Affirmative Action was White.*

A major hurdle for a black serviceman in the South looking to take advantage of the GI Bill's education benefits was to find an open slot in a black college. Black colleges could not meet the demand the GI Bill had created and since black servicemen were not admitted to white colleges in the South, many black soldiers who managed to get approved for education benefits were not able to use them after all.

When Southern black servicemen opted to pass on college and get trained in a vocational skill, they often fell prey to crooked schools that had been set up hastily to attract GI Bill money from blacks. There were many schools that made promises to black GI's in exchange for their GI Bill money. Katznelson explains that these schools didn't effectively teach the black servicemen the skills they paid to learn.

In the end, it wouldn't have mattered if blacks had received proper training in advanced skills because if they stayed in the South they would never have been allowed to use them in white-owned companies. Carrying such skills northward wouldn't have increased their chances at a good job either, since the more recent European immigrants were already very anti-black and would almost certainly protest a black hire for a skilled position.

College opportunities were marginally better for black servicemen in the northern and western US, but they were far from ideal. Many colleges outside the South still had racially-biased entrance criteria. If a black serviceman did manage to get into college, many professors were still biased, having encountered so few blacks in higher education. Finally, if and when a black serviceman graduated, he was still subject to racially biased hiring practices.

Black servicemen also had trouble getting the home loan guarantees provided by the bill. To make use of the Federal Housing Administration (FHA) or Veteran's Administration (VA) loan guarantees, a soldier had to find a bank willing to make the loan.

Blacks in both the North and the South were not allowed to buy in "white" neighborhoods. When a black serviceman found a house he was "allowed" to buy, it was always in a black neighborhood. Loan officers felt that houses in black neighborhoods were not good risks, so they refused to approve the loans.

In *Uprooting Racism*, Kivel writes:

> [T]he FHA specifically channeled loans away from the central city and to the suburbs... The FHA and the VA financed more than $120 billion worth of new housing between 1934 and 1962, but less than 2 percent of this real estate was available to non-white families.

During that time period, bank managers routinely took a map of their local area and drew a red line around districts that were considered bad places to invest.

Loan officers were expected to refer to the map when considering loan applications and deny those applications related to properties within the red-lined districts. The practice was actually called *redlining*. No one hoping to buy a home in a redlined neighborhood was going to find a bank willing to provide a mortgage loan, even with a federal loan guarantee backing it up.

The impact of this denial is immeasurable. A qualified black buyer who was denied a home loan was denied all the benefits that come with home ownership.

In their 1998 article, "Trends in homeownership: Race, demographics, and income," Lewis M. Segal and Daniel G. Sullivan state:

> For most Americans, a home is more than shelter. It is also their most valuable asset and an important savings vehicle. Moreover, a high rate of homeownership is often thought to create better citizens, enhance the stability of communities, increase the value of other property, and even improve the performance of children in school.

As Segal and Sullivan note, there are benefits that accrue to the homeowner's family, to the children, and to the neighborhood. For the family, the asset can be used as collateral for a business or education loan. Mortgage payments provide for tax code concessions. Equity in the home can be converted to home improvements and thereby further increase the families assets. Homeowners often pass their homes and equity down to the their children as an inheritance.

Segal and Sullivan's statement about the benefits of homeownership can be inverted to say that because of the low rate of home ownership in black communities, those communities suffered a lack of stability that encouraged crime and resulted in lower school performance.

We can list all those losses without even considering the additional costs of segregation. By not being allowed to move in to the suburbs their fellow (white) servicemen and servicewomen were flocking to, they lost chances to network with neighbors, therefore missing out on career benefits that can come out of casual conversations at neighborhood and school-related events. Their children lost out on the education provided by those well-funded suburban schools.

Curiously, when white GI's passed their home or equity to their children decades later, many were certain they had purchased and maintained their suburban homes by tugging long and hard on their own bootstraps. They conveniently forgot that critical role government had played in their financial lives while denying the same support to black servicemen.

Another Post-War Wave of White Mob Violence

Danielle McGuire, writing in her book, *At The Dark End of the Street*, sums up the second post-war wave of violence – a reprise of the violence that had taken place just after the first world war during what came to be called the Red Summer.

McGuire details the violence black servicemen attracted, as whites reacted to their spirited post-war activism:

> *The approximately one million African Americans who served in the armed forces...returned home with a new sense of pride and purpose and often led campaigns for citizenship rights, legal equality, and bodily integrity.*
>
> *Whites responded to the postwar black activism with a wave of violence that reasserted white supremacy.*

Within the first few weeks of 1946 alone, uniformed [white] officers [in Birmingham, Alabama] reportedly killed five black men, all veterans, because they had taken part in voter registration drives.

On February 12, 1946, Linwood Shull, the chief of police in Aiken, South Carolina, jammed his billy club into Sergeant Isaac Woodward's eye sockets after the black serviceman, home from a fifteen month stint in the South Pacific, got into an argument with a white bus driver. The beating permanently blinded Woodward. After an all-white jury... acquitted Shull of any charges, white spectators in the crowded courtroom roared with approval.

Whites were especially concerned about blacks voting in the 1946 election and the Klan was active in spreading the message that black voting would not be tolerated.

McGuire related an incident that took place in Taylor County, Georgia:

On July 17, 1946 — Election Day—veteran Maceo Snipes walked past armed thugs patrolling the ballot box to cast his first and last ballot. Later that night, four white men dragged him out of his house and murdered him.

She writes about yet another incident, this one in Mindin, Louisiana in August of 1946:

[P]olice...arrested and jailed John C. Jones, a twenty-eight-year-old black veteran, and his seventeen year old cousin, Albert Harris, for acting "uppity" after they protested an unfair land deal.

However, police claimed the two men were "prowling" around a white woman's window, though she refused to press charges. After several days in jail, police released them into a mob of armed white men. The mob drove Harris and Jones down a country road where they tortured and beat Harris until they believed he was dead. Then the mob mutilated Jones with a meat cleaver and a blow torch. When they were satisfied with their work, the mob left the mangled men in a ditch, ostensibly dead. Jones died, but Harris managed to survive and eventually identified five of the murderers in court, though an all-white jury acquitted them.

Here it was, eighty years after slavery had ended and blacks in the South were hardly in any better position than they had been as slaves. When it came to ensuring that white supremacy remained in place, and blacks would continue to work hard for very low wages, whites were as pathologically cruel and every bit as prone to maniacal marauding as they had ever been.

Black-Owned Businesses Over the Decades

An overwhelming majority of the GI Bill's small business loans went to whites. Blacks who managed to get GI Bill-backed small business loans had to be very careful not to attract too much attention from whites. Whites were still willing and able to put blacks out of business by not renewing licenses, increasing taxes in black business districts until they were high enough to be untenable, and any number of other manipulations. The creativity of whites' machinations to put black and brown people out of business will probably never be fully uncovered.

White suppression of burgeoning black businesses and the destruction of successful black-owned businesses had been around long before the GI Bill.

I haven't included a review of white efforts to undermine black businesses in each chapter because our black family members did not own businesses or attempt to start them. However, in looking at the grossly uneven benefits distributed under the banner of the GI Bill, I think it's important to note that whites did not limit their violence to successful black farmers and sharecroppers.

In this section I present a selection of examples, starting in the late 1800s, and spanning the twentieth century.

We can begin with Nicodemus, Kansas, one of the most impressive black-only towns to rise up in the first few decades after Emancipation. According to Quintard Taylor, Nicodemus was undermined in the late 1880s by its lack of a railroad line. Taylor states, "Nicodemus became an important symbol of the African American capacity for self-governance and economic enterprise."

The town tried to attract a railroad line, but despite their efforts, none of the three railroads opted to bring railroad tracks through the town.

> [T]own leaders placed their hopes, and sixteen thousand dollars in railroad
> bonds, in unsuccessful efforts to attract the Missouri Pacific, the Santa Fe
> and the Union Pacific railroads to their town. When all three railroads
> bypassed Nicodemus, its fate was sealed. After 1888 local boosters ceased
> trying to lure additional settlers, and prominent citizens...left the area.

Taylor's book, *In Search of the Racial Frontier*, doesn't delve into the
proceedings that led the various railroad officials to opt out of a railroad
line through Nicodemus. Given the documented evidence of other policies
and business decisions during that time period that were designed to
undermine black-owned businesses and enterprises, it would be less than
surprising to uncover proof that white businessmen from nearby towns
used anti-black sentiment to gain favor for their towns over Nicodemus. It
would have been such an easy ploy for the white mayor of a nearby city to
lure a railroad away by claiming that a stop in Nicodemus would subject
white passengers to unwanted interactions with blacks, thus sullying the
rail line's reputation.

Therefore, we can reasonably extrapolate that because of racist whites,
Nicodemus never had a chance with the railroads' decision makers.

Turning our attention to the first decade of the 1900s, we learn from
Leon Litwack's book, *Trouble in Mind*, the story of Isaiah Montgomery.
Montgomery was a black man, who, in 1901, publicly touted his conviction
that blacks could start businesses and thrive in accordance with their
dedication to good business principles.

Just three years later, Montgomery wrote a desperate letter to Booker
T. Washington outlining examples of ways in which black businesses were
attracting white backlash:

> *Rev. Buchanan has the best appointed printing establishment of any colored*
> *man in the State, and conducts a Baptist Newspaper...and was no doubt*
> *prospering, his daughter was his cashier and Bookkeeper, they kept a Horse*
> *and Buggy, which the young woman used frequently in going to and from*
> *work; they kept a decent house and a Piano; a mass meeting of whites decided*
> *that the mode of living practiced by the Buchanan family had a bad effect on*
> *the cooks and washerwomen, who aspired to do likewise, and became less*

disposed to work for the whites. A mob forced Buchanan and his family from the town...

Thomas Harvey runs a neat little Grocery, he kept a Buggy and frequently rode to his place of business, he was warned to sell his Buggy and walk.

Mr. Chandler keeps a Grocery, he was ordered to leave, but was finally allowed to remain on good behavior.

Mr. Meacham ran a business and had a Pool table in connection therewith, he was ordered to close up and don overalls for manual labor.

Mr. Cook conducted a Hack business between the Depots and about town, using two Vehicles, he was notified that he would be allowed to run only one and was ordered to sell the other.

Later, in Litwack:

Few individual cases, however, attracted as much notoriety as that of Thomas Moss of Memphis. He had saved his money as a letter carrier, and with two other black men—Calvin McDowell and Henry Stewart—opened the People's Grocery Company in the thickly populated black suburb, where it competed with a white-owned grocery. Moss and his partners were murdered by a mob because they had armed and defended themselves against white marauders threatening their property and because, as one of Moss's close friends surmised, "they were succeeding too well. They were guilty of no crime but that." After the murder of the three men, a [white] mob looted the grocery, creditors closed the place, and what remained of the stock was sold at auction.

We have to remember that the racial climate in the US at the turn of the century was terrible. Whites were still whipped up about the book *The Clansmen* so it's hardly surprising they would act out against black businessmen in such racist ways.

We can jump forward two decades to the 1920s and check to see if whites had more progressive attitudes toward black-owned businesses by that time. Oh wait, twenty years later the US was recovering from the Red Summer riots of 1919. Whites were whipped up about french-woman-ruined-black-GIs and all sorts of other imaginary threats.

There was a riot in Tulsa, Oklahoma in 1921 that wiped out the black business district known as "Black Wall Street." Tulsa had been home to the wealthiest community of blacks in the entire United States. Whites attacked and burned the business district to the ground.

Additionally, during the late 1920s and the 1930s, as blacks were more formally locked into "black" neighborhoods, the practice of redlining began to affect black business ownership as well. After whites abandoned a residential neighborhood, nearby shop owners would often shut down as well. New red lines were drawn and shops sat empty because banks refused to loan money to those interested in running a business in a black neighborhood.

City officials would be slower to send street cleaning equipment, pot hole repair, and other services that would keep the neighborhood bright and shiny. Empty shops led to vandalism, loitering, littering and other petty boredom crimes.

Later, Jews and Asians would come to provide most goods and services in black neighborhoods. These communities often started businesses using money collected from family, friends, and other connections. Since they did not rely on banks for loans, redlining practices did not serve as discouragement to them.

Commercial spaces in these neighborhoods had often sat vacant for such long periods of time their rental rates became highly negotiable. When people who could self-finance came along and inquired about starting a business there, they were able to take advantage of eager landlords and low rental prices. This was just another way non-blacks benefitted financially from the economic suppression of blacks.

Though the rental rates were low, insurance rates were not favorable because the businesses were in redlined neighborhoods. This meant some shopkeepers opted to go without insurance. Operating a business in a volatile neighborhood without insurance surely must have caused shopkeepers an immense amount of stress and angst.

Shop owners had legitimate reasons to maintain higher prices than those that might be seen in suburban stores. In much the same way, their patrons had legitimate reasons to protest those high prices. One form of protest would have been to simply avoid those stores, however because of the lack of transportation many ghetto residents suffered, they had little choice but to buy goods from the stores closest to their homes, even as they resented doing so.

Over time, blacks came to see these merchants as their exploiters. The merchants likewise saw their customers as hostile and corrupt.

Adding to the already tense relationships, these business owners tended to hire from their own families and ethnic groups, cutting off more job opportunities for blacks and increasing the perception that the owners did not care to be part of their community, they cared only to exploit it.

As Paul Kivel describes in his book, *Uprooting Racism*, the phenomenon of Jews and Asians owning businesses in black neighborhoods puts these three oppressed groups in contention with one another instead of encouraging them to form alliances that would help them work together to dismantle oppressive tactics. Intentional or not, these divisions serve white elites very well and is likely the reason whites didn't undermine the Asian and Jewish businesses that grew up in black neighborhoods the way they have undermined black businesses.

Yet another technique for discouraging black-owned businesses is the skillful application of a principle called eminent domain. This principle provides that the government can take control of any privately owned land if government officials decide it should be used for the good of a broad group of citizens.

Using eminent domain white officials could massage decisions about roads, parks, and zoning to ruin black businesses and black business districts.

A relatively famous race-based abuse of eminent domain took place in California in the 1920s. A black couple had developed a thriving resort for black people in Manhattan Beach, California. The resort was called Bruces' Beach. White residents decided they didn't want Bruces' Beach to remain in their community, so they used eminent domain to claim the community would benefit from having a park on the land instead. The town council pushed the Bruces off their land. The city's need for the park must not have been urgent after all because the city officials didn't get around to building the park until thirty years after they kicked the Bruces off the land.

So, again, that happened in the 1920s. Let's keep moving and once again jump two decades forward hoping to see progress. We can once again find that by the 1940s, black-owned businesses were still being undermined.

A 1946 race riot in Colombia, Tennessee, resulted in whites tearing through the black-owned business district there, demolishing the black-owned businesses, arresting business owners and patrons, and miring them in legal battles when they should have been tending to their business affairs.

Even with whites continuing attempts at sabotage, there were some blacks who managed to get rich. There weren't many of them in each generation but some broke through. Those blacks who did become rich generally did so because they created products that were purchased and used by the black community. Maybe that formula worked because whites often did not notice that such products were being sold at all.

A great example of this business model was the hair care products company founded by Madame C.J. Walker. Walker was the first woman to become a millionaire in the US. She invented hair care products for black women. She sold her hair softeners and straightening combs through a network of her trained agents.

As with many historical figures that are celebrated during Black History Month every February, to celebrate Madame Walker's accomplishments is not to celebrate straightening combs and creams, instead, what makes Walker a celebrated figure are the following facts:

- Whites were not able to steal her inventions and formulas and take credit for them.
- Whites were not able to put her out of business through trickery or some other nefarious plotting.
- Whites were not able to otherwise orchestrate her personal or financial ruin.

With all odds against her, Walker not only invented products but was savvy enough to manufacture, market and sell her products. Walker was

You do not have to experiment when you use Madam
C. J. Walker's Preparations.

Figure 21: An ad for Madame C.J. Walker's company products as it appeared in a 1912 edition of *The Crisis*.

not the first, nor was she the only black person to use this business model of catering to other blacks.

Writing in *Black Bourgeoisie*, E. Franklin Frazier explains that most blacks who gained relatively significant wealth in the earliest decades after Reconstruction did so by creating black banks, insurance companies, mutual aid societies, and black newspapers.

The same could be said of black moguls who came later; perhaps their successes were "allowed" because whites didn't know what was happening until it was "too late" to do anything to undermine them.

When, in 1942, John H. Johnson started building the publishing empire that would create and distribute *Jet* and *Ebony* magazines, he was most likely left unmolested because whites either didn't notice or didn't think he'd make much money at it.

Sadly, small business owners, especially in the South, are vulnerable to racist attempts to undermine them even in this new millennium. A high school friend of mine, who is black, shared a story with me recently about several whites who sabotaged a small business he and his brother were developing.

They'd leased a property in a shopping district of my hometown in

Texas. This district was the old "downtown" that had been abandoned by whites in the 1970s in favor of the city's first shopping mall. After the abandonment, the district had been redlined. From the 1970s to the end of the century, the area had contained businesses that catered to black and brown residents who lived nearby. Nightclubs, "soul food" restaurants, and various other businesses limped along, funded by savings accounts, high interest-rate credit cards, and family loans.

In the earliest days of the new millennium, the blighted area started to undergo a revival. While the area still adjoined the "black" residential area of town, it was gaining attention from white patrons and shopkeepers.

My friend Anthony and his brother Carleton opened a night club there just as many nightclubs had opened before, not realizing that in the minds of whites, the district had changed.

The new white business owners, with their cupcake shops and paint-it-yourself pottery studios, felt the nightclub didn't fit the *je ne sais quoi* of the district. Never mind that the *je ne sais quoi* of the business district had been black for decades by that time.

The white shop owners banded together in an attempt to come up with some way to legally force the nightclub out of the district. They considered some sort of zoning change but couldn't find one that could be used to their advantage.

Anthony and Carleton began to get regular visits from local police because the surrounding shop owners were lodging complaints. The white shop owners claimed that the nightclub's patrons were littering and vandalizing their shops. Anthony and Carleton made repeated appeals to their customers and the customers repeatedly agreed to comply.

One quiet Saturday morning, Anthony parked in the back alley, entered through the back door and was working through receipts and bills when he heard a ruckus near the front entrance.

Going to investigate he spied two white female shopkeepers smashing beer bottles along the sidewalk in front of his nightclub and trailing trash along the sidewalk toward their own shops.

Anthony confronted the women but they denied that any such thing had happened. The police were called once again and the conflicting accounts were entered into the record.

The nightclub was a side business for my friends, each of whom had a stable day job. They decided, in the end, that fighting the battle would create too much stress and take away from their familial priorities too significantly.

Anthony and Carleton's story gives us a glimpse into what the undermining of black business looks like today. Was it racial? Or was it just that these women ran "family" establishments and my friends did not?

I'm guessing these white shop owners believe they are not motivated by racism. They would claim, and sincerely believe, that it was the nature of my friends' business that made it unwelcome, not the fact that the owners and patrons were black.

The problem is that these white shop owners believe it is their absolute right to decide which businesses are "best" for the area and which should be shut down. This is a common blind spot for whites; it would be hard to convince them that their opinions on which businesses fit best should not carry more weight than the opinion of my friends. They might claim that any *reasonable person* would agree with them and not my friends. Yet if you dug into their definition of "reasonable person" you (and they) would quickly realize that by "reasonable person" they actually mean "middle-class, thirty-something, white person."

The Summer of 1949

In the summer of 1949, my Grandpa Otto was 50 years old, my grandmother was 46 and their daughter, my mother, had just turned six.

Even though the economy was in a recession, Otto's finances must have been healthy because he bought a boat and christened it the "Kay Joy."

The boat was kept at Lake Coeur D'Alene, across the state border, in Idaho. On the weekends they could drive 90 miles to Spokane, visit Otto's mother, then drive another 45 miles, or so, over to the lake where their boat was docked.

Only six years before, in the Summer of 1943, Otto had gone to Greenville, Pennsylvania with a plan. Arriving there, he would speak with every man in his son's chain of command. In other words, he'd follow Plan A to its natural end. During the many solitary hours he'd endured on the road, he'd also come up with a Plan B. He vowed to himself that only after he'd made every possible appeal, would he resort to Plan B. Plan B would only be necessary if *they* forced his hand.

In the wee hours of June 25th, 1943, Otto told his son about Plan B. But, when the sun rose that next morning, the two men hugged goodbye.

Figure 22: A boat, christened "Kay Joy." Lake Coeur D'Alene, Idaho, 1949.

For the rest of his life, Otto would review in his mind things that were said, and not said, done, and not done. Otto had seen a way to save his son and he'd let it slip away.

So while Kay Joy enjoyed the summer sun and the relaxing rock of the boat on the water, Otto wished he could give it all back. The boat, the houses, the land, their cars: all of it – because none of it gave him any joy anymore.

THE 1950s

The 1950s are usually remembered as an exuberant time for the United States. The war was in the rear-view mirror and the economy was booming. Rural towns were getting electricity and indoor plumbing and city dwellers were purchasing televisions.

Suburban (White) Utopia

Because the GI Bill caused the market to be flooded with government-backed home-loan money in the late 1940s, the early 1950s were a frenzy of homebuilding. Housing developers purchased large tracts of land and created satellite towns that came to be known as "suburbs."

In *American Apartheid*, Massey and Denton write:

> As home construction skyrocketed during the late 1940s and 1950s men and women began to marry and have babies...growing families of the 1950s sought large houses and spacious lots in areas with good schools and plenty of room for supervised play, conditions that were more easily met by constructing new homes on inexpensive land located outside of central cities. The suburbanization of America proceeded at a rapid pace as the white middle-class deserted inner cities in massive numbers.
>
> In making this transition from urban to suburban life, middle-class whites demanded and got massive federal investments in highway construction that permitted rapid movement to and from central cities by car.

White city managers often designed the path of highways to take care of other "pesky" problems, especially as those problems related to black people.

From *American Apartheid*:

White flight was enabled by massive federal investment in freeways, often constructed strategically to form barriers between black and white areas. Federal urban renewal programs and public housing projects were used by local governments, with federal acquiescence, to contain and isolate urban blacks.

For instance, if there was a booming black business district that city officials preferred didn't exist, they could route a new freeway right through the middle of it using eminent domain.

Writing in *White Like Me*, Tim Wise notes:

[F]rom the 1950s to the 1970s, urban renewal and the interstate highway program had devastated black and brown communities in the name of progress, with hundreds of thousands of homes, apartments, and businesses knocked to the ground.

In New Orleans itself, the I-10 had sliced through the city's largest black communities in the 1960s, the Tremé and the Seventh Ward. The Tremé— [was] the oldest free black community in the United States.

Once completed, the I-10 had destroyed what was, for all intents and purposes, a public park sixty-one hundred feet long and one hundred feet wide, along with hundreds of businesses and homes.

Additionally, George Lipsitz, in his essay, "The Possessive Investment in Whiteness,[33]" spoke of the highway construction used strategically to undermine black neighborhoods:

Federally funded highways designed to connect suburban commuters with downtown places of employment also destroyed already scarce housing in minority communities and often disrupted neighborhood life as well. Construction of the Harbor Freeway in Los Angeles, the Gulf Freeway in Houston, and the Mark Twain Freeway in St. Louis displaced thousands of residents and bisected neighborhoods, shopping districts, and political precincts.

---

[33] I found Lipsitz' essay in Paula Rothenburg's *White Privilege: Essential Readings on the Other Side of Racism*.

Manufacturing and Marketing Whiteness

Writing in *Crabgrass Frontier: The Suburbanization of the United States,* Kenneth T. Jackson explains that suburbs were more than just places to live, he makes the case that "the physical organization of neighborhoods, roads, yards, houses, and apartments set up living patterns that condition our behavior."

The behavior that many have claimed rose out of the suburbs was first conformity, and later, isolation, depression, and quiet, seething dysfunction. The conformity began from the moment a family chose a house from the four to six available models. I've heard more than a few friends tell anecdotes about getting lost in various suburban communities because the long streets of matching residences can be so disorienting.

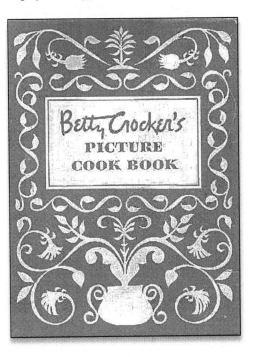

Figure 23: First published in 1950, Betty Crocker's Picture Cookbook is the best-selling cookbook of all time. Both my mother and my grandmother had copies, dog-eared and grease stained. This cookbook was more than a cookbook though. It was a manual for suburban wives. It enabled soon-to-be-called whites to cook and eat the American way and present themselves to neighbors as red, white and blue Americans instead of as German Jews, Italians, Poles, or Irish.

Not only were the houses the same, some of the earliest residents delighted in the startling uniformity. Jackson quotes a suburban newsletter from 1949:

[O]ur lives are held closely together because most of us are within the same age bracket, in similar income groups, live in almost identical houses and have

common problems.

The move to the suburbs radically changed women's lives. First, they were asked to forget about the independence they might have enjoyed during the war when they were needed in the factories.

Rather than celebrating American women's strength and independence, ad campaigns were designed to shame middle-class white women back to being dependent on their breadwinning husbands.

This complete dependency on the husbands' ability to earn a good paycheck altered men's roles as well, and greatly increased the stress that middle-class white men suffered.

Women were targeted with ads about new appliances and ultra-modern cleaning formulations.

New suburban homes (as well as urban renewal programs that wiped out ethnic neighborhoods) drew young couples away from the "old neighborhood" where their parents, uncles, aunts, cousins and many long-time acquaintances lived. They picked up and moved to a brand new house, on a brand new block, in a brand new suburb.

If the couple had been heavily influenced by the traditions of ethnic parents, they often left their ethnicity behind as they tried to fit in to the new suburban culture.

For instance, a Greek-American housewife would use Betty Crocker's cookbook, instead of her mother's recipes, because she didn't want to call attention to her ethnic roots. Better still, food manufacturers were offering frozen and canned items that fit right into the self-image they were encouraging her to embrace. By using their products she could prove she was a modern American woman who knew how to leverage science and technology in the running of her household.

When her first born started teething, she would not call her mother for advice, instead, she'd reference Dr. Spock's book. The 1940s hit had been updated for the 50s and was just as popular among the mothers of the 1950s as it had been with the mothers of the 1940s.

For housecleaning, these young wives likewise eschewed their mother's old-world tips and tricks. Modern appliances and formulations were calling out to them from the pages of their favorite women's magazines and across the airways of their new television sets.

George Lipsitz explains:

> *During the decades following World War II, urban renewal helped construct a new "white" identity in suburbs by helping to destroy ethnically specific European American urban inner-city neighborhoods.*
>
> *Consequently, ethnic differences among whites became a less important dividing line in US culture, while race became more important. The suburbs helped turn Euro-Americans into "whites" who could live near each other and intermarry with relatively little difficulty. But this "white" unity rested on residential segregation, on shared access to housing and life chances largely unavailable to [blacks.]*

In other words, I've often heard people of Italian, Irish, Cuban, Latvian, Polish, or Greek origin brag about how their ancestors arrived with nothing and within one generation had been able to achieve middle-class status. These stories often have a "therefore" attached to them. "Therefore," they often add, "Blacks must be lazy because they've been here for generations, and so many of their families are still in poverty."

Those arrived-in-America-with-fifteen-dollars-in-his-pocket stories tend to be raised during informal discussions about America's race problems. Unfortunately, rather than illustrating black laziness, they highlight how the label of whiteness has given less-brown people license to step on blacks as they climb upward.

But let's go back to the suburbs of the 1950s where everything was new and shiny and perfect and resident-approved skin tones ranged from translucent to only-those-brown-shades-lighter-than-the-suburban-breadwinner's-lunch-sack.

The new American culture was being manufactured by the advertising agencies popping up along Madison Avenue in New York City. The lessons in human psychology and the power of propaganda that had been perfected during World War II were being carried to those advertising agencies and converted into newspaper ads, magazine ads, and later, television commercials.

For a Latvian immigrant, learning to be *white* became as simple as reading advertisements and buying the right products. Consumerism and whiteness went hand in hand.

Advertisers made an offer most could not, or simply did not, refuse. In exchange for their willingness to give up their ethnic traditions and identities, they could have a suburban home with a large, private backyard.

They could enjoy that backyard, with its concrete slab patio, barbeque grill, red-white-and-blue plastic decorations, hot dogs, hamburgers, potato chips, and best of all, smart, like-minded couple friends who lived within walking distance.

Summer barbeques were lessons in conformity. The men would discuss business and news, carefully seeking out the least controversial positions to heartily agree on. Talking about business allowed them to network with their neighbors thus increasing their access to better jobs.

The women would trade recipes and gossip. The gossip allowed the women to further conform to the new American culture.

In their lifetimes, those who were conflicted about the abandonment of their ethnicity kept quiet about it. Whiteness was a gift. Embracing the chance to become white was what kept you from becoming black.

Many of their children, however, and generations after (including, certainly, me and mine), would often struggle to understand why they (we) felt so bereft of cultural authenticity.

1950s Youth Culture & Interracial Anxiety

The 1950s was the first decade in which American society acknowledged a life-stage distinct from both childhood and adulthood. Since that decade, children in each generation have been allowed to pass through their "teen years."

After the war, televisions became the focus of living room gatherings. As radios were cast aside and largely forgotten by parents, teens picked them up, plugged them into their bedroom wall sockets, and explored the dial. Small independent radio stations, now the nation's afterthought, began casting about for an audience by playing records from across the spectrum. As white teenagers started listening, they called in to request replays of black artists' records.

Writing in *All Shook Up: How Rock 'N' Roll Changed America*, Glenn C. Altschuler explains:

> The more attractive R&B became to white youth, the more controversial it became... It's easy to see why. Since whites, as Brian Ward argues, "had long reified black culture as the perpetually fascinating but feral, alluring but alarming, sensual but sordid antithesis to the dominant white one," rhythm and blues gave them nightmares that their teenagers would live out the fantasy described by Jack Kerouac in On the Road: "At lilac evening I walked with every muscle aching among the lights of 27th and Welton in the Denver colored section, wishing I were Negro, feeling that the best the white world had offered was not enough ecstasy for me, not enough life, joy, kicks, darkness, music, not enough night."

Jack Kerouac was not alone in his belief that somehow blacks had tapped into the best of what life had to offer. As whites continually tried to buy happiness, blacks seemed to always have access to it.

By enforcing black poverty, whites had almost guaranteed that black artistic expression would bubble and boil and eventually bust through some kind of cultural escape valve. White teens couldn't get enough of what Kerouac called the ecstasy, life, joy, darkness, and night of black music and culture.

Since one could not *become* black, copying blacks dance moves, phrasing, fashion choices and hairstyles was going to be as close as any white person could get.

Even as their parents tried to purchase a satisfactory and fulfilling life, these teens recognized in black music something deeper and, in many ways, not for sale.

Elvis crafted impersonations of black culture and was not ashamed to proclaim the roots of his persona.

From Altschuler:

> In public, and in the South, [Elvis] acknowledged his indebtedness to the music of African Americans. "The colored folks been singing and playing [rock 'n' roll] just like I'm doing now, man, for more years than I know," he told the Charlotte Observer in 1956.

161

"They played it like that in the shanties and in their juke joints and nobody paid it no mind until I goosed it up. I got it from them. Down in Tupelo, Mississippi, I used to hear Arthur Crudup bang his box the way I do now and I said that if I ever got to the place where I could feel all old Arthur felt, I'd be a music man like nobody ever saw."

Sam Phillips believed that Elvis was without prejudice and that "sneaking around through" his music, but clearly discernible to his fans, was an "almost subversive" identification with and empathy for blacks.

Later, the Beatles, the Rolling Stones and many other iconic white musicians would credit Rhythm & Blues artists as their earliest and deepest inspirations.

As white parental anxiety reached a fevered pitch, someone realized they might re-package the entire experience by having wholesome white kids, like Pat Boone, record the hits of black artists (changing any lyrics parents might find unsavory).

Copyrights and royalty payments aside, Pat Boone's persona was a deliberate attempt to erase black artists from the minds of white teens. The idea was that teens only loved the music, so if Pat Boone sang it instead, maybe white teens would forget that it had come from blacks and stop listening to black radio stations. For many white teens, Pat Boone *was* sufficient and their parents could sigh in great relief[34].

Leah Tyler's White Ancestors in the 1950s

Otto's mother, Eliza, lived on for another fourteen years after her husband Ai's death. She died in 1953. Upon her death, Otto received the rest of his land inheritance.

Otto and Leah now had more than enough land to make a comfortable living. Otto had handed over most of the day-to-day farm operations to his son, Lester, in the early 1940s.

---

[34] American popular culture has dictated the world's trends for decades because black culture generates fresh sounds and sights so quickly, and with such richness and variety, white appropriation machines can cherry-pick at will and sell re-packaged, white-washed culture at a premium, all the while complaining that black culture is broken.

Otto still liked to contribute to the farming operation in a constructive way though, so he stayed busy searching out and forcibly removing interloping plant species.

While Otto sprayed weeds out at the farm, his wife and daughter stayed in town. Kay Joy learned domestic crafts like cooking, baking, sewing, crocheting, and ironing. She learned to set the table for formal dinners and she participated in setting up teas for Eastern Star events. She was also given plenty of free time to explore and create on her own. If she got bored she might ask for permission to walk two blocks down to the small, local grocery store or a similar distance over to a friend's house.

Her childhood experiences were rich and varied, and they were all undergirded by the baseline security provided by the wheat land and the money it reliably produced.

The farming schedule meant an uneven workload across the seasons. When the family farmed winter wheat, they planted in October and then had the rest of the fall and the winter months off. Many farmers in the area had winter homes in southern California where they relaxed and waited out the cold season.

That year, the same month that Otto's mother died, the winter wheat seed was planted, and Otto took his wife and daughter to Hawai'i.

My mother enrolled in the local Hawaiian school for her fifth grade studies. Before that trip to Hawai'i she'd lived in a place where "diversity" was understood as the happy mixture of the Norwegians, English and Welsh. Now, she found, her race made her a numeric minority.

Present day Hawai'i can be rough for white teens. Discrimination against "haoles" can be intense. Back in 1953, things were evidently different, because fifth graders at the Jefferson School treated my mother in such a way as to generate for her only the fondest memories of her time there.

Eventually, Otto, Leah, and my mother returned to their lily-white, small-town, farming community. Otto began a long tradition of buying a new Cadillac every few years. They vacationed at their lake house and took friends out on their boat.

Figure 24: My mother is in the second row, standing slightly left of center with her hands clasped in front of her. She is wearing a red dress with puffed sleeves and a sweetheart neckline. In a class of 30 students, my mother was an ethnic minority. This experience shaped her worldview.

Camps Are Enjoying Hawaiian Weather

Word comes from the Otto Camp family that they arrived OK on the Islands and having lovely weather with Christmas decorations like our home towns. Kay enrolled in the Jefferson school Nov. 30. They are all enjoying swiming surf riding and plenty of sunshine.

Dec 4 53

The luxury of her Hawaiian sojourn wasn't an anomaly. Throughout my mother's life she had endless opportunities. As she grew older, she participated in scores of activities. She was a majorette, a cheerleader, and a twirler. She owned horses and participated in 4-H. She played an instrument in the school band.

In high school she was elected as one of the harvest festival princesses. This meant she wore a fancy ball gown and rode four-hundred feet on a parade float, waving at the townspeople, nearly all of whom she knew by name.

In short, there were no activities her parents could not afford to provide her experience in, or access to. Additionally, her every accomplishment was announced in the local newspaper, as were the accomplishments of the other landowners' children. Her parents encouraged her to take advantage of the many entitlements that came with being a member of the upper class.

This constant attention and praise would teach my mother that the world was her oyster, even during an era when, as a woman, she was taught to defer to and cater to the expectations and needs of men.

The privileges of her childhood also exposed her to so much information about life that, as my mother, she seemed Encyclopedic in her ability to answer questions about how the world worked, why things were a certain way, or where to buy some obscure object.

My mother could make a diorama for a school project, fix a toilet, run a brownie troop, sew a costume for a school performance, tutor us in math, make and decorate stunning cakes, and advise us on how to handle drama in our friendships. She knew how to hula dance and how to perform CPR. She taught us to baton twirl and do front and back flips off diving boards. She gave us advice on how to go back to sleep after a bad dream and how to let an unfortunate suitor down easy.

She such resourceful, creative, can-do person. How much can those qualities be attributed to the fact that she was raised under such privileged

Figure 25: Otto and Kay Joy outside the hotel they lived in when they took a long vacation in Hawai'i.

circumstance wherein she was exposed to so much that life had to offer?

Leah Tyler's Black Ancestors in the 1950s

When the 1950s began, my husband's father Bill was four-years old. Bill lived with his parents, Beatrice and Sampson and his many siblings. We know from family oral history that Beatrice gave birth to lots of children—probably nine.

It goes without saying that Bill wasn't enjoying a life of leisure in Hawai'i. His father, Sampson, did not receive a home loan even though, as a veteran, he should have qualified for one. Sampson did not receive unemployment benefits. He didn't get a small business loan, and he didn't receive training in a job skill that would garner him a higher wage. Bill's parents were poor not because they were stupid or lazy; They were poor because whites in Louisiana had succeeding in their mission to make sure blacks remained poor.

Neighbors from Monroe who remember Sampson and Beatrice have told me they were as poor and hardworking as any of the other families in the area. They, like their neighbors, were hourly workers and still subject to white manipulations of wages and living conditions.

Sampson died when Bill was eight years old. The widowed Beatrice was denied Social Security payments that any white widow would have received to help her keep the children fed and clothed. Once the situation became dire the children were taken away to group homes. Those group homes were like orphanages we often see in movies.

When *Brown* was ruled on, Bill was ten years old. He was one of the very students being discussed by Kenneth and Mamie Clark; one of the many black children who weren't getting the education they deserved.

The year the Montgomery Bus Boycott began, and Emmitt Till was murdered, Bill was eleven.

When the Little Rock Nine moved to desegregate Little Rock Central High School, he was twelve.

Regardless of whether Bill was aware that civil rights protests were gaining ground, I doubt he would have pinned his hopes on the idea that a Supreme Court decision in the nations' capitol, or a bus boycott in another state would have any effect on his daily life.

Even as progress was made on paper, whites worked to ensure that as a little as possible changed in the way blacks and whites related to one another locally. In fact, in many localities, whites tightened Jim Crow in angry, petulant, tantrums triggered by *Brown* and other federal decisions.

No matter what civil rights news Bill was privy to, whites would be successful enough in their efforts to maintain the status quo that Bill would develop an itch to leave the South as soon as he was old enough and had a plan in place.

THE 1960s

Leah Tyler's White Ancestors in the 1960s

When it was time for my mother to attend college, she chose Washington State University (WSU) just forty-five miles away from her hometown. By attending college my mother was nearly certain to meet a college-educated man to marry.

She joined a sorority her first semester there, something that cost considerable money, but that allowed her to create an upper-class social network for herself. Were she to move to another state or city, she could use her sorority affiliation to identify women of similar social class, wealth, and education, and thus ease herself into a ready-made social circle in her new location. If she remained single past college graduation, which was not likely, she could have counted on her sorority sisters to identify potential suitors on her behalf.

In 2011, I found a box in the basement of my parent's home. The label, in my grandmother's handwriting, said, "Kay's Letters," and the box contained letters my mother had written to her parents, starting in college and continuing for decades.

In one of her earliest letters home from college, she wrote:

I've met a lot of nice girls. But guess what? One of my roommates and my counselor—both the nicest girls—guess what religion? Both good ole Catholic. My luck I guess.

I asked my mother about these lines in her letters and she explained that Catholics were considered unrefined by the Protestants in her hometown. What I find interesting about her bigotry back in 1961 is that she seems to be saying it's *too bad* they can't be friends. She isn't expressing any outright hatred. She doesn't add a bigoted diatribe to her regrets.

I also take comfort in the fact that she isn't afraid to tell her parents that she likes these Catholic girls. It helps me infer that Otto and Leah might only have been bigoted in a practical way, not in any virulent, hateful way. But maybe I read what I want to into the words because I love all the people involved.

Another thing that makes me smile is the realization that just by going to college my mother had her horizons expanded. College is supposed to be a place where you meet and interact with people you might not have interacted with otherwise, and it seems that was exactly what my mother was gaining from her college experience.

In her next letter home, she wrote:

I've had two dates with Bud Morrison from Spokane...Bud's the guy whose father raises thoroughbred [horses]. I like him—so naturally he's probably Catholic.

My mother and her best friend/sorority sister, Jane, decided it would be fun to go to the University of Hawai'i for the summer semester between their freshman and sophomore years at WSU. They told their parents it was necessary that they take difficult math and economics classes at U of H in order to keep their grade point averages in good shape. My grandparents agreed that a semester in Hawai'i sounded perfectly reasonable.

Kay Joy returned from Hawai'i tan, relaxed, and ready to begin her sophomore year at WSU. Otto and Leah bought their daughter a brand-new Chevy II Super Sport convertible. They felt the car made sense because it would enable her to drive back and forth every few weeks to visit them.

It was during her sophomore year that my mother caught the attention of a young graduate student, my father. My father admired my mother from afar for a while, but then, finally, during the summer break following her sophomore year, showed up in her wheat farming hometown, and asked her out for coffee.

Figure 26: My mom on the deck of the ship that would take her to Hawai'i for a summer semester at the University of Hawaii.

They were married in 1965. My mother, having found her college-educated husband, dropped out of college and began having babies. My father finished his master's degree at WSU in 1965. Our family moved to Texas shortly after that because my father was slated to begin studying for his PhD.

I was born in Texas, in 1968. That was the same year my father completed his PhD and accepted a job as a professor at Texas A&M in College Station, Texas.

In 1988, the year I turned twenty, *Time* magazine did a retrospective celebrating the twentieth anniversary of the year 1968. It talked about the death of MLK, the actions of Tommie Smith and John Carlos at the Olympics in Mexico, the rise of the Black Panther Party, and various other protests and events.

When I read through the retrospective I became invigorated by the idea that I had been born in such a radical year. I asked my mother what her memories were of that time period. She said she remembered the assassination of JFK in 1963, but didn't remember the Civil Rights Movement at all. I found her answer disappointing. She had raised me to so respectful toward people of all colors and backgrounds and I'd never heard her say anything bigoted. I couldn't understand how anyone, a college-educated young woman, least of all, could have missed the entire Civil Rights Movement. It was hard for me to accept that she had truly been oblivious – it did not seem possible.

In 1998, the year I turned thirty, she gave me a book called *1968*. I was living in Kansas City, Missouri at the time and I received the book in the mail. She'd written a note to me just inside the cover of one of the books. In the note, she wrote, "As the years have passed and things are brought up about events in '68, I think 'where was I when that happened?' It was like I'd been in another world. I guess I was rather self-centered. I couldn't worry about our country or the world because I have having a tough time taking care of me and mine."

Though I wouldn't realize it until after she'd passed, my mother was trying to apologize to me for the disappointment I'd expressed in 1988. My disappointment that she wasn't a Freedom Rider or march participant was low grade – it didn't affect our relationship on a daily basis— but it did rear up anytime I began preaching self-righteously about some topic in the news or some cause or that had captured my attention.

I wondered if perhaps she'd done something she was ashamed of, instead. Whenever I looked at the photos of the Little Rock Nine I always focused in on the rabid white girl in the background, screaming and spitting hatred. I often wonder if there are people today, descendants, who are ashamed of how their ancestors acted during those pivotal moments. That snarling woman most likely went on to become a mother, and then, a few decades later, a grandmother. Had my mother done something like that?

After finding the box of letters in 2011, the question again lodged itself in the forefront of my mind. How could she have missed the entire Civil Rights Movement? Could she be hiding something?

When I found a letter postmarked April 8, 1968 I was sure I'd hit the jackpot. MLK had been assassinated on April 4. I reasoned that of all the events of the '60s, surely MLK's death or the uprising that followed would have to have captured my mother's attention.

It had not.

In her April 8th, 1968 letter, she talks about picking out fabric for curtains, and there is no mention of MLK, uprisings, marches, black people, white people, or anything even remotely resembling current events.

Writing in the book, *The Feminine Mystique*, Betty Friedan actually explains both my mother's blind ignorance of the Civil Rights Movement as well as her probable reason for dropping out of college as soon as she was engaged to my father. Back then, Friedan explains, women who stayed in school after marriage were considered unfeminine and were attacked for emasculating their husbands.

As for the Civil Rights Movement, Friedan explained that young wives of the 1960s were pressured to focus solely on their husbands and children. Friedan had written for women's magazines during that time and was privy to her male editors' choices and opinions:

> I started writing for women's magazines, in the fifties,[and] it was simply taken for granted by editors, and accepted as an immutable fact of life by writers, that women were not interested in politics, life outside the United States, national issues, art, science, ideas, adventure, education, or even their own communities, except where they could be sold through their emotions as wives and mothers.

Friedan relates that Thurgood Marshall, the lead attorney in the Brown desegregation case, made himself available to explain the Civil Rights Movement to the editors and writers of the top women's magazines at a get-together.

Marshall and other NAACP officials hoped the magazine editors would publish articles that would inform suburban housewives of the movement and possibly get them interested in being supportive. Friedan tells of how all of the women's magazine editors passed on developing articles about civil rights because they were convinced that white suburban mothers would be unable to process the ideas and principles of the movement, and even if they did, they wouldn't care.

Friedan helped me see how extraordinary it would have been for my mother, as a white suburban housewife, to have had any awareness of Supreme Court decisions, marches in Alabama, or protests in Mississippi. Furthermore, she helped me see that when my mother did finally begin to take anti-racist stances in the 1970s, it was not too little too late; it was awesome.

Leah Tyler's Black Ancestors in the 1960s

Bill, my husband's father, was fifteen-years old when the 1960s began. In 1963, when he was 17 years old, Bill fell in love with a thirteen-year-old girl named Diane. One of Diane's sisters told me that while no one believed Diane was old enough to be involved in a mature relationship, "You couldn't keep them away from each other, so we gave up trying." Bill and Diane continued to see each other, even with the older family members clucking their tongues. Diane became pregnant, and my husband was born in 1964, in the small town of Jonesboro, Louisiana, forty-five miles southwest of Monroe.

As a telling illustration of the racial climate William was born into, the same year he was born, three Northern college students had gone to the neighboring state of Mississippi to register blacks to vote as part of Freedom Summer. Two of the students were Jewish and the third was black. The three students were killed by white racists who didn't appreciate Northerners meddling in the affairs of Southern life. The murders of Schwerner, Chaney, and Goodman and the subsequent Federal Bureau of Investigation inquiry are detailed in the movie *Mississippi Burning*.

A year after welcoming his son into the world, Bill bid his mother goodbye. Beatrice died in 1965, at the age of 53. Her death at that relatively early age was due in large part to her inability to afford healthcare. Bill's parents were gone so, unlike my mother, he could not depend on them to send him to college or pay his fraternity dues. Bill, the seventeen-year old husband and father, soldiered on, trying to make a living repairing cars for black folks.

The problem with black customers in the Jim Crow South was that they had a strong need for car repair services, but very little money to pay for those services. Once, a black customer who couldn't pay cash gave Bill a black-and-white television as payment. My husband, four or five years old at the time, remembers that he was excited to see the television arrive in his father's arms.

Soon, he learned that the tuner on the television was fried. Bill intended to use the television not for receiving TV shows but for providing warmth in their home. That night, and many nights after, the television was placed in the family bed to warm them.

Diane was approaching eighteen around that same time and probably hadn't begun to work as a maid, yet. She might soon be pressed into service by the family's poverty. This would mean she would be subjected to her employers' sexual advances. I imagine that Bill, seeing the same inevitability, might have been desperate to find a way out of the South.

The Projects

Since Bill and Diane were living in the small town of Jonesboro, Louisiana, they wouldn't have witnessed blockbusting, white-flight or the formation of what George Clinton and Parliament Funkadelic would come to call, "The Chocolate Cities and the Vanilla Suburbs."

To deal with the problems whites had created in the cities by directing all the GI Bill money out to the suburbs, Congress passed housing acts in 1949 and 1954 that provided federal money to any city that would provide inner-city residents with affordable housing. These redevelopment projects were often called simply "the projects" by locals.

According to Massey and Denton in *American Apartheid:*

During the 1950s and 1960s, local elites manipulated housing and urban renewal legislation to carry out widespread slum clearance in growing black neighborhoods that threatened white business districts and elite institutions.

Massey and Denton describe how federal funds, allocated for housing development projects in almost every major city, were used to destroy the existing dwellings of at least two black neighborhoods. One of the neighborhoods would be selected because it was creeping in a direction that threatened white business interests or a white institution such as a college or hospital. The other neighborhood would be selected because it was *not* threatening white interests in any way.

Once two neighborhoods had been identified, the neighborhood that was causing problems for whites would be razed and retail stores catering to whites, or some other structural buffer would be built in its place. The other area now needed to somehow hold residents from both of the destroyed areas. The best way to double the amount of residents on a small piece of land was to create a multi-story apartment complex. Thus, housing projects were often more than one story high. The taller the structure, the more land could be reclaimed for buffer zones that benefited whites.

In retrospect, the highest-density housing projects are considered to have been massive failures. Housing projects often came to be ruled by gangs. Alex Kotlowitz' book, *There Are No Children Here* tells the story of two brothers growing up in a Chicago housing project. Through Kotlowitz' narrative we see the myriad dysfunctions of a large, inner-city, housing complex.

I also found a research brief called, "A Brief History of Public Housing," written by J.A. Stoloff, in 2004, for the Housing and Urban Development Agency (HUD). According to Stoloff, by 1968, HUD recognized the issues created by the large, highly-concentrated housing projects and prohibited the further building of high-rise dwellings for low-income families. They also discouraged the further building of housing projects that took up two or three city blocks. This policy move by HUD was in direct response to the emergent problems they were seeing in the large footprint and high-rise communities.

Since shifting away from the large projects, HUD has favored and funded scattered-site developments with fifty or fewer units each. They have also favored and encouraged the use of housing vouchers since these programs integrate low-income families into functional, family-oriented neighborhoods.

Interestingly, Stoloff's paper overturns a common misconception about one shortcoming of those large-scale housing projects. Many people believe (and repeat the fallacy) that the housing projects fell into terrible disrepair because the tenants did not care about their living conditions. Those murmurings were propagated to buttress the argument that people who are given "entitlements" (like affordable housing) are ungrateful and lazy and show these traits in the way they maintain their homes.

The HUD paper details that, in fact, when many projects were built, project managers tried to make up for budget overruns by switching out appliances and building materials, replacing them with sub-standard items. The cheap appliances and shoddy building materials wore out and broke down more quickly and more often than quality versions would have. Then, local governments opted not to repair or replace the items because they wanted to focus instead on paying off the construction debt and declaring the project a financial success. Residents quickly learned that a broken dishwasher was going to remain broken, and they worked around the inadequacies because they had no real recourse for remedying the situation.

It's hardly surprising that many public housing projects were poorly designed. Too many were designed not by considering the quality of life for future residents but with the goal of packing as many black people as possible into small spaces.

Rather than using "urban renewal" funds to benefit the black and brown people abandoned in the inner cities, funds were manipulated in ways that made life even harder for the black and brown poor.

When my husband's parents finally left rural Louisiana for Denver, Colorado, they would find a ghetto waiting for them, complete with the requisite Federally-funded, poorly-designed, housing projects.

Civil Rights Legislation

President John F. Kennedy was assassinated in 1963. Because of the president's death, the vice president, Lyndon Baines Johnson, became president.

Progressive Congressmen had been trying to pass a civil rights bill since the 1950s, but Southerners used their *States' Rights* power coalition to block the bills or remove all the important provisions every time it came close to passing.

It was now LBJ's turn to give it a go. LBJ knew exactly which strings to pull to get a strong civil rights bill passed. He had experience with how the timing of a bill's introduction affected its chances of being held up by other legislation. Having been a masterful Senate majority leader, he understood exactly how to finesse not just the procedures, but also the people.

The Civil Rights Act of 1964 outlawed segregation in schools and in public places like waiting rooms and public transportation.

The Voting Rights Act of 1965 outlawed literacy tests and poll taxes for voters.

The Fair Housing Act of 1968[35] made it illegal to deny people the chance to live in certain areas of town based on their race. It also made it illegal to charge people different rental amounts or demand higher deposits based on a tenant's race.

The problem with this third act, unlike the two previous, was that Congress didn't include any way for the act to be enforced. If a landlord was caught breaking the rules, nothing could really be done to punish that landlord. The weakness of the Fair Housing Act would enable cities to continue locking blacks into their inner-city ghettoes for another two decades. That continued segregation would set the stage for the devastation caused by crack.

These three civil rights acts of the 1960s were important, but they didn't immediately bring about changes. Rich whites worked at finding loopholes in all three acts so that they could continue to exploit black labor. Less powerful whites looked for loopholes as well since they'd been brainwashed by decades of fear-mongering and othering into believing that living beside black families or working with them on the job could

---

[35] It was actually called the Civil Rights Act of 1968 but it had important provisions aimed at ending housing segregation.

only cause them harm.

The Law And Order Movement

As high-profile Civil Rights Movement successes made the news and attracted sympathy from many Northern and Western whites, some white leaders began to claim that when blacks held sit-ins at lunch counters or protested discrimination by marching in the streets, there was nothing noble about it. It was crime, pure and simple.

Richard Nixon, who became vice president under Eisenhower in 1952, seems to have been the first white leader to recognize that to keep the racial bribe in place, there would need to be a new way of talking about issues. The new way would have to hint at race, without ever mentioning it outright. The new language would be "colorblind," because racist language was effectively against the law.

Nixon decided that the phrase "law and order" could be used as a coded anti-black phrase that would keep poor whites mad at black people and therefore keep the important bond between rich whites and poor whites in place.

Instead of talking about black versus white, Nixon's idea was that messages should be coded into "law abiding citizens" versus "lawbreakers."

MLK, Rosa and the throngs of women who walked to work for a year to change Birmingham's busing system were simply a bunch of lawbreakers breaking the law.

In her book, *The New Jim Crow: Mass Incarceration in the Age of Colorblindness*, Michelle Alexander explains that Nixon emphasized to his key advisors privately that:

> "You have to face the fact that the whole problem is really the blacks. The key is to devise a system that recognizes this while not appearing to." That subliminal appeal to the anti-black voter was always present in Nixon's statements and speeches...using coded anti-black rhetoric.

With that, Nixon conjured a new common enemy for poor whites. This new, terrifying *other* had the code name "lawbreaker." The scary new lawbreaker enemy was the really the same Giant Negro that it had always been, roaming around looking for a white woman to rape, it was just illegal to call that monstrous *other* "black" anymore.

Just as the Scientific Racism of the early 1900s required that blacks not be allowed to get too much education, or speak too fancy, the new law and order framing would require that black crime be encouraged, highlighted and exaggerated.

What Nixon started, Reagan would perfect beyond anyone's wildest dreams.

Suburban Myopia

A decade after the suburban rush had begun, the luster began to wear off for its residents. Some suburban mothers began to recognize the things they'd lost when they accepted the grand bargain of consumerist life in the suburbs.

Friedan, in *The Feminine Mystique*:

Millions of [white] women lived their lives in the image of those pretty pictures of the American suburban housewife, kissing their husbands goodbye in front of the picture window, depositing their stationwagonsful of children at school, and smiling as they ran the new electric waxer over the spotless kitchen floor.

They baked their own bread, sewed their own and their children's clothes, kept their new washing machines and dryers running all day. They changed the sheets on the beds twice a week instead of once, took the rug-hooking class in adult education, and pitied their poor frustrated mothers, who had dreamed of having a career.

Their only dream was to be perfect wives and mothers; their highest ambition to have five children and a beautiful house, their only fight to get and keep their husbands. They had no thought for the unfeminine problems of the world outside the home; they wanted the men to make the major decisions. They gloried in their role as women, and wrote proudly on the census blank: "Occupation: housewife."

But, Friedan also noted:

> Sometimes a woman would say "I feel empty somehow . . . incomplete." Or she would say, "I feel as if I don't exist." Sometimes she blotted out the feeling with a tranquilizer.

> Sometimes she thought the problem was with her husband, or her children, or that what she really needed was to redecorate her house, or move to a better neighborhood, or have an affair, or another baby.

> Sometimes, she went to a doctor with symptoms she could hardly describe: "A tired feeling . . . I get so angry with the children it scares me . . . I feel like crying without any reason." (A Cleveland doctor called it "the housewife's syndrome.")

Friedan quoted one young mother who said:

> I've tried everything women are supposed to do—hobbies, gardening, pickling, canning, being very social with my neighbors, joining committees, running PTA teas. I can do it all, and I like it, but it doesn't leave you anything to think about—any feeling of who you are. I never had any career ambitions. All I wanted was to get married and have four children. I love the kids and Bob and my home. There's no problem you can even put a name to. But I'm desperate. I begin to feel I have no personality. I'm a server of food and a putter-on of pants and a bedmaker, somebody who can be called on when you want something. But who am I?

I believe that my mother felt the weird sadness that Friedan describes. I also believe that she misdiagnosed her sadness and decided that it came from her lack of beauty. I think she believed that if she could improve her looks and lose weight, she wouldn't feel that sadness anymore.

Her low regard of her physical appearance haunted her. She coped with the vacuous suburban culture not by rejecting consumerism, but by gorging on every advertising scheme aimed at women who wanted to lose weight.

I can see her in my mind, smoking a Virginia Slim and drinking a TaB soda while she waited patiently in our passenger van just outside my school. Of course, the highly consumerist weight loss industry is self-perpetuating— designed to never put itself out of business – so even though she devoted endless time and money to her self-improvement, she would never really be happy with the outcomes. This meant she retained that weird, unexplainable sadness Friedan described. It wouldn't be until the 1970s that she would find a supplemental *raison d'etre* when she came to the rescue of a boy named Baby Joe.

Raising Privileged Children

In the late 1960s, my mother was using whatever edition of Dr. Spock's book was current as a guide for assuring our physical and mental health.

Betty Crocker's cookbook, television commercials, and local grocery store marketing displays dictated our diet.

Then there was our moral and ethical training.

My mother had been raised Methodist, but had willingly accepted my father's Baptist religion[36]. The Baptist interpretation of the bible was supposed to provide our moral lessons but it did not provide guidance for navigating the modern world. Those rules were left to interpretation.

American frontier tenacity had, by now, morphed into a certain arrogant, high-horse, self-righteousness that was being passed down through white, middle-class[37] parenting techniques.

Consciously or subconsciously, my mother understood her duty to teach us about ethics and justice. She was unaware that her idea of justice had been skewed by her upbringing. She was raised with the sense that the world owed her special treatment and that if she didn't get it, she could appeal to higher and higher authority until it was awarded to her. She certainly wasn't alone in this. This sense of entitlement pervades the white middle class.

My mother taught us these lessons of inevitable justice by intervening

---

[36] In our Texas town, being a Baptist provided a far more lucrative social network so her conversion turned out to be a lucky coincidence.

[37] When I make references to middle-class the reader is invited to assume I mean "middle class and all higher classes." Certain privileges begin to accrue at the middle-class level and only become more lucrative as families move into upper-middle class and then upper class.

in our early childhood squabbles. She taught us that when things were not going our way, we could ask for an intervention from her and she would study the problem and deliver an equitable decision. What passed as equitable often served to make everyone happy. In other words, justice wasn't as important as the appearance of justice and the outcome seemed to reinforce the idea that we all deserved something pleasant as a reward for seeking counsel and intervention from a higher authority.

Furthermore, she encouraged us to ask for adult intervention everywhere we went: at church, at school, and at friends' houses. The lesson we learned, time and again: *Ask for justice and a pleasant outcome will nearly always be arranged for you by the adults in your life.*

When children are successful enough in securing "justice" for themselves, they go on to develop a sense of entitlement around fairness and justice even if the bulk of what they end up being awarded is neither fair, nor just.

We learned that we could bend interactions to suit our needs. I believed that when any rule was presented to me, I deserved to have the reasoning behind that rule explained to me. I was also certain that I deserved to be thought of as a unique and valuable individual at all times, and under all circumstances.

An eye-opening book, *Unequal Childhoods: Class, Race, and Family Life,* by Annette Lareau, outlines the differences in childrearing techniques she observed in families of different races as well as of different social classes. She paid special attention to lessons and outcomes related to self-advocacy, entitlement, and the pursuit of personal justice.

She found that middle-class parents train and encourage their children to negotiate with authority figures so that policies and rules will be amended or revised in their favor.

From Laureau:

> In general, the children of middle-class parents have a sense that they are special, that their opinions matter, and that adults should, as a matter of routine, adjust situations to meet children's wishes. Thus, one of the benefits of middle-class status appears to be the transmission of exceptional verbal skills that enable children to make special requests of adults in

positions of power.

Consider this example scenario:

> Your child has an oral report due, but you have her scheduled for a dentist appointment the morning she is to deliver the report. You cannot change the dentist appointment. You anticipate that your daughter's mouth might still be numb in the afternoon. Do you tell your child that nothing can be done and that even though she might get a bad grade, she will just have accept the unhappy coincidence?

> When she says that isn't fair, do you tell her, "Life isn't fair"?

> Or do you encourage your child to talk to the teacher, explain the situation, and ask her teacher if the oral report can be delivered the following day instead?

The middle-class way is the latter. Parents with middle-class values encourage their children to reason with their teachers and ask for special treatment based on their special circumstances.

People who embrace the middle-class model of childrearing will believe that such a request would be perfectly logical and reasonable. The teacher, also middle-class, will likely think the request is reasonable as well and cheerfully grant the request.

Lareau:

> *The white and Black middle-class children...exhibited an emergent version of the sense of entitlement characteristic of the middle-class. They acted as though they had a right to pursue their own individual preferences and to actively manage interactions in institutional settings. They appeared comfortable in these settings; they were open to sharing information and asking for attention.*

> *The working-class and poor children, by contrast, showed an emerging sense of constraint in their interactions in institutional settings. They were less likely to try to customize interactions to suit their own preferences. Like their parents, the children accepted the actions of persons in authority (although at times they also covertly resisted them).*

Lareau notes that today's middle-class black families were much more similar to middle-class white families than they were to working-class black families. In short, when children of any color or ethnicity are raised to self-advocate, they will likely be successful at getting special treatment and then become likely to develop a similar sense of entitlement.

Unfortunately, she also noted that when families don't believe they have a right to self-advocate, they often believe they have no choice but find un-sanctioned ways for getting what they feel they're due. For example, working-class parents might encourage a child with a same-day oral report and dentist appointment to simply skip the rest of that school day and report to the school that they are sick. By encouraging the child to lie to their teacher, the child ends up with the same special treatment but without the practice in stepping up to authority and requesting that special treatment. In other words, the outcome would be the same, but the experience for the child of working-class or poor parents would be far less empowering.

Laureau found that working-class parents talked as if teachers and administrators cared nothing about their special needs and circumstances so rather than appeal for special treatment, working class parents treated dishonesty as a tool for creatively attaining fair outcomes.

When Leah began the second grade, I volunteered at her school to help serve breakfast in the cafeteria for the first two weeks. At the time that I volunteered I had just finished reading Laureau's book. As it turned out, during that cafeteria work, I would come to understand Laureau's work on a visceral level. It happened this way:

Over the course of those ten days I looked for various ways to streamline the process so that the children could get through the line more quickly. One major bottle neck was an area where the children were supposed to use a metal turner to get a slice of "bread." The bread was actually apple raisin cake so most of the children liked that bread better than any other breakfast offering. The official cafeteria lady and I noted that we kept running out of bread before everyone had been served. I began posting signs, "One Piece of Bread Only," but kids continued to try to get away with taking more than one. Finally, I decided to pull the bread out to its own station and personally serve each piece.

In the course of serving the bread one day, I recognized a boy that I thought I'd already given a piece to. "Didn't I already give you bread?" I asked, eyeing the flimsy tray he held aloft as he shook his head no. I paused, observed his pleading eyes, and turned a piece of bread over onto his tray.

As I leaned toward the outer edge of my bread station, I saw it. There was his original piece, smashed flat on the floor. He'd dropped his piece and circled back attempting to pass himself off as a newcomer. A few weeks earlier I would have thought to myself, "Well that little liar!" but having read Laureau's work, I had a very different reaction.

I got *it*, and *him* and the *situation* and the understanding hit me like a punch in the gut. He'd lied because he didn't trust that by telling the truth, he would be awarded justice. Had someone taught him *that life isn't fair and if you are dumb enough to let your apple cake slip, then you get what you deserve, which is nothing?* Or had they taught him that *life isn't fair so you have to find ways to get ahead that aren't exactly advertised as options?*

When children are honest it's because they've been taught that honesty pays off. When they're dishonest it may be that they are testing limits, but it may also be because they've been taught that they don't deserve justice. In that lunch situation, the little boy had no way of knowing whether to expect justice from me. He must have figured that he had one chance to approach me for that replacement piece of bread and trusting me to deliver justice was simply too risky. He was hungry so he chose to take the route that seemed more likely to result in a new piece of bread.

When a person has consistently been treated unjustly, why are we surprised that they don't even bother to play by the rules anymore? They look for loopholes, short cuts, and indirect means to desired ends, while we fold our arms across our chest, shake our heads in disapproval and *tsk tsk* what we have decided is evidence of their degraded morals.

Then, we feel sufficiently superior to them, never acknowledging that we've had the luxury of living in a mini-world where justice can be requested and special happy results are granted to everyone on a regular basis.

THE 1970s

Figure 27: Me on my grandmother Leah's lap and my sister on my grandpa Otto's lap. This picture was taken in the College Station, TX, airport. My grandparents were flying in and out to see us at a time when middle-class people could not afford to fly.

The Jim Crow South in the 1970s

Sure, the Civil Rights Movement had been making the national news since 1954 and some important laws had been passed in Washington D.C. in the mid-1960s, but my husband's parents had seen almost nothing change in Monroe, Louisiana.

They still couldn't check out books from the local library; that was a privilege reserved for whites. They still weren't allowed to try on clothes and shoes in department stores; whites wouldn't buy things if they knew they'd draped or shod black bodies, even momentarily. Poor whites still insisted on being deferred to by blacks in every conceivable way.

From Kenneth Young's *Jim Crow Narrative* we can see how white doctors and white patients expected blacks to only receive medical care after any and all white patients had been catered to:

> I carried my mother to a white doctor… I didn't have an appointment. That man saw every white patient he had. As long as they came he'd see them, and as they closed, we'd been there since nine o'clock in the morning, and around four-thirty the whites stopped coming, then he turned to me and said who wants to see the doctor. I said my mother would like to see him. "Well, come on." He saw her then. Been sitting there since about nine-thirty.

These were the kind of incidents the federal government couldn't legislate, so these were the kind of things that continued. When whites could not control how much money blacks made, they tried to control any luxury items blacks might buy. In Walter M. Caver's *Jim Crow Narrative* he talks of how the whites in Charlotte, North Carolina tried to bully him out of owning a luxury car:

> I had a gentleman call me up, the richest person we have here in Charlotte. I knew him very well. I came home for dinner and while I was at dinner the phone rang. I answered it. He told me who he was.
>
> "Was that your car you were driving this morning?"
>
> I said, "Yes."
>
> He said, "Sell it. I don't want to see it on the street no more."
>
> So I said, "Well, whatever a person wants to drive, if they've got the money, [they] can drive it."
>
> A friend of mine, had to go to Pennsylvania and get a car. It was the biggest Chrysler they were making back then. They wouldn't sell him one

here. I got [my Lincoln] through a person in another state. When I built this house, wouldn't a bank in town loan me one dime. I had to build it from scratch.

Though it was the 1970s whites continued to insist that blacks should never be given the honorific of "miss," "missus," "mister," "sir," or "ma'am." In one *Jim Crow Narrative*, a man recalled speaking about one of the black teachers at the local school and forgetting the rules. In speaking to a white person he referred to his teacher as "Miss Jones." The white person became upset, saying, "Don't you Miss her to me!" The white person not only refused to call a grown black person Miss or Mister, they wouldn't even allow the honorifics to be used in their presence.

In Dr. Emery L. Rann's *Jim Crow Narrative* he tells about a conversation with a white man wherein he forgot to show the appropriate level of deference. The incident happened after he'd been to college, but before he put himself through medical school and became a doctor:

"Where is the place?" [the white man asked.]

I told him where it was.

"Do they have a phone there?"

"Yes they do."

He said, "Do they have a phone there?"

I said, "Yes, they have a phone."

*"God damn it, [N****r], when you talk to a white man, you say 'sir'!"*

I said, "Sir," and went out of the door, and lo and behold, there was a group of white men waiting, and I ran and jumped in my car. I mean I didn't run, but I made haste to my car and left that town just as fast as I could.

Among those who still hadn't left the South by 1970 there were some who, more than ever before, felt primed to either buck the system or catch the next bus out of town; or, having done the first, felt compelled to do the second in short order.

From the *Jim Crow Narrative* of Olivia Cherry:

My name is Olivia, which I feel is a very pretty name. My mother thought that way. That's why she gave it to me. And I had trouble with my name.

I would be upstairs cleaning the bathroom. One white lady [I worked for] said, "Susie."

They loved to call me Susie. "Susie."

I didn't answer. I was a spunky kid then. I was like 13 or 14.

Finally, she come to the steps and said, "Olivia, you hear me calling you?" I said, "Now I hear you. Now you said, 'Olivia.' That's my name."

[T]here was this white man and his girlfriend. They had a raspberry farm. They wanted us to pick the raspberries. I didn't really like [it] because it was backbreaking.

So here we are picking the raspberries, and here goes my name again. The man said, "Hey, Susie. Susie. You missed some on your row."

I knew he was calling me because this was my row, but I just kept on working. He said, "Susie, don't you hear me talking to you?"

I said, "I told you before, my name is Olivia. Olivia. Can you say that?"

He said, "Don't be so damn smart."

I went back and picked what he said I missed. It wasn't that I was working badly, I just overlooked it. Well, another day he did the same thing. "Susie, I want you to work down this end, and I want you to work with them." I just kept on working.

He said, "Do you hear me telling you?"

I said, "Do you know my name? Can you learn my name?

He said, "All right, whatever it is. I want you working down there."

So one day we went through this again. He said, "Get the hell off my property! I don't want you working for me at all."

I said, "Fine, because I don't want to work for you, but you have to pay me for the work I have done." I already computed the amount.

He told his girlfriend, "Pay her. Let's get rid of her."

I said, "No, this is not right. You owe me such-and-such cents."

"Pay her. Give her anything so we can get rid of her." So she paid me, and I stepped out on the highway.

I said, "Come on, you all, you don't want to work for him. He doesn't know how to treat you." They was standing there working and scared.

He said, "Get away from here! Get away from my property!"

I said, "Wait a minute. I'm on the highway. My mother and father paid taxes for this highway. This is not your highway." I said, "You leave me alone." And I went home and told my mother.

She said, "Oh, Lord! They're going to kill my daughter. I know they're going to kill my daughter."

Leah Tyler's Black Ancestors in the 1970s

My husband's parents, Bill and Diane, didn't want to wait until they lost their tempers and had to skip town in a rush. They wanted to save up their money and drive out of town before an incident arose.

Diane had an aunt who had been living in Denver for a decade or more. Diane's aunt offered Bill and Diane a temporary landing pad that made Denver hard to pass up.

My husband was six years old when the 1970s began, and sixteen when they came to a close. He was seven years old when his family arrived in Denver, all of them full of hope about their new life.

His father, Bill, was probably the most optimistic of all. He had a young beautiful wife and three bright, talkative, clever children. William was seven when they made the trek to Denver. Theresa was six and Tammy was four.

They arrived at Diane's aunt's house, tumbling out of a gold station wagon. Diane's aunt showed the children where they would sleep and helped them begin putting what little they owned into the drawers of a dresser. Bill went back out to fill the car with groceries. When he transferred those groceries into the cupboards and refrigerator a half hour later, he did so in a show of gratitude to Diane's kin for taking them in.

The next morning, Bill went down and signed himself up at the Ford Motor Technology Institute. When he wasn't attending classes or studying, he was looking for paid work so his family would not create an undue burden for Diane's aunt and uncle.

Bill knew a lot about cars. Back in Monroe, he had a reputation for being able to diagnose and fix *any* car someone brought to him. Car problems that stumped others were solved in short order once they were put in front of Bill Tyler.

He'd enrolled at the Ford school in Denver not so much to learn about cars, as for the better job opportunities that would become available once he had Ford's stamp of approval.

He bet his heart on Denver. He was certain that, unlike Monroe, an automotive shop in Denver would pay him for his expertise and then give him a raise when he completed the Ford program.

The first auto shop he visited offered him a position as a janitor. He brushed it off. The second shop did the same. This treatment was rooted in racism and he knew it. He told himself he'd never thought Denver would be perfect, even though he had.

Bill was starting to understand that, in Denver, no one mentioned race, but the outcomes were the same. Denver's racism was hidden under lies while Monroe didn't bother to fake it.

Bill completed the Ford program and was awarded his Certified Mechanic license. The program had promised job placement services upon graduation. The program seemed to be much better at placing white graduates than black ones.

He was not welcome in local unions and was never called back when he applied for jobs at the many shops that were on Ford's list of partner employers. He couldn't prove there was any racial discrimination, yet he still couldn't get a job that paid him for his advanced skillset.

Before long, Diane gave birth to another boy, Tyrone.

Whenever Bill's frustration leaked out, Diane was unsympathetic. She wondered aloud whether he was imagining things. She and the children got along fine with both black and white neighbors.

These white people in Denver we different, Diane explained, and Bill had to be brave enough to find that out.

After a few maddening years and some ill treatment by Denver police, Bill decided he wanted to go back to Louisiana. He told Diane he couldn't bear to stay in Denver any longer.

Diane was determined to stay. She'd found work as a teacher's aide for the Head Start program. If she went back, she'd almost certainly have to work as a maid. She felt it was in *her* best interest, and in the best interest of the children, to stay in Denver.

After discussions turned to arguments and arguments lapsed into fights, Bill left the family, returning to Monroe.

Leah Tyler's White Ancestors in the Early 1970s

Figure 28: My grandparents gave us money to purchase an above-ground pool. I am the little one with the pigtails.

I was two-years old when the seventies began and twelve when they ended. While my husband had to be grateful for a television that gave off heat, my family had several watchable televisions and central air.

My grandparents, Otto and Leah, were a force and

Figure 29: We drove from Texas, all the way up to see my grandparents in Whitman County, Washington, nearly every summer. If we visited during the wheat harvest, my mom would take us out to one of the trucks and let us play in the grain.

a fixture in our lives. They helped us settle into a four-bedroom, three bathroom brick house with a sliding glass door that opened onto a concrete slab patio. They did this by providing my parents with the 20% down payment. Then, about a year later, my grandparents pitched in even more money so that we could get an above-ground backyard pool.

Since we were still young, my mother would fill it to baby-pool height and we would run around in water up to our knees or lay down and pretend to swim.

The pool, no doubt, eased my mother's stress level. My siblings and I would play ourselves to near exhaustion, then, fall asleep in the early evening without being nagged. My mother enjoyed many a peaceful summer evening because of that pool.

My father was a hardworking young professor. He wasn't making much money, but my parents' marriage wasn't strained by money woes because my grandparents were happy to supplement my father's income. If my mother began feeling depressed or overwhelmed she could shop her way to a better mood (just as Madison Avenue had taught her).

Because my mother managed her own happiness, my father was free to focus on his career—working long hours and travelling as needed.

My father had put himself through college before he met my mother, and that achievement can't be diminished, but once he'd married my mother, her wealth allowed him the latitude to continue focusing on accolades and awards.

Had my mother made the mistake of marrying a man who turned out to be intensely unhappy and frustrated with his life (perhaps someone dispirited by a low-wage job or supervisors who didn't give him a chance to succeed), that husband might have tried to take out those frustrations on my mother. In such a situation, my mother's wealth would have protected her.

Anyone my mother might have married would have been obligated to treat her gently and lovingly, because at any time, my mother could have called her parents, and they would have whisked us all back to Washington to live with them.

My grandparents also made sure our family had two solid, reliable cars at all times. My mother could ferry us to school and after-school activities, always knowing that if any car trouble arose, she could count on her parents to make sure things got fixed quickly, so our middle-class activities and ambitions could continue uninterrupted.

Diane's Life as a Single Mother

Diane was left in Denver to raise their four children without Bill and without his financial support.

After Bill's departure, the new man of the house, ten-year-old William, did well enough in school to enjoy it, but he also did a good job of stealing, drinking liquor, and smoking cigarettes.

Diane began drinking socially and continued to do well in her job even though the pay was low enough that she continued to qualify for government assistance. She began dating a white man who lived nearby.

The white man, named Eddie, was a convict. He'd just returned from prison when he began dating Diane.

Unlike my mother, who found her suitable mate in college, my husband's mother found her new boyfriend in the crime-ridden inner city. Segregation forced Diane to live in the poorest of neighborhoods. Her job was in the same poor neighborhood. She had no chance of meeting a man who could provide her with a three-bedroom brick home and a middle-class life, so, she dated someone who treated her nice and was fond of her children.

When Diane was at work, she left her children in Eddie's sister's care. Eddie took William and Tyrone around the neighborhood, teaching them how to hustle.

The kids were always hungry, and neither Diane nor Eddie's sister were able to keep them fed. Eddie would take them to the grocery store and have them crawl under the produce tables. In those days, a lot of the produce tables at grocery stores looked almost like flying saucers. They were made of green plastic and had a futuristic shape that provided for a large, round hollowed out base. William, Theresa, Tammy and Tyrone could wait comfortably inside these produce spaceships without anyone noticing they were there.

Eddie would go around the store picking up lunch meat, crackers, cookies, and fruit. He would discreetly pass everything to them and the children would feed from their own private smorgasbord until their stomachs distended. When the kids came out from under the fruit stands, the five of them would casually exit the grocery store and go on about their day.

Hustling quieted a growling stomach.

William had begun having asthma attacks around age nine, and his mother routinely gave him weed and whiskey as a remedy. She couldn't afford to take off work to sit all day in the free clinic close to their place. She had no idea that early exposure to drugs and alcohol would damage William's brain in ways that made him far more susceptible to addiction.

William got really good at stealing cars. He would steal a car, go for a joyride, get arrested, be put in juvenile detention, have a call placed to his mother, be released into his mother's custody, go home, take a nap and go out to steal another car.

He loved driving cars.

Diane was struggling mightily to keep her job and keep her boys out of trouble. Social workers threatened to put them in a group home if they didn't attend school on a more regular basis and stay out of trouble.

Diane quit her job, sold what she could to raise money, and bought three frozen chickens from the grocery store. William watched her, tiptoeing around and looking for clues that might reveal her intentions. She fried up the chicken and packed his school bag with clothes. When the chicken had cooled, she wrapped them in tinfoil, put shoes on Tyrone, handed the bag of clothes to Theresa and the bag of chicken to William.

They left their apartment in the projects, not even bothering to close the door behind them, and began a march toward the tall buildings of Denver's core.

As they approached the regional bus station hub, they encountered the usual crowd on its outskirts. Some had suitcases and were simply catching a cigarette break during a stopover. Others were begging for money, trying to raise enough to buy a ticket to their next stop. Still others were locals who used the pretense of travel to beg from passersby.

Diane pushed through the smokers, the travelers, and the faux travelers, opening the door to the bus station and settling the mystery in William's mind.

They were going somewhere; most likely Louisiana.

It took three days to reach Jonesboro, Louisiana where Diane's mother and sisters shared a home. Along the way, all they had to eat was cold chicken. When the bus stopped and other families disembarked, returning with chips, soda and candy, William worked hard distracting the younger children, hoping they didn't see the luxuries being enjoyed by the other travelers.

They would stay in Jonesboro for six weeks. While they were there, Diane's mother, Hazel, seemed constantly in motion as she busily gathered herbs, boiled concoctions, and slathered sour-smelling pastes onto his mother's feet. Still, it seemed to William that Diane's gout and gangrene were getting worse, not better.

He hated Jonesboro. His asthma had gotten worse in the lush, humid South. His attacks were more frequent and were now so violent that he soiled himself in their throes. He began pressuring his mother: *When would they return to Denver?*

One afternoon he came into a quiet house only to be jolted by the sound of a slap followed by the wail of his young sister. Then, his aunt's voice came, accusing someone of being "just as saditty as your momma." He froze in the hallway and listened as his aunt continued, "Diane think she can run back to the city and leave us here to scrape by. We got enough trouble without taking hers."

It was Tammy who drew the wrath of the various aunts. Though she hardly spoke, the aunts seemed to roil with hatred toward her. When that morning finally came, Tammy seemed to sense her fate. Every time Diane moved, Tammy was underfoot. William watched Tyrone, checking in on him from moment to moment, but what Tammy seemed to sense had not registered with Tyrone. Instead, he was out on the porch, arranging rocks with such studied intensity he never looked up long enough to realize his mother couldn't bear even a glance in his direction.

Diane, William and Theresa boarded the bus back to Denver in much the same way as they'd come. Theresa with the bag of clothes hugged to her chest, and William with a bag of chicken.

Back in Denver, Diane was put on government disability by a case worker. William continued hustling to make ends meet. To hustle meant to combine resourcefulness with ingenuity and tenacity. To hustle also meant to find some *thing*, somewhere, recognize some kernel of value, then, find a way to convert that value into cash. In some people's minds, hustling is synonymous with breaking the law, but for those who know what it's like to grow up where want is stacked on top of need and sandwiched in between desperation and last resort, hustling is a venerated skill.

William's intelligence made him exceptional as a hustler. His mother depended on him and he came through for her again and again.

Leah Tyler's Parents Go to (Desegregated) School

I started first grade, in 1974, in Texas. Even though the *Brown* decision had been decided almost twenty years before, my Texas town didn't get around to integrating the schools until two years before I walked through their doors.

It had taken at least four additional Supreme Court Cases after *Brown* to finally integrate most schools. That was true for the South as well as the rest of the country.

It was a case decided in 1971[38] that finally triggered the integration of my town's schools. In that case, the Supreme Court ruled that busing *could* and *should* be used to achieve integration.

Thus, starting in the fall of 1972, black students were bused into my local elementary school, the school less than a mile from our house.

When I started school in 1974, I was part of the third never-segregated class. Unlike larger cities, where whites could move to suburbs to avoid integration, in a city too small for suburbs, there was nowhere for whites to go. Some white families in our town reacted by finding it in their budget to place their children into private schools. My father had attended integrated schools in California and Washington so he was neither alarmed nor worried.

In those early years, whenever I spoke about school, if I told my parents a story and began by saying, "This black girl in my class..." my father would interrupt, asking me whether the girl's color was relevant to the story.[39] I was instructed that if race was germane to the story I could mention it, but otherwise I should leave it out.

It was rare for me to see black people anywhere off the school grounds, so I easily absorbed the idea that black people at our home might be unwelcome. My mother countered that by actively encouraging us to include any friends who happened to be black when we made out the guest lists for our birthday parties.

We were also encouraged to have black girlfriends over for sleepovers. My mother saying, "If your best friend is black, then invite her

---

[38] *Swann v. Charlotte-Mecklenburg Board of Education.*
[39] Yes, he actually used the word *relevant*, and yes, I knew what it meant.

for a sleepover just as you would a white friend." I remember at least two occasions when I had black girl friends over for sleepovers during elementary school.

In the second grade, my best friend Jackie came to spend the night. We swam from noon until dusk. My mom took home movies of us splashing around in the water. Later that night, my mom granted us a special treat. We had two big bean bags in our living room, and she okayed Jackie's and my request to fall asleep in front of the TV, spending all night in our swimsuits, asleep on the bean bags.

When, a little later in that second grade year, I told my parents of my crush on a black classmate named Derrick, then told them of my plans to ask him to be my boyfriend, they expressed no reservations at all[40].

In third grade, I had a new best friend. She was black also and around Easter of that year she came for a sleepover just as Jackie had the year before and I remember the details of her visit just as vividly as I remember Jackie's sleepover.

For some reason, I gravitated toward my black classmates – girls and boys—and I'm not sure why. My best guess is that I was attracted to their self-confidence. Within the dynamics of my own family, my position among my siblings was one of weakness. Perhaps because of this, I sought out friends who weren't bossy, but that were very self-assured. Perhaps I was attracted to them because I wanted to be more like them. The black children in my elementary school classes seemed to have a sense of themselves that the white children didn't. They seemed to know their own strength and I felt desperate to find mine.

My desegregated school experiences were very positive. My husband also has fond memories of his elementary school, but if you let him tell it, Denver schools had never been segregated, all the children danced around maypoles holding hands and all the beautiful, kind, supportive teachers farted rainbows.

Okay, he wasn't *that* delusional about his school experiences, but he *had* believed his mixed-race schools were far superior to mine. He

---

[40] I'm guessing they shared at least a sideways glance but nothing was said to discourage me

repeatedly claimed to me that Denver schools had *never* been segregated.

The actual history of Denver schools does not align with his recollections. An article in the New York Times, written by James Brooke in September of 1995, belies my husband's idyllic recollections of Denver schools in the 1970s. While poor whites in Denver *did* live in the same housing projects as poor blacks, just as he had claimed, those whites would have been free to live in other areas. If they got good jobs and could afford an apartment in one of Denver's suburbs, they could move out of the inner city and their children could attend predominately white schools. That was not the case with blacks. In fact, when the Tylers arrived in Denver, a desegregation case that had begun in 1969 was wending its way up to the Supreme Court. The case was *Keyes v. School District No. 1, Denver, CO.*

Denver residents had voted an anti-busing majority onto the school board thinking that board would protect them from bus-based integration. Instead, a class-action lawsuit was filed with Wilfred Keyes, a black father, as the lead plaintiff. Denver whites responded by setting fire to the city's school buses and bombing Keyes' house.

When my husband William was nine years old (1973), the Supreme Court ruled that Denver had to desegregate its schools by beginning busing immediately. The Colorado legislature quickly passed racist provisions to ensure that the suburbs would not be included in the busing plans. Integration would take place only within Denver County and whites could move to suburbs if they wanted to avoid integrated schools.

There was massive white-flight. The *Times* article included the following quote:

> *"We lost 7,000 students in the summer of 1975," recalled Naomi L. Bradford, a white busing opponent who was elected head of the [Denver] school board in 1985. "In the fall, we lost 100 students a week -- probably as soon as their homes were sold."*

In the fourth, fifth, or sixth grade, (he can't recall exactly) William began riding a bus fifteen miles away from home to a Denver school in a predominantly white neighborhood.

After reading about Keyes and burnt buses, I ask him again about school segregation. This time as he tries to brag, I delight in interrupting him to correct his faulty memory and point out that, in fact, there was a battle raging all around him. "Remember when you started riding the bus? Why do you think that happened?"

Suddenly, he breaks into a broad smile. I watch his expression as things fall together in his mind and he recognizes why he'd gone from attending a school a few blocks from home, to riding a bus to a school miles away. He can't stop laughing. "Man!" he says, several times.

"So?" I say, "What does it feel like to be Ruby Bridges and not even realize it for like, thirty years?"

"Man! That's crazy. Yeah. But see, we saw the buses as an adventure. We were black!! And we were goin' over to that other school to have fun! We were black!!" he recalled, emphasizing the word "black" with such delight that I took a moment out of our conversation to teach Leah to chant the James Brown mantra, "Say it loud! I'm black and I'm proud."

Back in the mid-1970s William and his friends had obviously absorbed the messages of the Black Pride movement.[41] They loved being black and they spent very little time or energy thinking about how whites felt about them.

Each morning, as William and his friends boarded the buses, they looked forward to seeing fifteen miles of city beyond their neighborhood. They loved the smiling, supportive teachers at the white schools, even while they thought of them as gullible. They loved recess and physical education classes where they felt they were able to dominate the games and activities. They also felt that when they got in trouble, the punishment was almost non-existent: There were almost never whippings and often they were just taken aside by a nice white lady who smiled and told them they were good kids and they should try harder to stay out of trouble. When they did something bad enough to warrant a paddle or two it never approached the severity of the wailings they got at home or the physical pain of fights they got into with one another as a sport of sorts.

Later, William figured out that if he didn't board the bus for the trip home in the afternoons, he could walk through the surrounding

---

[41] The Black Panther Party even had a Denver branch led by a man named Lauren Watson.

neighborhoods, find a bike laying in a front yard, or sitting in an open garage, and ride it home.

Back in his own neighborhood, it wouldn't be long before the bike would get taken from him in much the same way. That was life: It was his life anyway, so, he'd shrug it off, skip the afternoon bus the next day and get himself another one.

Whites with missing bikes probably felt doubly justified in their opposition to integration once a hooligan like my husband pricked the bubble that had previously enveloped their lives.

I asked him if, at that time, he'd ever stopped to consider how the white kids felt when they found their bikes stolen. He said, "I didn't really think about them because everyone I knew had their bikes stolen. If you had a toy, it would break quick or get stole quick. Wasn't any use in getting' sad about it 'cause it happened all the time. I figured they was just like me. They let it roll off their backs because that's what *we* did. That's all you could do, really."

But the whites were indignant. They lived in a world where rules were followed and fairness was valued. William's mother hadn't bothered to teach him about fairness. Nothing in Diane's life, the life of her parents, grandparents, cousins, neighbors, friends or acquaintances had ever been "fair" in even the smallest way. Black parents in the Jim Crow South couldn't talk about "fair" to their children, it would only remind them just how little fairness they'd ever encountered.

In the white neighborhoods, children were taught that bikes were prize possessions. Bikes were either awarded to them by Santa after a year of good behavior or they were something their parents helped them purchase after they'd worked long and hard at some task. Children of the suburbs ceremoniously used the money from their piggy banks to make their bike purchases at the local department store. For white kids, bikes were full of lessons about how "anything worth having is worth working for."

But now, because of William, there was a white kid who was devastated and grief-ridden. And this poor white kid had white parents, who were also seething with anger about those...those...*black people.*

Maybe they sat around the dinner table that evening, the evening the bike went missing, and tried to remain calm while they discussed a move to the suburbs, after all.

In their clenched-jaw hysteria they could not see that *they* had created him. Had they allowed blacks with middle-class values to move into their neighborhoods, *those* black kids wouldn't have stolen *their* kids' bikes. Those black kids would have been instilled with the exact same value system *they* had, because the middle-class value system is what would have enabled that black family to buy the house and move their children in. The very presence of middle-class black neighbors would have protected whites from forced busing. Had it not been for the racist, exclusionary acts carried out by whites; my husband and his friends would never have been bussed into their neighborhoods in the first place .

Instead, whites in Denver used restrictive covenants to keep blacks out of their neighborhoods and schools. They locked them in ghettos where they had to rely on survival-of-the-fittest rules. Whites forced blacks to develop strategies for getting by even as they were denied adequate educational opportunities and wages. The strategies developed by blacks in direct reaction to the conditions whites created, then came back to haunt whites.

Oops?

Lessons in Getting By

My father liked awards and formal recognition. He would have liked for us, his children, to win awards, too. He used verbal praise and verbal admonishment to try to guide us. However, because of his professional pursuits, and traditional gender roles in place at that time, he wasn't the person paying attention to homework and other school programs.

That role, of course, was administered by my mother. She had mixed feelings about how much pressure she should put on us to excel in school. Early in our lives, when she dressed us all alike in patent leather shoes, white socks, and color coordinated outfits, people came out of the woodwork to praise us. We were beautiful and clever and a source of joy, even to strangers.

Once we entered grade school, she continued to encourage us and bask in the praise from our teachers and others. When an essay contest came up, my mother gently coaxed us along in our writing and we swept the contest. When a poster contest followed, she guided our efforts and we swept that contest, as well.

During these same years, she began volunteering at our school and came to know some of the black children who were struggling to keep up.

When I was in the third grade, she was assigned to help one child in particular. When "Baby Joe" came to our school in what was supposed to be his third grade year, he could not recognize or even name the letters of the alphabet[42]. He was small in stature and still sucked his thumb. Yet, on the playground with me and my friends, he was bright, funny, clever and very good at sports.

It was obvious that more than one person had failed him, miserably.

What the hell had happened in kindergarten? Didn't anyone notice? What about his first grade teachers? His second?

The school asked my mother to tutor him for extended hours. She accepted the challenge. She poured her heart into his lessons and was thrilled by even the smallest improvements.

By day she was his elementary school tutor. By night she worked with him at our town's Boy's Club. That meant, a few nights a week, she loaded us into our family's passenger van and took us to the "black" side of town.

When her tutoring sessions were over on those weeknights, five or six boys would ask for rides home. She would wend our van through the back streets and dirt roads. Sometimes the boys would make fun of each other's houses and my heart would ache for them. We didn't care what anyone's houses looked like, my mom would reassure them.

When she was featured in the local newspaper for her work at the Boy's Club I was intensely proud. I had a sense that many whites probably didn't approve, and that made me even more proud.

Her tutoring efforts spanned my third and fourth grade year, and then, Baby Joe's mother moved him away from our town.

---

[42] I feel comfortable sharing his story because I've learned from mutual friends that "Baby" died years ago. Drugs, guns, murder – something along those lines.

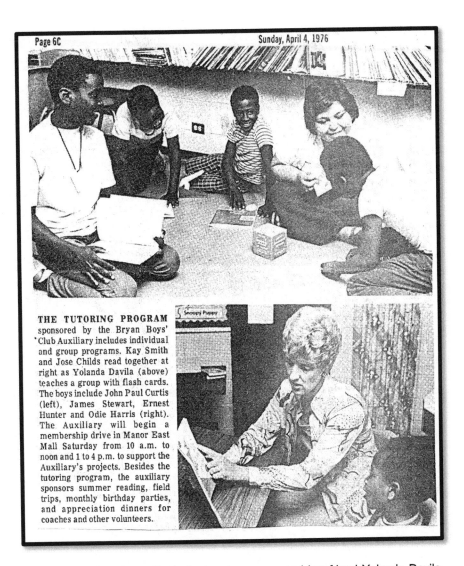

THE TUTORING PROGRAM sponsored by the Bryan Boys' Club Auxiliary includes individual and group programs. Kay Smith and Jose Childs read together at right as Yolanda Davila (above) teaches a group with flash cards. The boys include John Paul Curtis (left), James Stewart, Ernest Hunter and Odie Harris (right). The Auxiliary will begin a membership drive in Manor East Mall Saturday from 10 a.m. to noon and 1 to 4 p.m. to support the Auxiliary's projects. Besides the tutoring program, the auxiliary sponsors summer reading, field trips, monthly birthday parties, and appreciation dinners for coaches and other volunteers.

Figure 30: The Bryan Eagle featured my mom and her friend Yolanda Davila for their work at the Boy's Club in 1976.

I think Baby Joe changed my mother. After she met him, she saw us, her own children, as grossly advantaged. Further, she saw that her encouragement was giving us an even greater edge. She took a step back from our school activities. After Baby Joe left, it seemed like she decided we were on our own. We would either do good things or we would not, and it was not her place, she felt, to intervene.

Even though my mom kept her distance when it came to our school achievements, I remained convinced that I was the smartest person that had ever lived.

William was fairly confident in his level intelligence, as well. His mother was distant in a different way. Once Diane was on her own, she didn't parent William at all. She was stretched too thin. She struggled to pull together the right resources at the right time to maintain a stable home life. She was always more likely to worry about bills and groceries than grades and extra-curriculars.

When William stole things and sold them, he took the money home to his mother. Diane needed the money, so she didn't ask questions. She didn't want her son to break the law, but the money was a relief to her and she didn't have the luxury of considering whether her son was mortgaging his future.

Claude Brown, writing in his autobiography, *Manchild in the Promised Land,* had this to say:

> *Mama's favorite question was, "Boy, why you so bad?"*
>
> *I tried many times to explain to Mama that I wasn't "so bad." I tried to make her understand that it was trying to be good that generally got me into trouble.*
>
> *I remember telling her that I played hookey to avoid getting into trouble in school. It seemed that whenever I went to school, I got into a fight with the teacher. The teacher would take me to the principal's office. After I had fought with the principal, I would be sent home and not allowed back in school without one of my parents.*
>
> *So to avoid all that trouble, I just didn't go to school. When I stole things, it was only to save the family money and avoid arguments or scoldings whenever I asked for money.*

William could have done well in school despite the instability of his home life. In fact, he could have done exceptionally well because he had self-confidence and a very bright mind. Unfortunately, he had attention deficit hyperactivity disorder (ADHD), just as I did.

We were both advanced in our use of vocabulary and were able to handle complex logic. We were also both fairly incapable of sitting still long enough to complete assignments and we both often made careless mistakes.

William and I both went undiagnosed. We were both called *unfocused*. Somewhere along the way, his lack of focus was classified as typical (for a black boy), whereas mine was seen as a side effect of my superior intelligence.

I remember sitting in my third grade class while everyone but me recited the multiplication tables. I thought to myself, "How do they all know this weird sequence of numbers they're chanting?"

The other students knew what to chant because multiplication tables had been assigned as homework. Homework I'd not bothered to do. Not only did I not do the homework; I didn't even understand the concept of

Figure 31: Me with my mom on a beach in Maine. That summer we drove all over the New England states. We visited all kinds of sites important to US history. Our stops included New York City, Philadelphia, Boston, and many other cities and attractions.

multiplication.

By that time, I'd already established the pattern I'd follow for many years. Each day when I got home from school, my mom would ask if I had any homework. I would say no, and that would be the end of the discussion.

By the end of the third grade (1976), my parents had instituted a twice-yearly ritual where they would call me into a private meeting, away from my siblings, and explain to me, while holding my report card, that all my teachers said I was smart, and I had high scores on intelligence tests, so my grades could only mean that I wasn't trying. They wanted me to try harder, but the message I walked away with each time was very different from the one they had attempted to convey. My thought process went like this:

If everyone, including me, believes I'm smart, then why would I work any harder just to prove something we all already know and agree on?

Gifted? Or Troubled?

The more I was assigned homework and didn't complete it, the less I was able to keep my grades up.

One school morning, in the fourth grade, realizing that I had a report due, I decided to copy a section out of the World Book Encyclopedia on sloths[43]. Grabbing the *S* encyclopedia on my way out the door that morning, I decided that rather than taking the time to copy the entry, I would cut a hole in a piece of notebook paper so that it formed a window on the section I had planned to copy. I was too attention-deficit, it seemed, to properly plagiarize.

Later that morning, I stood at the front of my classroom, opened the encyclopedia and appeared to be reading from the piece of notebook paper. In reality, I was reading the encyclopedia through the hole I'd cut.

I was sure that my teacher knew what I was doing, but for whatever reason she chose not to embarrass me.

---

[43] The irony of the topic was lost on me back then

A new program was starting the next school year and fourth grade teachers had been asked to be on the lookout for kids who would be well-suited for it. It was called STEP or the STudent Enrichment Program. STEP was a gifted and talented program (GT).

I remember my fourth grade teacher giving me the STEP test. She gave me a list of words and asked me to read them. With each successive

Figure 32: I am seated in front. My grandparents could have given us money to help us get a built-in swimming pool, but they didn't. We didn't need their money. My parents, by that time, had a great credit rating and had equity in our house. They easily qualified for a home improvement loan with a nice low interest rate. During the same time period, banks discriminated against black homeowners, denying home improvement loans.

word, she grew more excited, smiling, nodding, and asserting, "Yes!" The list was a lot of fun to read. I would start looking at a word, never having seen it before, but as I sounded it out, I would hear my father's voice, and I would know the word. I made it through the entire list, which was designed to be progressively harder and I nailed every single word.

My father always used big vocabulary words around us. Mainly he did it because he wasn't very attuned to what words children our age would understand. My mother would point out to him that we couldn't understand him, but he didn't believe it was necessarily better to talk at our level. In retrospect, his use of the advanced vocabulary probably helped us far more than it hurt.

So in the fourth grade, because I had a father who used big words, and because I thought IQ tests were a lark, I knocked it out of the park on a test for the fifth grade GT program.

I don't know if Denver schools had a GT program. In the earliest days of GT programs, only select schools were venturing into this new area.

My husband was being taught by white teachers who were more than likely in the throes of culture shock because of the busing.

There was an additional difference between us. I spoke the accepted, mainstream, middle-class English dialect. My English had a less pronounced Southern dialect than my teachers and fellow students because my parents had been living in the Northwest just a few years prior, and my mother had not yet developed a strong Texas accent.

Conversely, my husband spoke a rural Louisiana dialect—but in Denver—where it likely would have caused him to be prejudged as simple-minded in the eyes of Denverites.

When I got to the fifth grade, I learned that, based on my fourth grade teacher's recommendation and my test results, I'd been tracked into the STEP program.

When lobbying for the creation and funding of GT programs in the late 1970s, psychologists claimed that the program was necessary because those of us who were gifted, if left in mainstream classes, would certainly be at risk for failing due to the lack of challenge presented. In retrospect, I think the designers of the program, when they originally conceived it in the early 1970s, had unknowingly lumped together kids with ADHD and Asperger's Syndrome (a high-functioning form of autism). Those diagnoses were not fully understood back then, and teachers saw some kids who excelled in some ways, but fell woefully short in other ways.

Kids like me, with ADHD or some other attention problem, were at risk, but it was because we had trouble concentrating in a traditional classroom setting. If you had ADHD, you also had to test well, talk "right," and it didn't hurt if you could draw or had otherwise shown creativity.

I definitely showed creativity. I could draw and when any project involving arts or crafts was assigned I had a great time coming up with creative expressions. My teachers always gushed over my arts and crafts work. Sometimes my crafts met the project requirements but sometimes they didn't. If they didn't, it was because I'd decided I simply didn't care to meet the requirements or I'd decided my ideas were better than the guidelines.

Creativity requires confidence. You have to believe that you can come up with a solution that no one else seems to have thought of. Sometimes the creative solution is one that initially seems out of bounds. As a middle-class white child I had been encouraged to trust my instincts and present my ideas without fear of ridicule or recrimination.

Many of the kids in STEP seemed to me to be nothing more than nerds. Early in the first semester, we were tasked with doing a mock trial based on the story of Little Red Riding Hood. The two students who stepped up begging to be the attorneys did so because they both had already decided they wanted to go to law school. Of course, Leslie and Justin both became attorneys and practice law today. These two were traditional high achievers. They didn't need any special program. They were going to do well regardless of what English class they ended up in. There was nothing at-risk about them.

When I arrived in my fifth grade STEP class that first day, I noticed right away that everyone in STEP was white and middle-class. Eight months before that day, in January of 1977, my mother and us kids sat glued in front of the television as *Roots*, the mini-series, was broadcast for the first time. In my nine-year old view of the world, slavery explained why the kids at the Boy's Club were poor and everyone in our white neighborhood was not.

Seeing *Roots* was a big, big deal for me. It changed me. If that weren't enough, I'd also seen *Cornbread, Earl & Me* so I knew the truth about modern society: *Black people were just trying to get home in the rain with a bottle of orange-flavored soda while white people were over-reacting to fear and misunderstanding and f&*king everything up.*

Walking into that GT classroom and seeing only *us* and no *them* I was conscious enough to know that something was very wrong.

A few weeks in, my GT teacher began waxing about our class getting a new student. Our teacher talked about her so long and so lavishly I became suspicious, wondering what the big deal could possibly be.

When the student arrived the next week, the mystery was solved. Our new classmate, Trisha, was black. It seemed obvious to me, even at that young age, that my teacher's intensive introduction was due to guilt and overcompensation[44].

Then, I wondered how it had happened. I imagined that when we all arrived that first day, my teacher looked at us and felt the same way I had.

I imagined that a call must have gone out to all the fifth grade teachers, asking them to take a hard look at their students and try to find non-white, non-middle-class kids who could be pulled into STEP.

We also got a rural, working-class, white girl named Belle a few weeks after that.

In all the years I was a member of STEP, we never had another black student. Certainly we would not have had an ADHD-type black boy. It just wasn't the kind of behavior a black boy could exhibit and be seen as smart in our Texas town in the late 1970s and early 1980s.

I remembered recently, that a boy in my fourth grade class, a black boy named Byron, had once given a suspiciously creative oral book report in our fourth grade classroom. He stood exactly where I'd stood a few weeks prior when I read my fake sloth report out of the encyclopedia. He'd given an oral report on a book I'd read, and his account was nothing like the actual book.

His report was full of interesting and entertaining details and he had the whole class laughing. After he finished his report, I pulled him to the side. "Byron, I read that book," I said. His face registered surprise and then worry. "I'm not going to tell on you. Besides, I liked your report. It was funny."

So Byron, being smart and creative, fit the first part of the criteria for STEP. The fact that he had not done his reading in time to give his book report meant he was at risk for squandering his talent by not being focused. If I was a prime candidate for STEP, he should have been a shoo-

---

[44] Don't get me wrong, my teacher's guilt was totally justified, as was my own. Guilt was good. It moved that teacher to action and she got results.

in for STEP as well. My guess is that he was never tested.

When I remembered this story, I immediately needed to know how things turned out for Byron. Did he end up like my husband? Did he drop out of school and end up in prison? I checked my high school yearbook. In his senior photo, he's wearing a suit and tie. This wasn't a common outfit among the seniors that year. Seeing that he'd held things together into our senior year, I felt confident that he was probably doing well. I checked in with a mutual friend who assured me he's living a middle-class life.

The real question isn't about Byron; it's the question of how many other little black boys, like my husband, would have been significantly more productive and successful if they'd been nurtured by the school system instead of labeled, tracked remedial, and stigmatized by it.

In Texas today, GT programs have morphed into something like a private school experience within the public school system. People lobby to get their children into these programs. They pay for prep classes to improve their children's chances of making the cut. If their kids don't get accepted, they go through another round of preparatory activities and apply again the next year. To think that funds in a public school system are being diverted so that an elite group of children can have an enriched experience above and beyond that of the general population seems to me to be a travesty, and a distortion of the original intent.

But that's a topic for another day.

What's more important to point out here is the fact that racial prejudice and bias led teachers and administrators to fail my husband. The same prejudices and biases led them to elevate me.

It's also interesting to consider how much more of a privileged life I could have led if I'd just taken advantage of the opportunities that were practically forced on me. I could have used the GT program to garner significant additional advantages. By doing so, I could have layered one advantage on to another, concealing the origins and claiming that all my successes had accrued to me because of my endless hard work and unflagging dedication.

William The Violent Juvenile Offender

Three years after the trip to Louisiana that ended with Tyrone and Tammy staying behind with their grandmother Hazel, Theresa died. William heard the story six different ways before he slammed open the door to his mother's apartment and found her sobbing.

William turned on his heel and demanded that anyone who knew where to find Rocket had better share that information. Rocket was the one who'd encouraged her to keep sniffing even after she complained of a splitting headache. He was also the one who failed to seek help when she collapsed.

After assaulting Rocket with a brick and putting a gash into his head that spurted blood like a bad horror movie, William officially transitioned from a pesky joy-rider to a violent juvenile offender.

Sentenced to a group home, he immediately became a staff favorite. He was smart, polite, and kind. He earned his General Equivalency Diploma (GED) easily, despite his spotty school attendance over the years.

When he was released from juvenile corrections, William enrolled in high school. He did even better in that formal setting than he had as a child. One day, he came across a cheerleading practice in session. He'd taught himself to do gymnastics tumbling years before on a discarded mattress. He could do standing back-flips, handsprings, and he could walk on his hands.

The school's cheerleaders were impressed and asked him for help learning to tumble. His work with the cheerleaders led to him being recruited for the school gymnastics team. As the paperwork was being filed to get him on the gymnastics team, his GED came to light. The principal barred him from returning to the school.

Being kicked out of high school was disappointing. He was young and wanted to socialize with kids his own age, yet he was being punished for having earned his GED.

Within a few months of being kicked out of school he began to rely on alcohol more and more. It was a cure for boredom more than anything else.

The School-to-Prison Pipeline

A side effect of the forced integration of schools seems to have been the creation of something many now refer to as the school-to-prison pipeline.

In elementary school, I remember hearing the black boys talk about getting paddled at the principal's office. I recognized even back then that the black boys were far more likely to get sent to the principal's office while the black girls and white children would get a short lecture in the hallway.

What strikes me in retrospect is that I don't have any recollections of black boys acting unruly. They didn't raise their voices or talk back to the teachers so what in the world were they being paddled for?

Did the white teachers send the black boys to the principal's office because they feared them? Did fully grown white women fear elementary-school-aged black boys?

As research on implicit bias[45] clearly shows, a person can, in every rational way, want to believe that blacks and whites deserve a level playing field, but that doesn't mean they can avoid over-reacting and feeling fear when they interact with blacks.

Remember Zimbardo's words:

> Dramatic visual images of the enemy on posters, television, magazine covers, movies and the Internet imprint on the recesses of the limbic system, the primitive brain, with the powerful emotions of fear and hate.

In other words, with the decades of Giant Negro tales being drummed into white Americans' heads, teachers were, and are, very vulnerable to over-reacting to the misbehavior of black children.

As early as 2005[46], scholars were recognizing that black children's behavior was much more likely to be seen as criminal while white children behaving similarly were seen as merely disruptive or as having emotional

---

[45] See Harvard's http://implicit.harvard.edu

[46] "Breaking the School to Prison Pipeline: Identifying School Risk and Protective Factors for Youth Delinquency" appeared in *Exceptionality: A Special Education Journal* Volume 13, Issue 2, 2005

problems. In her book, *Lockdown High: When the Schoolhouse Becomes a Jailhouse*, journalist Annette Fuentes notes the increasing criminalization of school children:

> Zero tolerance [policies have] triggered a process that pushes the most vulnerable and academically needy students out of the classroom and into harm's way—what many now call the school-to-prison pipeline. Failing schools breed failing students and place them at risk of falling into the juvenile justice system, especially as policing and the practices of that system increasingly make their way into the schoolhouse.

> [The] entrenched interests—political and economic—...together have promoted and profited from the transformation of our schools into prisonlike institutions where children are treated like suspects. These interests have clout and will pose a challenge to those seeking change. But there is hope and a growing movement to end the zero tolerance, lockdown approach to public school safety.

Lockdown, zero tolerance policies are far more likely to exist in inner-city schools where the students are black and brown, even though suburban white boys are the prototypical school-site mass murderers.

In March of 2014, the US Department of Education released a brief[47] on school discipline practices. The brief highlighted data that showed racial bias beginning in preschool and becoming more marked as students get older. Education Secretary Arne Duncan and Attorney General Eric Holder held a press conference to announce the release of the brief and call attention to the mounting evidence that racial bias and criminalization are limiting opportunities for black and brown children as early as three and four years old.

Illegal Housing Practices in the 1970s

Even though the trio of LBJ civil rights acts had been passed in the mid to late 1960s, discriminatory housing practices still abounded in the 1970s. The laws now stated that discriminating against my husband's

---

[47] U.S. Department of Education Office for Civil Rights, CIVIL RIGHTS DATA COLLECTION, Data Snapshot: School Discipline, Issue Brief No. 1 (March 2014)

parents when it came to housing, was illegal. Yet blacks trying to move out of the city center were still hitting invisible walls.

According to *American Apartheid*:

> Black home seekers [since the Fair Housing Act was passed] face a more subtle process of exclusion. Rather than encounter "white only" signs, they face a covert series of barriers. Instead of being greeted with the derisive rejection "no [blacks] allowed," they are met with a Realtor with a smiling face who, through a series of ruses, lies and deceptions, makes it hard for them to learn about, inspect, rent, or purchase homes in white neighborhoods.

Differences in the treatment of white and black home seekers were often uncovered using a technique called a housing audit. Two sets of auditors, one white couple and one black couple would dress similarly, report the same income, report similar jobs and education levels. They were trained to ask questions in ways that would not arouse the suspicions of the leasing agents.

A Denver housing audit conducted in the 1980s found that blacks were treated in a discriminatory way about half the time. Let's imagine, for a moment, that Bill had not come up against so much job discrimination in Denver. Let's pretend that after he got his certificate from Ford, he found work as a fairly-paid and well-respected mechanic.

Let's assume then, that he would have stayed with Diane and they would have raised their children together. Then imagine that Bill decided his boys were being influenced in the wrong ways by living downtown. Perhaps he and Diane would start looking for a stable, working-class apartment complex in the suburbs. That would be something they could do to get their children away from high crime, drug availability, and other deleterious influences that were growing more intense in the inner cities during the late 1970s.

They should have been able to rent in any neighborhood they could afford, but, as Denver housing audits showed, Bill and Diane most likely would have found their applications to suburban apartment complexes denied. Eventually, they would have been channeled right back into the same neighborhood, regardless of their income, because they were black.

Next we can imagine that Bill and Diane together, after a few more years, would have built the credit history and the income that would qualify any white couple for a home loan. In this scenario, imagine that the boys have gotten into some trouble already and Bill and Diane are now desperate to get them into a suburban school where they will have a fresh start.

Real estate agents would not be able to find them a home to buy. They would face the catch-22 of black homeownership: Blacks could only find housing in "black" neighborhoods, and banks wouldn't give mortgage loans for houses in "black" neighborhoods.

A few years ago I had some friends who had become increasingly concerned about their teenage daughter. They didn't like her boyfriend or her other friends and they believed she needed to be separated from those friends so that her grades and attitude would improve. They were aware that I'd been a terrible high school student and a college dropout so they asked my advice.

They opened the conversation by telling me about the many options they were considering: They could move her to a different local public high school, enroll her in a local private school, send her away to a private boarding school, or homeschool her. These white people had so many options for getting their daughter back on track it could almost be called an embarrassment of riches.

When poor and working-class black parents see their children making bad choices, their options are strikingly limited. This is in part because their finances are so limited, but also because, historically, their ability to move out of their assigned neighborhoods was so severely restricted by redlining and housing discrimination.

Federal Intervention to End Redlining & Housing Discrimination

After Richard Nixon left the presidency and Gerald Ford took over, several key reforms helped push black homeownership and black business ownership forward.

In 1974, Ford signed into law the Equal Credit Opportunity Act

(ECOA). This act made it illegal for banks to deny loans to people based on age, sex, race, or marital status.

The problem with the ECOA was that telling banks not to discriminate wasn't going to be enough. With history as their guide, those who wanted black and brown people to actually get approved for home and business loans knew that someone would have to be able to look at the paperwork within each bank and check for discrimination.

An overseer would want to dig around in each bank's records to answer questions like :

- Who did the loan officers meet with? (race, age, gender)
- What did their applications look like in terms of their credit rating, salary, and other factors?
- When a black person's application looked like that of a white person who'd applied and been approved, did the black applicant also get a loan?

A new law was needed to allow this kind of digging around.

That law was signed in 1975, again by President Ford. The Home Mortgage Disclosure Act (HMDA/Humda) required banks to report the number and dollar amounts of loans, categorized by neighborhood. The statistics could then be used to charge banks with violating the Equal

Figure 33: Geraldine Toliver-Hester integrated our neighborhood in 1976 and I'm proud to report that no one noticed.

Credit Opportunity Act.

In 1976, a black woman purchased a home in my family's formerly all-white neighborhood in Texas. I was eight years old when she and her twelve-year-old daughter moved into a house five houses away from ours. I could see their driveway from our driveway. According to Google maps, we were 479 feet apart.

Our new neighbor was Geraldine Toliver-Hester. She'd grown up in our town and had gotten her college degree at nearby Prairie View Texas A&M University. She'd been living in Oakland, CA and working as the Director of Compensatory Education for the Oakland Unified School District. When her elderly mother needed help, she retired from the Oakland School District and returned to Bryan.

Her twelve-year old daughter, Faith, had come from a childhood in the epicenter of the Black Pride movement. Oakland was a place where little black girls were successfully taught to love being black and to understand that they could *be* and *do* anything they wanted. It would have been a sad thing indeed if my Bryan neighbors had robbed her of that pride and confidence by burning crosses or protesting on her new lawn.

I don't remember how I learned that they'd moved in. They kept to themselves and so even though I knew a black family owned the house, I could never seem to confirm it for myself until years later, when I was in high school and I got to know Faith's younger siblings who were four or five years behind me in school. Toliver-Hester owned the home until 1993 and never experienced any kind of segregationist pushback.

The combination of Toliver-Hester's middle-class values, education, and the opportunity to situate her family in a middle-class neighborhood meant her children enjoyed a degree of protection from the problems that plagued the children in the "black" section of our town.

In this way, even though Toliver-Hester's son graduated from Bryan High in 1991, at the height of crack and gang activity, he was not affected or influenced by either.

Conversely, some of those black parents who fought mightily to keep their children out of gangs and safe from crack, even though they were still stuck in the segregated neighborhoods, still lost children in drive-by shootings and other random violence.

Thanks in part to the housing legislation passed during the Ford administration, Toliver-Hester never had to suffer the pain of losing a child to the side-effects of segregation.

Toliver-Hester's story is a story of the way the world is *supposed* to work. When a family values education, and lives by the middle-class tenets of industry and thrift, they should be able to build solid, humble, temperate lifestyles. They should be able to purchase a home, save for retirement and imbue their children with the set of values they choose. They should not be forced to live in an environment that directly contradicts their value system simply because of the color of their skin.

Once the EOCA was passed, Toliver-Hester was poised to benefit from it. She qualified for a home loan based on her credentials both before and after the legislation. Before the legislation was passed the only barrier would have been the fact that she was black. Once the federal government required banks to lend to people regardless of their color, she was in a prime position to benefit. Unfortunately, in 1976 Toliver-Hester was still exceptional. Because of racism, few blacks in my Texas town were as educated and credentialed as she was.

The EOCA and HMDA were making a difference, but racial disparity still existed, so policy-makers began looking for more and better ways to open loan opportunities to blacks. It was turning out to be true that blacks, who made up 14% of the population, were not applying for 14% of the loans, and, those that had applied, did not have the credentials that whites did. Black had been denied access to jobs and education for decades so their applications would logically be expected to feature lesser credentials.

Lawmakers understood it was time to try a different approach. While blacks might not have résumés that looked like white people's résumés, they did keep their money in banks and there were plenty of them that deserved an opportunity to own a home.

Lawmakers found that banks were taking in deposits from low-income people but only giving loans to middle-class people. That might have been a sound business practice, but because of the history of discrimination and racism, this meant black money was being lent to whites but not vice versa. It didn't seem right that blacks could support banks by being their depositors but the banks had no obligation to support them in return.

Because of this injustice, later in 1977, Congress passed the Community Reinvestment Act (CRA). The CRA required that investments from a particular community had to be used to provide credit to members of that same (often geographic) community. If a bank branch sat in a low-income black neighborhood, it was now required to issue home loans for houses in that very neighborhood.

The EOCA and HMDA opened up new opportunities for those blacks who had gone to college and managed to find a good job or for those who ran small businesses and had higher income levels. The CRA was more likely to benefit working-class folks who saved their money and made substantial sacrifices in order to afford a home.

It's great that the CRA recognized that many blacks were not going to have the incomes and resumes that my parents had, but it was too late for William. His father was gone, and his mother was disabled and defeated. Other black boys might get out of the ghetto in time to turn their lives around, but he would not. Though he had no idea crack and gangs were coming, even if he'd looked to escape the inner city before they arrived, there was no where he could have gone.

Illegal Hiring Practices in the 1970s

The Civil Rights Act of 1968 had outlawed job discrimination based on race. The act could only be enforced, however, as blacks were able to file court cases and attempt to prove that they had been discriminated against. Businesses could be very careful to discriminate only in the most subtle ways. When a case did meet the burden of proof required to garner financial and legal support from the NAACP, a worker who believed they had been discriminated against was often left with no option but to forget about it and get on with their life.

The other thing that anti-discrimination laws could not overcome were the advantages that whites, like my parents, had accrued over the years in terms of education and job experience.

While Bill and Diane could finally apply for jobs and be somewhat less likely to be legally discriminated against due to their race, they still didn't have the schooling or advanced training to get a job as well-paying as my father's. They also didn't have rich parents like Otto and Leah to support them if they wanted to go back to school and train up for better opportunities.

The Wheat Land in Jeopardy

In the latter half of the 1960s, my mother's brother was still farming my grandparents' land. For some reason, he just decided to stop paying his taxes.

On February 16, 1971, my uncle was charged with failing to pay taxes for five years in a row, starting in 1965. I knew about the tax evasion before he died, but I would never have asked him about it. He was known to have quite a temper, and it wouldn't have been worth the fallout to ask questions. I probably wouldn't have learned much anyway, as his anger would have outsized his interest in self-reflection or sharing.

My grandmother saved everything, even the bad news, and I have her clippings about his trial. The newspaper articles published during the different phases of the trial included a report of his income for those years.

He made $27,356.61 in 1965. He made progressively more each year, and by 1969, he made $33,536.91.

I looked up the average income for US residents in 1965 and found a Census Bureau report published in January of 1967 called *Income of Families and Persons in the United States*. That report indicated that anyone making more than ten thousand dollars a year was in the top bracket. In other words, people making more than ten thousand a year were "rich."

Of course the numbers reported for my uncle may have been his gross income in those years. They might not have taken into account his operating costs; things like the cost of seeds, fertilizers, machinery, and hired help.It's hard for me to know just how much of this became his net income. Even if I presumed his net was just one-third of his gross, he was making enough to be either in the highest income class or very close.

Another table in the same report shows median income broken out by the color of the family. That table shows that the median income for black families that year was $3,971.

We know that blacks in the South were paid even less than blacks outside the South, so Leah Tyler's black ancestors were most likely making even less than the $3,971 figure shown.

Figure 34: The summer of 1967, one of the years my uncle didn't file taxes. The family is pictured on the balcony of my uncle's lake house in Coeur D'Alene, Idaho. Pictured (L to R) are my aunt, my grandpa Otto's sister, my grandmother, my uncle holding my sister and my mother holding another of my sisters.

The sentencing guidelines for my uncle's offenses, as reported in the newspaper, outlined that my uncle could receive up to one year imprisonment and a $10,000 fine for each year he didn't pay. That would have meant a maximum of five years in prison and a maximum of $50,000 in fines. The fines would be owed in addition to whatever taxes he owed and hadn't paid.

In the end, my uncle's total fines, including back taxes and penalties, came in at $80,000, and his prison sentence was thirty days in jail.

Otto and Leah, as well as my uncle and aunt, must have breathed a collective sigh of relief. There would not be a monetary sentence punitive enough to force some drastic financial measure, like selling the land to pay the fines.

And just in case a thirty-day absence might put the farm at risk in any way, my mother recalled that he was actually allowed to serve out his sentence on the weekends. He reported to the jail on Friday evenings and left the jail on Sunday evenings. He did this for fifteen weekends in a row.

My uncle's sentence was a far cry from the way cases were used against black landowners for over a hundred years in the South. In the South, any farmer owing taxes on his land would have been an easy target for those wanting to wrest away the land. The sentence for any Southern black man would have been designed to remove the him for a period long enough that the land could be confiscated. Alternately, the judge could set the penalties high enough that the land would have to be sold in order to settle the penalty debt.

Not so with my white uncle. His need to keep the land going was given such high priority that even thirty consecutive days away from it was seen as too extreme. A judge, inclined for whatever reason to empathize with my uncle, made sure his sentence would have very little impact on our family and our farm's operation.

In Retrospect: My Life as a *Good White Person*

As I've already noted, when I was in elementary school, my parents encouraged me to have my black girlfriends spend the night just as any white friend would have. I have to admit we felt really good about ourselves. We were *Good White People*.

But did a visit to our house actually make those girls' lives better? They were from poor families. What was that experience like for them? Did they seethe with anger over the injustice of what they saw? Or worse, did they see me, or my family as somehow more deserving of a luxurious life? In other words, did they buy in to white supremacy because of the life we enjoyed?

My third grade year, when my best friend came to spend the night, I remember that it was the Friday after Easter. In my Easter basket several days prior, I had received a plush rabbit. He was small, soft, and intricately stitched. My friend arrived carrying a thin, washed out plastic bunny baby toy – also, presumably, an Easter prize.

When she left, my plush toy was gone, but her plastic toy remained. In my plush bunny's wake, nestled in with my other plush toys, I found the pink plastic bunny.

We had not made a trade, but she had placed her toy in such a way that she suggested we had. It made me very sad for her. It made sense to me that she would want my plush bunny because I believed it was clearly superior. Then, after processing what had taken place, I was immensely proud of myself for not characterizing her actions as stealing, even though clearly, she'd either been dishonest or delusional.

What I didn't see back then was that I had created the conditions that made her feel that her little plastic bunny was inadequate. Had she brought it with her because she was proud of it and wanted me to see it? Certainly, that is the only scenario that makes any sense.

Back then ,I saw her visit to my house as a net benefit to her. I figured she had a great time, enjoyed the company of my family members, and went away with a soft, beautiful bunny toy. But did she even need to know that the plush version existed? Had she not come over, she surely would have continued to cherish her plastic bunny.

This was a pattern I would engage in throughout my life. I often created situations or conversations within which my *Good White Person* status would be highlighted.

It's only been in the last few years that I've come to recognize how, when I worked to prove myself good, I often forced situations that weren't beneficial for others. Back then, I saw injustice from my own perspective, and didn't take into account that things might have looked a lot different to someone on the opposite side.

The black guy that I told my parents I had a crush on in the second grade fared better[48]. Derrick was pretty aloof when it came to my attempts

---

[48] I actually confirmed it with him via Facebook.

to get his attention, but I did exploit him in a way. I was not the cutest girl in our grade, but I was able to get the largest share of his attention, probably because I was white and he attached a value to my whiteness. I also had blonde hair, and he, like many others, recognized the America's obsession with a shade of blond that only appears on children and Scandinavian women. He attached a value to that, just as he'd been taught to do by American media.

I was fixated on Derrick for three years of elementary school. In the spring of our fourth grade year he often called me on the phone after school. We considered ourselves pretty mature for talking on the phone, even though our conversations were beyond banal. During one of those phone conversations he broke some bad news. He told me his mother had gotten a job in Atlanta and the family was moving.

I was heartbroken. I cut the conversation short so he wouldn't hear my voice quiver. After we hung up, I closeted myself with a record player and listened to "Emotion" by the Bee Gees, over and over.

My summer of heartache was arduous, but as the new school year drew near, I began to look forward to meeting new friends and getting a fresh start. I would be going to a school that combined kids from every elementary school in the city. That meant there would be some social rearrangements. My Hello Kitty diary from that year reveals that on the first day of school I chose a black girl named JoEddie as my new best friend. No surprise there, based on my record. Over the next few weeks I began to focus on a black boy named Patrick as my new love interest.

But then something weird happened and the people mentioned in my diary started shifting. As it turned out, I had the right clothes and a few key connections through church such that I found myself pulled into the popular crowd through no actual effort on my part.

I was gangly and hadn't started developing breasts yet so I was recruited as one of the sidekick popular girls. I wasn't running things. My job was to stand behind one of the queen bees and back them up through fawning approval of everything they did and said. We had lunch together and that was followed by a recess where we were allowed to stand around outside.

When a black girl friend from elementary school approached me one day at recess, I got nervous. This popular group couldn't know about Derrick. My elementary school friend didn't seem to notice that I casually walked our conversation away from my group, hoping to move our exchange out of their earshot. Margaret asked me about Derrick and I told her he had moved to Atlanta with his mother and brother. She asked if he and I were still *going together*, I laughed nervously, quietly answered no, and prayed my clique hadn't heard her question.

I made some excuse to get away from her and return to where my friends were standing. As I walked back over, one of them asked me about Derrick.

I denied everything.

I was ashamed of my lies even as they came out of my mouth. That shame is probably what seared the memory of that moment so indelibly in my memory. I was melting, morphing, shape-shifting from a strong-minded individual who embraced the full spectrum of humankind, to a pawn for someone else's idea of what was cool and what was not.

The full transformation from *Good White Person* to *Despicable White Person* took only seconds. Somehow that sacrifice of individuality and character seemed worth it at time.

THE 1980s

The eighties are often called *the Reagan Era*. They are also called *the Me Decade*. The eighties were all about Wall Street, greed, fast cars, and conspicuous consumption. Men in the eighties wore brightly colored "power ties." Women wore big hair and shoulder-padded "power suits."

Greed Is For Those With Impoverished Ambitions

The movie *Wall Street* came out in 1987 and with the famous Gordon Gekko quote, "Greed is good," epitomized the attitude of the era.

Within my family, greed was still not considered good. My father set the example that what mattered most was that people pursue meaningful work. It was better to make less money and be purpose driven in your work than to make more and be miserable[49].

Though he wouldn't say it until several decades later, Barack Obama captured the essence of my parents' and grandparents' teachings about money. Obama said, "Focusing your life solely on making a buck shows a poverty of ambition. It asks too little of yourself. And it will leave you unfulfilled."

"What if you could travel back in time and change one thing about your life?" I asked.

"Well," my Grandpa Otto forced out a chuckle. "I guess I'd wear the

---

[49] Of course all of this was meant and understood to be "less" within middle-class to upper middle-class numbers. The idea that work must be purposeful and fulfilling is a very middle-class idea. For those making the least in our society, the higher purpose of work is that it results in a paycheck that can be used to feed and shelter one's family.

right sized shoes." He pulled his foot out of a slipper and showed me that his two smallest toes were twisted toward his big toe and nested in a crevice on the top of his foot. It was that way on both feet.

"Grandpa! What happened?"

He chuckled again. My mother...mumble mumble...but then Cleon...mumble mumble...and then they said...mumble mumble...too small.......mumble mumble...huh, huh, huh.

He talked so quietly I could catch only a few words of each sentence he spoke. I was trying to write a history paper. The assignment was to choose an historical event and tell how my own family experienced that event. I had decided to work time travel into it because I thought the assignment sounded really boring.

"Hold on Grandpa, I'm gonna turn off the television."

I came back to where he was sitting and asked him again about the one thing he would change if he could travel through time.

When he started talking again I couldn't believe my ears.

"Grandmother?" I whispered. She was easily startled, especially when she was busy in the kitchen so I always whispered to get her attention. She looked up from the pie crust dough she had rolled out on the counter and was sprinkling with cinnamon.

"Grandpa just told me that if he could go back in time he'd make a run for Canada."

"Oh, lord," she said, "Yes, he would. He sure would. I guess you might be a little Canadian teenager right now instead. But then your mom wouldn't have met your dad. So actually, instead of being Canadian you wouldn't even be here today."

"Why did he want to be Canadian?"

It took both of my grandparents and my mother to fill in all the gaps. As soon as one of them get choked on a sentence another would jump in to keep the narrative going. About a half-hour later, I had the whole story.

I wrote up my paper about World War II and the loss of my uncle. Then I wrote about my grandparents' willingness to give up everything they had, if only they could have saved him by convincing him to go AWOL. That night in Pennsylvania, in 1943, my grandfather had begged my uncle to get in the car with him and go across the border to Canada. My uncle was tempted. They discussed the pros, cons and consequences for hours. The family might lose everything – the land, their home, everything.

My grandfather had assured him that they (himself and my grandmother) were okay with losing all their material possessions, as long as they didn't lose him. My uncle worried about prison, and my grandfather said he was okay with that, too.

In the end, my uncle refused to go along with Plan B. He thought it was too much to ask of his parents.

When I wrote up my paper that evening, I told the story of my uncle and grandfather, then, I launched into something resembling a sociological analysis of greed and empathy. *What makes some people so indifferent to money and others so indifferent to human suffering? And has anyone but me noticed that those who care about money end up in power and those who care about people end up giving everything away, including their power to make the world a better place?*

Back then, the day I turned in my paper, I was convinced that what I'd written was 100% Boo-Yow. *What a deep thinker I was! What profound thoughts I'd put to paper!*

A few weeks later, when the papers were handed back, there was a bright red "C" on my paper's cover sheet. The teacher wrote that I'd posed some thought provoking questions, but that I had diverged so far from the paper's requirements she could only give me a C.

Leah Tyler's White Mom in the 1980s

I was twelve when the 1980s began and twenty-two when they ended.

Throughout middle school I continued to be a problem student. Even though I was in STEP class for English, and that protected me from failing grades, I was a terrible student in every other class. I didn't want to do my schoolwork. I didn't listen to my teachers. I spaced out assignments. I failed tests. I skipped class.

Once, I got caught skipping class with two other white girls. We were hanging out in the school bathroom instead of sitting in music class. I remember feeling so ashamed at the moment we were caught. The disapproval of authority figures was not something I was accustomed to experiencing. Curiously, my teachers didn't report us to the principal. They didn't tell our parents. They talked to me and the other girls, and we promised not to do it again. They must have reasoned that we were *good kids, from good families,* and there was no need to stigmatize us by reporting us to the principal's office.

As I progressed in school each year, my STEP teachers would threaten to kick me out. That would have forced me back into mainstream English which was exactly where I wanted to be. Somewhere along the way, I realized that if they kicked me out of STEP, the school would get less money. The teachers wanted me out. The principals wanted me in.

I wondered if kids who were in the remedial track suffered the same fate. Did they hit their heads against a remedial ceiling? Once they were tracked lower, did they find it impossible to get back into the mainstream classes because the school was being paid extra money for each student enrolled in a special program?

I wasn't just a bad kid during school hours. I did some shoplifting but never got caught. I probably didn't look like a shoplifter, and that must have helped me escape notice.

I always had money; either from work, my parents, or my grandparents. We got money from Grandpa Otto and Grandmother Leah on birthdays, Christmas, Valentine's, Easter and Halloween. In one particularly fruitful year, I actually received a card and ten dollar bill for Arbor Day.

My grandmother always sent a check to my mom for our back-to-school shopping, so we always had cool school clothes. Having cool clothes and going to the right church more than secured my place in the popular crowd.

My first formal job was a paper route for which I delivered newspapers by roller-skating around the neighborhood at dawn. Almost all the people in my neighborhood had enough money to subscribe, so my route was geographically small enough that I could get it done before school.

In a poor neighborhood a paper route would have been out of reach for a kid because subscribers would be rare enough to make the route geographically impossible without a car.

In junior high school I babysat for a number of families and it seemed like I could hardly keep up with all my clients, my list grew so fast.

In poor neighborhoods even today, teenage girls are regularly asked to watch children for little or no pay. Not so with me. I had rich families to babysit for, and I reaped the benefits in the form of solid hourly wages and high profile references. My clients picked me up in their cars and dropped me off back at home at the end of the night.

Much of my babysitting network originated from our church, and our church discouraged those of color from continuing to attend. I know this because darker-skinned families would show up but they would only attend a service or two before they disappeared. Of course, the custodial and food services staff were black, but they were not allowed to join.

Food services may strike some readers as an odd service for a church. My church was actually a big church, a pre-cursor to the mega churches that would develop later. We had a Christian Life Center which was really a social club where we could roller skate, play volleyball and bumper pool, attend makeup classes (yes, that happened) and many other activities. I don't know how much our church gave to the poor, but I know we had yearly ski trips and amusement park trips for the youth group.

Because my network originated from a classist and racist church, my network acted to advantage me in ways that my husband simply couldn't have hoped to compete with.

I began babysitting for a woman who worked for a local upscale women's boutique. My mom suggested I ask the woman about openings at the shop. The woman connected me with the owner, who gave me a job unpacking clothing shipments and getting them ready for the sales floor.

Over time I became a good, reliable worker who used my middle-class ideas to please my boss. For example, one day when I had done all my regular duties I decided to clean out a small refrigerator that was in the back room with me. I didn't ask anyone if that would be a good use of my time. I took a gamble in the hope that it would be something that surprised and impressed my boss and my co-workers. It was a huge hit. The owner, the manager, the assistant manager and the other saleswomen talked about it for two weeks, at least. The build-up of frost was gone, the old moldy containers and slimy spills wiped out. At work I had become a superstar and every day I looked forward to going to work, even though at school I was still a wreck.

My academic performance in high school was bad. The STEP program ended after the sophomore year. The high achievers transitioned to a special college prep program. I was not invited to join that group. Now that I was in mainstream English classes I wasn't protected by the "gifted" label. In junior English, I got in an argument with the instructor over a test question I felt was poorly worded. The question was multiple choice, and I insisted none of the answer choices was accurate enough to merit my pencilling-in. If I'd had a perfect score in the class, this question might have been worth arguing about. As it stood, I had a C average. Fighting over a single multiple choice question was much more an exercise in arrogance than a matter of any import or substance.

During my first semester of Senior English, I actually received a failing grade. I was completely astonished. No matter how many times I'd been warned, I hadn't expected to actually receive an F grade. After all, when I was in STEP, no matter how poorly I performed, I'd never come home with less than a B. My mom went to talk to my teacher, and he explained all the ways he'd tried to help me get back on course. When my mom questioned me about his attempted interventions, I explained that I had not outright rejected his attempts to help; frankly, I just hadn't noticed.

Late in the spring of my senior year, my mom informed me that I had been accepted to Texas A&M.

"Did I apply?"[50] I asked.

My mom reminded me that I had taken the SAT and written the application essay. She'd filled out the form and put it in the mail.

---

[50] I know this sounds like an exaggeration of what really happened. Over the years when I've told the story, people have questioned how I could have written an application essay and been unaware of what I was doing. It does seem crazy to me now, but I really was that oblivious.

I did remember taking the SAT. She'd woken me up one Saturday morning, drove me to the school, handed me two sharpened Number 2 pencils, and instructed me to "go to room 112."

I'd had fun taking the test. In fact, just thinking about the SAT makes me smile and wish I could take it again.

I've always been a confident test taker. I was so certain of my intelligence that tests did not represent, to me, high stakes events. If I did poorly on a test, someone would assure me that my dismal showing was borne out of the fact that I was simply "too smart" somehow for that test. If I did well, someone would tell me it was because I was "so smart."

When my SAT scores came back, I found out I'd done fairly well.

So with pretty good SAT scores, terrible grades, few extracurricular activities, and an average essay, I had managed to get into a top school.

But how, exactly, had that combination been a winner?

I was a legacy.

Legacy admissions are awarded to kids whose parents went to the same school. My father had gotten his PhD at Texas A&M, so that made me a legacy.

Affirmative Action for Me, Yay!

Given that my father was enrolled at Texas A&M during a time when there were very few black and brown students enrolled, a legacy admission for me was like being rewarded for being born white. Legacy admissions are affirmative action for the middle- and upper-classes. Legacy admissions are the reason George W. Bush got into Yale. He was a terrible student like me, but Papa Bush was an alumnus.

In many admissions departments, legacy consideration comes well before any federal affirmative action considerations. In other words, rich whites kids come first.

On November 14, 2013, the *Wall Street Journal* ran an article by Josh Freedman. The article was entitled, "The Farce of Meritocracy" and it detailed just how disgusting legacy admissions really are. Freedman is an alumnus of Stanford University.

He tells us that, as a legacy, a Stanford applicant it three times more likely to be accepted as is someone from the general population. He explains that an applicant whose parents donate to the school is even more likely to gain admission.

Freedman writes:

> *If alumni have donated money, the admissions office will know about it. In any other circumstance, this would be considered bribery. But when rich alumni do it, it's allowed. In fact, it's tax-subsidized.*

> *The case against legacy admissions is very strong. Children of alumni already have an incredible built-in advantage merely by being the children of college graduates from elite universities. They are much more likely to grow up wealthy, get a good education, and have access to the resources and networks at the top of the social, economic, and political ladders. Legacy admission thus gives them an added advantage on top of all of this, rewarding those who already have a leg up at the expense of those who do not have the same backgrounds. William Bowen, Martin Kurzweil, and Eugene Tobin put it more succinctly: "Legacy preferences serve to reproduce the high-income/high-education/white profile that is characteristic of these schools."*

So Harvard, Yale, Princeton, Brown: all of these schools recycle scion privilege like cows chewing their cud.

Freedman goes on to explain that the system actually creates a strange tax side-effect:

> *As non-profits, these elite universities – and their enormous, hedge fund-esque endowments – are mostly untaxed. Both private and public universities that use legacy admissions are additionally subsidized through student aid programs, research grants, and other sources of federal and state money.*

> *In addition, as Elizabeth Stoker and Matt Bruenig explain, alumni donations to these schools are also not taxed and therefore subsidized by the general population.*

> *They write, "The vast majority of parents do not have an educational background that enables them to benefit from the donation-legacy system. Yet these parents are forced, through the tax code, to help fund alumni*

donations that intentionally militate against their own children's chances of admission to the elite institutions they may otherwise be well qualified for."

This, while black and brown students are given what seems like a scatter of birdseed to peck at. The federal affirmative action program seems a lot less worthy of so much ire once it's compared to the legacy system.

Only poor whites are left out altogether and yet, who do they see as the bad guys? Black people, of course. They keep lodging these lawsuits against black people who get into law school when *they* don't. They need to look at all the sons and daughters of privilege who cost them their spot by grabbing the lion's share before black applications even get a look-see.

Poor whites are disadvantaged beyond comprehension when it comes to gaining admission to a top school, but it's the rich white legacy students that pull the rug out from under them, not black students who get a little boost right near the end of the admissions process.

There are plenty of blacks who get into college based purely on their GPA's, extra-curriculars, test scores and application essays. Then, at some point, affirmative action kicks in and additional blacks get in. Every black who gets in under affirmative action has been accepted because the admissions office believes they have a chance to succeed, but some won't. That's okay, because affirmative action is about giving black students a chance, it's not about giving them a cake-walk. Plus, with each passing generation, there are more black kids who are legacies.

The affirmative action kids join the legacy kids (like me) in the gaggle of Mediocres. I call us the Mediocres because we didn't have the home run college apps.

Once we Mediocres are in, things can go in any number of directions. If an affirmative-action Mediocre's grades fall too low, they no longer qualify for federal grants and loans. Affirmative action kids are often from working-class or poor families so without grants, they have to drop out and go home. I'm sure sometimes the black Mediocres are relieved to go home. College can be alienating and lonely.

Some portion of the Mediocres figure things out, buckle down, and make good on the chance offered to them.

I wasn't one of the ones who buckled down. I sat in class, writing poems about how college wasn't "real" and how I needed to get out in the "real world," live through some hard times, and test my own mettle. I didn't even make it through a my first semester before I stopped going to class.

Many of the white, legacy, Mediocres tend to stay in school, though they may have to go on probation with their fraternities and sororities. They continue enrolling in classes, rarely showing up, barely studying, partying every night, and praying for Ds. Their parents get mad at them every semester when the grades are released, but unlike the government (in the case of the affirmative action Mediocres), the parents continue to foot the bill.

After all, these parents might reason, it's not about whether you learn anything in college, it's about whether you get that piece of paper at the end. They tell each other and even themselves: *No one puts their grade point average on their resume, anyway.*

Their parents settle on lowered expectations after a lifetime of struggle with their child's lack of dedication and follow-through. I know this because if I would have just stayed at Texas A&M, my parents would have had that attitude. They were exhausted with me. They just wanted me to get the piece of paper and get on with it.

I wasn't in a sorority but many legacy Mediocres join the Greek system. The parents of those men and women might reason that if they just keep paying the sorority and fraternity dues, their low-performing children will at least be able to use their Greek connections to get a job someday.

Kay Joy Inherits Some Wheat Land

At some point during the 1980s, my grandparents started transferring half of their wheat land to my mother. The other half of Otto and Leah's land went to their son, my uncle, Lester. The land transfers were arranged as a series of yearly gifts. My grandparents trusted my mom enough to give away their livelihood, knowing that if they outlived the money they'd set aside, my mother (and her brother) would pay to cover their needs.

This trust between my grandparents and mother came out of the long, wonderful, mutually beneficial relationship they had enjoyed. Financial stability had ensured that my mother and her parents had never had to borrow money from each other. My mother requested money from them often, but with the knowledge she wasn't expected to pay it back.

They never had their relationship strained by financial crises. If my grandparents had worried about trusting my mother's intentions, they would have had to allow their land to transfer to her only upon their deaths. Transferring the land as an inheritance instead of as incremental gifts would have meant that my mom's inheritance would have been taxed.

My mother's brother lived on the land and had taken over Otto's equipment many years before. Otto had agreed that his son, as the farmer and manager of the land, would keep two-thirds of the profits from the yield each year. The other third was paid to Otto and Leah. That was the standard arrangement in Whitman County between the farmers and non-farming landowners. My grandfather entered into that arrangement willingly. After all, it was his son, and he wanted the best for his son.

Each year, when wheat is harvested, the trucks full of grain are driven into town and taken into a community grain elevator. The elevator personnel then give the driver a receipt showing the weight of the grain delivered.

At the end of harvest, the farmer has an accounting of the total weight of the wheat he harvested and delivered to the community grain silo. My uncle had been farming some land on behalf of my great-aunt Hazel for a number of years. He and Hazel fought a lot. He decided to have silos put on the land so that he could do his own accounting of the harvest.

Not going to the grain elevator meant he could cheat my great-aunt out of her share of the money if he wanted to. As it turned out, that's exactly what he wanted to do. He proudly revealed that plan to other men in the family.

Years later, when he and my mother inherited the land, she saw no reason to change the general terms of the agreement her parents had made with her brother. Her brother would continue to farm her land on her behalf and would get two-thirds of any profit. She would then receive her third after the books were settled at the end of each year. Of course, whether she got what was actually due or not was always an open question because of the silos. The best she could hope for was to stay on good terms with him so that she could get more of her rightful share—probably not all, but more.

After the transfer of Otto and Leah's wheat land to my mother, every other year, around Christmas, my mom would get about $20,000.

Our family came to call that money, "the wheat money," and conversations in our house went like this:

"Are we getting the wheat money this year?"

"Can't we just pay for that with the wheat money?"

"When is the wheat money supposed to get here?"

Leah Tyler's Black Dad in the 1980s

William was sixteen when the 1980s began and twenty-six when they ended. For most middle-class people these are the years they look back on most fondly. Even if they aren't the best high school students, they often find a way to get back on track by their mid-twenties. Those who do not falter, and instead follow their ambitions, enjoy the financial and emotional support of their parents as they move from high school to college and on to a career or continued schooling.

Ages sixteen through twenty-six were nothing like that for William. After being kicked out of high school for having a GED, he hung out around labor pools.

Some days he was selected for labor gigs with end-of-day cash payments, but there were many days when there were far more laborers than jobs and he was left loitering when the last trucks rolled out. One day, as he stood among the other leftovers wondering how he was going to get food for his grumbling stomach, he ran into Eddie.

Eddie had just returned from yet another stint in prison and he quickly recruited William into a new "business" partnership.

Eddie would dress up in a suit and carry a clipboard. William would wear coveralls and navigate a dolly. They visited office buildings in downtown Denver. Eddie would lead the excursions, studiously consulting his clipboard, scribbling notes, and pointing out equipment to his younger assistant. William would then load the equipment onto his dolly, and the two would leave.

They would cart the equipment to nearby pawn shops, sell the merchandise for cash, and head back downtown for another dolly's worth of equipment.

William would always split his earnings in half, taking one half by his mother's place, and using the rest to purchase food, alcohol, and cigarettes. Only on the coldest nights was he willing to pay for a hotel room. If the weather was reasonable, he'd sleep under the stars.

At some point, William got spooked about the police being wise to the scheme he and Eddie were running so lucratively. He began having nightmares about a sting operation. He decided it was time to leave Colorado.

He called his dad and asked if he could move to Monroe and live with him. His dad said yes, but within months of William's arrival, there was significant tension in the household. He was finding it hard to get along with his father's new wife. The wife wanted him gone and would snoop around in this things trying to find evidence of an eviction-worthy offense.

His younger brother, Tyrone, had been living in Louisiana since being left behind at his grandmother's as a toddler. Shortly after William had arrived at his fathers, he'd made the trip to nearby Jonesboro, visited his grandmother's house, and inquired about his little brother. His grandmother, Hazel, told him Tyrone had been put in a group home for the latest in a series of delinquencies.

Weeks later, on the day Tyrone was scheduled to be released, no one in the family was planning to go pick him up. William was astonished that the family would be so callous. He rode his bike thirty miles to the group home and carried his brother back home on the handlebars of the bike.

Reunited, William began telling Tyrone how much their mother missed him and how anxious she was for the brothers to return, together, to Colorado.

William and Tyrone didn't have any money, and they knew their father would refuse to give them any, so they decided to try to ride bicycles from Louisiana to Colorado. Before leaving, they filled a bed sheet with ten or so cans of beans, soup, and vegetables. Tyrone rode on the handlebars, clutching the sheet full of cans, while William pedaled.

They stopped to eat, using a large rock to push a screwdriver through the metal top of the can. Then, then drank vegetables and soups straight out of their cans.

As they sat eating, they also strategized: They needed to get a second bike for Tyrone to ride. They would steal one as soon as they could find a white neighborhood— where the bikes would be plentiful and often unattended. Tyrone took the first bike that looked sturdy enough to make it to Colorado.

When they got about fifty miles outside of Monroe, Tyrone was exhausted and begged to turn back. William objected, assuring Tyrone they could make it, but also allowing that Tyrone could go back if he wanted to. Tyrone turned back toward Monroe. William continued toward Denver.

After several days' exertion, not enough sleep, and not enough to eat, William arrived in Dallas and decided he would find something to steal and sell. Then he would use the money to buy a bus ticket to Colorado.

After hours of looking for a way to get some money, even more tired and hungry than before, he bent his own code of ethics and broke into a school.

He'd developed his code of ethics a few years before, as a thieving teen in Denver. He'd stolen a television from a woman on his block. He later learned that his victim had purchased the television on credit. Not only could she not afford a new television, but she would be forced to continue making payments on a television she couldn't even watch. After hearing of the situation he'd created by stealing the woman's television, he'd vowed not to ever steal from homes, churches, or schools. He knew stealing could sometimes hurt people, and the least he could do, he figured, was to find some way to keep from hurting people or institutions that he perceived to be on *his* side.

242

That night in Dallas, he broke into a school looking for electronics he could pawn, but found, by chance, the keys to a school maintenance truck. He loaded tools and electronics into the back of the truck and went around Dallas looking for a buyer.

A man agreed to look over his haul, but when it came time to pay up, the man tried to jack him instead. William ended up getting in a fist-fight with the would-be buyer. During the scuffle, his ID fell out of his pocket. He didn't notice he'd dropped the ID and drove off in the truck. The beat-up would-be buyer reported him to the police and gave them William's ID. Meanwhile, William had purchased liquor and was drinking and driving his way toward Colorado. The lack of sleep and alcohol combined to make him too drowsy to continue. He pulled over on the highway shoulder and went to sleep. He awoke to a policeman's flashlight shining through the truck window and into his eyes.

Once in custody, he took a plea deal and was sentenced to seven years in a Texas prison.

Ronald Reagan's Racist Presidential Campaign

During the 1980s, the blacks I grew up with were doing well. They were still underrepresented in my high school's college prep track and over represented in remedial and vocational programs, but for the most part they were staying in school and staying out of trouble. They were not drug addicted. Many were excelling on our high school sports teams. For so many blacks of my generation, men and women alike, sports were a ticket to college.

Other blacks in my Texas town were going to college on merit alone. Years later, I would learn through Facebook that so many of my black classmates who had grown up poor were able to carve out satisfying and stable middle-class lives.

When we were in elementary school, our teachers would announce to the class that anyone needing free or reduced school meals should come to the front of the classroom for an application. Every single black and brown child would get up and go to the front while all of the white children would look at one another, still seated.

Public assistance, in the form of school meals, was a program that made a big difference in the lives of my classmates. When the schools had been segregated, the black schools had been under-funded in every conceivable way. That was the point, after all.

So knowing all of my black classmates, I look back on Reagan's campaign in 1978 and '79, and it's strange to me that my classmates' families generated such a racist backlash. At that time, my classmates' families had been receiving benefits for less than ten years. There was no evidence that black families would lose their ambition to work because of the assistance, yet people like Reagan were claiming it had already happened.

In *The New Jim Crow*, Michelle Alexander explains:

> *Condemning "welfare queens" and criminal "predators," [Reagan] rode into office with the strong support of disaffected whites—poor and working-class whites who felt betrayed by the embrace of…the civil rights agenda…[Reagan's] "colorblind" rhetoric on crime, welfare, taxes, and states' rights was clearly understood by white (and black) voters as having a racial dimension.*

Reagan's presidential campaign platform seemed to ignore all the evidence that the programs were making a difference. My reality told me that those programs were necessary and effective and they were working. Yes, my black classmates qualified for free and reduced lunch. You know what they did with that benefit?

They used it to eat lunch.

But even as that was reality for myself and my classmates in 1979, he preferred to dig up that lame, old, 1866 freeloader thing.

He did it so he could get poor white people to decide they were being victimized by the aid being given to blacks. Whites got free and reduced lunch too, especially in rural areas, yet somehow, even *those* white people were pissed about the programs.

Reagan used very particular language to stir up resentment in poor and working-class whites. Alexander explains that Reagan often talked in campaign speeches about welfare and food stamp "abuses:"

> *The food stamp program [in Reagan's speeches] was a vehicle to let "some*

fellow ahead of you buy a T-bone steak" while *"you were standing in a checkout line with your packet of hamburger."*

What Reagan understood but couldn't put a name to (because it didn't have name yet) was that he was capitalizing on the last-place aversion of working-class white people.

Last-Place Aversion

In the summer of 2011, a group of four economics researchers[51] released a working paper called "Last-place Aversion: Evidence and Redistributive Implications." Their study demonstrated that people have a deep fear of being in the last place of any ranking. The researchers talk about something they call "positional anxiety" and they show how many people's positional anxiety becomes more intense the closer they move toward last place. Second-to-last place is pretty triggering it turns out.

In their study, the authors used a computer game to assign users a random amount of computer money. Players were then shown where their amount ranked among other, imaginary, users. Each ranked player was separated by only one dollar.

Players were commanded to give their money away. They were given the choice of either giving money to the person directly above them in the ranking or directly below. Players, on average, were more likely to give money to the person below them, presumably in an act of imaginary charity.

The key finding, of course, was the change in behavior when players were in second-to-last place. In that scenario, players were more likely to give to the person above them, presumably because giving it to the person below them would have put themselves in last place.

Ilyana Kuziemko and her co-authors also found evidence of last-place aversion in the real world. They created a survey to test the public's support of a minimum wage increase. Eighty percent of those surveyed supported a raise. Curiously, those people making just a little more than minimum wage (say twenty to fifty cents more per hour) were *against* a

---

[51] Ilyana Kuziemko, Ryan W. Buell, Taly Reich, Michael I. Norton

minimum wage increase.

Kuziemko and her co-authors explain that if the last place aversion paradigm can explain this phenomenon, it does so thusly: When workers start at minimum wage and are rewarded with a raise, it puts them one step above last place in wages. If the minimum wage is raised, the workers making a little more than minimum wage must reason that the increase will put them back in the position of being tied for last place again.

It's astonishing to think these workers can't see how the raise would be better for everyone, even themselves. Yet somehow these workers continue to oppose the minimum-wage increase.

When Reagan used the steak versus ground beef analogy, he was implying to working-class whites that people on welfare were living a better life than they were, and that they were doing so by willfully choosing welfare benefits over a job.

Since the stereotyped image of the welfare recipient was (and is) a black person; poor and working-class whites recoiled from the thought that blacks had figured out a way to live better than them.

Though food stamp recipients live on very small payments and more of them are white than black, anti-welfare types tend to imagine them as blacks who are eating steak, buying huge flat-screen televisions, and driving luxury cars.

Last-place aversion explains much more than Reagan's burger-eating voters. Last-place aversion also gives us answers to conundrums like:

- Why some house slaves looked down on field slaves
- Why some free blacks in the time of slavery owned other blacks as slaves
- Why some American Indians owned slaves
- Why recent immigrants to the US develop negative attitudes toward blacks and undocumented workers
- Why people who are targeted by bullies don't help other victims when they witness them being bullied

Ronald Reagan's Racist Policies

We've already seen how racist people in the South used a variety of methods to kick blacks off their land. Not surprisingly, the government had its own programs for doing the same. The USDA separated blacks from their land by ignoring them in times of strife. These were times during which the USDA gave a helping hand to white farmers.

The website of the Institute for Southern Studies states that:

> Any discussion about race and the USDA has to start with the crisis of black land loss. African-Americans were able to establish a foothold in Southern agriculture. Black landownership peaked in 1910, when 218,000 African-American farmers had an ownership stake in 15 million acres of land.

> By 1992, those numbers had dwindled to 2.3 million acres held by 18,000 black farmers. And that wasn't just because farming was declining as a way of life: blacks were being pushed off the land in vastly disproportionate numbers. In 1920, one out of seven US farms were black-run; by 1992, African-Americans operated one out of 100 farms.

The USDA was able to help farmers at risk for losing their land; in fact, that was very much part of their mandate. They chose to help white farmers and ranchers instead of black ones. This meant that my grandfather and uncle would have been given loans if they'd applied for them, while a black farmer would have found his applications for similar loans denied.

A movement to dismantle racist practices in the USDA was gaining steam in the early 1980s, and black farmers were having their cases heard. Some were getting restitution payments.

Then, in 1983, President Reagan acted to hobble efforts to recognize and rectify the USDA's past racist abuses. Again, the Institute for Southern Studies:

> In 1983, President Reagan pushed through budget cuts that eliminated the USDA Office of Civil Rights—and officials admitted they "simply threw discrimination complaints in the trash without ever responding to or investigating them" until 1996, when the office re-opened [under Clinton]. Even when there were findings of discrimination, they often went unpaid— and those that [were paid] often came too late, since the farm had already been foreclosed.

Reagan didn't just stick it to black landowners, he also undermined all the work done under presidents Ford and Carter to end housing discrimination.

From *American Apartheid:*

> The Reagan Administration...worked closely with the National Association of Realtors to undermine HUD's already limited enforcement authority.

Massey and Denton describe the many ways Reagan made it easier for real estate agents and landlords to discriminate. His administration made it illegal to conduct housing audits that aimed to uncover discrimination. Reagan also attempted to use a paperwork reduction act to restrict HUDs data gathering efforts, removing data collection for race, age, and sex but leaving the rest of the form's data collection fields intact.

Additionally, there was Reagan's War on Drugs, as explained by Michelle Alexander in her book, *The New Jim Crow:*

> In October 1982, President Reagan officially announced his administration's War on Drugs. At the time he declared this new war, less than 2 percent of the American public viewed drugs as the most important issue facing the nation. This fact was no deterrent to Reagan, for the drug war from the outset had little to do with public concern about drugs and much to do with public concern about race. Crack hit the streets in 1985, a few years after Reagan's drug war was announced, leading to a spike in violence as drug markets struggled to stabilize.

Also in Alexander:

> [T]he President signed the Anti-Drug Abuse Act of 1986 into law. Among other harsh penalties, the legislation included mandatory minimum sentences for the distribution of cocaine, including far more severe punishment for distribution of crack—associated with blacks—than powder cocaine, associated with whites.

> Congress revisited drug policy in 1988. The new Anti-Drug Abuse Act...eliminated many federal benefits, including student loans, for anyone convicted of a drug offense...and imposed new mandatory minimums for drug offenses, including a five-year mandatory minimum for simple

possession of cocaine base—with no evidence of intent to sell. Remarkably, the penalty would apply to first-time offenses. The severity of this punishment was unprecedented in the federal system. Until 1988, one year of imprisonment had been the maximum for possession of any amount of any drug.

Reagan's War on Drugs continues today. Stop-and-frisk policies practically ensure that poor black and brown young men will end up in jail sooner or later, and once they're in the system, they'll have trouble exiting the revolving door. Having seen this happen to so many young men I know, I get angry just thinking about the phrase "stop and frisk."

Reagan is practically worshipped by some people today. I had a mildly positive opinion of him myself. It was only in doing research for this book that I learned just how much he had done to undermine black families and how different the United States is today as a direct result of his racist policies.

The Ghetto's Back Door

Racial tensions around housing segregation were still alive and well in the 1980s. Several incidents in southwest Philadelphia, Pennsylvania made national news.

In November of 1985, Charles Williams and Marietta Bloxom, a black couple, bought a house in the white, working-class Philly neighborhood of Elmwood. A mob of 400 whites gathered, protesting their presence. The following night, a similar mob surrounded the home of Gerald and Carol Fox, a mixed-race couple who lived a few blocks from Williams and Bloxom.

Even with racist tensions heating up the streets, those wanting to end segregation and housing discrimination were able celebrate the passage of some new fair-housing amendments. The 1988 amendments sought to rectify weaknesses in the original Fair Housing Act of 1968.

One amendment increased the amount of money that a discriminator could be penalized with. Other changes made it possible for Housing and Urban Development officials to enforce the laws.

With HUD's new enforcement role, if a citizen believed they'd been discriminated against, they didn't have to hire a lawyer or call the NAACP, all they had to do was visit a HUD office and file a complaint.

HUD investigations and the prospect of high-dollar penalties got the attention of those who might otherwise discriminate.

In the last two years of the 1980s and throughout the early 1990s, the back door of the ghetto opened just enough further for the flow of blacks to the suburbs to become noticeable to real estate agents, newspaper reporters, and white homeowners.

Black families were finally escaping the violence-riddled ghettoes in favor of the working-class neighborhoods they had long been able to afford, but had been locked away from because of racism[52].

Crack in Bryan, Texas

During the mid-eighties, as I finished up high school, I witnessed a few of my black male classmates smoking weed but most of my black male classmates did not, and many avoided even cigarettes and alcohol. My black female classmates either chose not to go to parties or weren't allowed to go. While I went to parties thrown by both blacks and whites, I never saw my black female classmates there[53].

While blacks were fairly conservative in their use of substances at parties, I saw powdered cocaine out in the open at house parties hosted by whites and attended by whites and Mexican Americans[54]. There were also many white and Mexican "potheads" at my high school, and every white and Mexican-American person I socialized with drank plenty of alcohol.

---

[52] My super smart but cynical friend Jamel pointed out to me recently that whites began allowing blacks to escape the inner city at almost exactly the same time that whites began wanting to live there. A sad, but true, observation.

[53] When I later learned that many whites stereotype black women as promiscuous, I was shocked. At my high school and later, in college, I can attest that white women were far, far more promiscuous.

[54] I understand that "white" and "Mexican American" are not two mutually exclusive groups, at least according to the US Census and other demographic collection instruments. However, when I was in high school, in Texas, in the 1980s, the two groups were considered mutually exclusive. In writing about that time period, I've chosen to use the names we all used to refer to each other and ourselves.

By the time crack was infiltrating the inner cities, my classmates had, for the most part, made their decisions about what drugs they would and would not be experimenting with. To this day, I've only heard of two classmates who got addicted to crack cocaine. I'm sure there must have been others, but I've only heard of two.

Gangs were unheard of in my high school during the late 1980s. Most of the people in my town didn't learn about Los Angeles gangs until the movie *Colors* came out in 1988. Shortly after kids saw that movie, Crip and Blood gangs formed all over the country. I'm guessing that once these amateur gangs were in place, drug dealers from the coasts were able to quickly identify through whom their supply of crack could be funneled, at least at the street level.

I probably learned of crack and its powerfully addictive qualities, when I saw the movie *New Jack City* in 1991. I suspect that was the first time *most* people in my hometown had heard of crack. Whatever effect crack had on my community, it didn't really affect my generation.

Since I was moving around alot during the late 80s and early 90s I guess it could have affected me in all the various cities and states I lived in. But it didn't. No matter what city I was in – Bryan, Texas; Kansas City, Missouri; Sherman Oaks, CA; Glendale, Arizona – I was never in harm's way. I chose to live in peaceful areas of town. I could have chosen to live in crime-ridden areas, I just didn't. I've *always* had a choice regarding where I've lived, because I'm white.

Crack in Denver, Colorado

Writing in their book *Freakonomics*, Levitt and Dubner note:

[S]ince the civil rights legislation of the 1960s, the telltale signs of societal progress had finally taken root among black Americans. The black-white income gap was shrinking. So was the gap between black children's test scores and those of white children. By the 1980s, virtually every facet of life was improving for black Americans, and the progress showed no sign of stopping. Then came crack cocaine.

By the time crack hit Denver, Colorado, William was in his early twenties and still serving prison time for felony theft. Four years after he'd taken that plea deal in Texas, he was released, and he made his way back to Colorado.

Once there, he found the crack wars raging.

Violence had never been his thing so he didn't join a gang. He tried to keep his head down and his spirits up. Many of those who became addicts were introduced to crack surreptitiously. Dealers routinely laced marijuana joints with crack. The smoker didn't know what made *that* joint so great, but they knew they'd found a new favorite dealer.

Over time, the smoker would learn that they were addicted to crack and would often then decide to go full bore with rocks and glass pipes. That's how William would eventually become addicted to crack.

While on crack, he committed any number of property crimes, trying to feed his habit. His life was a revolving door: jail, homeless, crack, arrest, jail, homeless, crack, arrest.

Looking back on all his prison time in the late 80s and early 90s, he reasons that being locked up during the worst days of the crack wars probably saved his life. Crack-related gang violence became so rampant in the early 1990s that he could have easily lost his life in a drive-by or other random shooting had he been out of prison, trying to piece together a living on the streets.

Divide and Conquer

As discussed in earlier chapters, the Southern economy of the United States was founded on teaching white people to think of themselves as white instead of according to their parents' or grandparent's nationalities. Whiteness was an invented concept based on creating solidarity *against* black people (and sometimes others).

In any society it stands to reason that there will always be more poor people than rich. The rich will always be outnumbered. This is the reason the rich must always use some sort of connivance to stay in power: Divide and Conquer is always the goal, only the particulars change.

When democracy and the concept of citizens voting was first developed in ancient Greece there was no belief that *every* citizen should be allowed to vote. In fact, the privilege of voting was reserved for those Greek men who owned land. In other words, only the rich would vote to create governmental policies (that favored the rich).

That was "democracy" to the Greeks.

During the 1800s, Westernized societies began to allow non-landowning men to vote. Since that time, the trend worldwide has been toward allowing more and more adults to vote. This idea is called "universal suffrage." In the US, race was removed as an exclusion in 1870 (though we know how that turned out) and women got their right to vote in 1920.

Rich whites in the US were hardly caught off guard by this trend toward universal suffrage. They understood the implications and tried to keep these amendments from passing. Unfortunately for them, the amendments did pass, so people who wanted our laws to continue favoring the rich had to come up with sneaky ways to keep the laws slanted in their favor.

As voting rights expanded, the rich knew they had to find a way to get some chunk of poor people to vote with them. It didn't really matter which chunk, it just had to be a big enough chunk.

In America, rich whites managed to do just that. They convinced poor whites to stick with them based on their shared skin color. If blacks had not been around to serve as a wedge, rich whites would have had to find some other way to convince a large group of poor people to vote in their favor.

Reagan's vilification of blacks encouraged poor whites to vote against government programs that would have helped their own families. Poor and working-class whites were so intent on making sure black families didn't get help, they ended up making sure they themselves didn't get any help either.

Perhaps it's hard for some to see racism as a strategy because racism is such an insidious force in American culture and therefore has become an emotional topic. We can actually explore the Divide and Conquer strategy as it could be played out along a non-racial dimension.

Imagine that the administrators of a middle school want to put together an anti-bullying campaign. They decide that the students know best what kind of message will be effective. The administrators announce a contest. The students are asked to come up with anti-bullying programs and the student body will vote to choose the best one.

Most students are skeptical. They doubt posters and slogans will change bully behavior. The bullies get together and decide they need the weakest possible anti-bullying campaign and policies. They want the winning campaign to allow them ample freedom to keep up their bullying behavior. They have a great deal of unofficial power at their school and they are not about to let some propaganda campaign change that.

They decide to develop a campaign that claims that some people deserve to be bullied but others don't. Their most rewarding experiences come from bullying the kids who seem destined to have the brightest futures. They like bullying kids who are good at math, science, and computers. Kids who are good at language arts, history or social studies are hardly worth their time.

The bullies reason that the computer kids are likely to have the most successful careers later in life, and that those are kids even the math and science kids can be convinced to hate.

The bullies put together flyers with the slogan, "Bullying is wrong, unless the target is a computer geek...they have it coming." The bullies then gather together the math and science kids and help them understand that while the bullies will still push them into lockers from time to time or abuse them with a random wedgie, they'll never again have to worry about the most brutal of the bullying tactics (like swirly shampoos in the toilet).

Vote for us, the bullies say, and your life will be better. Not a lot better, but certainly better than the lives of the computer geeks. The math and science kids agree to plan. Furthermore, the bullies notify the rest of the student body that if any other campaign beats theirs in the voting, the creators of the winning campaign will be bullied relentlessly from then on.

All the other entrants drop out of the contest.

The "Computer geeks have it coming" campaign begins getting a lot of buzz and that leads the alarmed administrators to cancel the contest.

Posters come down; no winner is announced.

It doesn't matter, the message has been sent. As long as the non-computer geeks are willing to side with the bullies, their lives will be better.

Soon enough, the bullies don't even have to risk detention or suspension because the math and science kids are now doing most of the locker slamming, pushing of heads into toilets, verbal harassment and a sundry of other bullying techniques. The bullies can just sit back and watch the harassment – all the delight, none of the punishment.

A math geek, having just tormented a computer geek might be lightly shoved against a locker by a passing bully and take it as an "atta boy" from his former enemy.

If this scenario seems ridiculous, understand that poor whites have accepted this very agreement. Rich whites have told them that some people deserve to be poor and they bring it on themselves. Other poor people (whites) don't deserve to be poor because they work hard and are only poor because of bad luck and temporary setbacks. Rich whites tell poor whites, *you're most likely still going to be poor, but at least you won't be hated and blamed for your own poverty like the blacks.*

Poor and working-class whites accept that deal wholeheartedly.

It All Started With The Music

Within each decade, I've told the story of the economic and other privileges my family accrued and passed down. What I haven't yet explained is how a daughter of privilege like me could possibly end up married to a crack-addicted felon. In order to shine light on how naturally that came to pass, it's important that I add a second biographical telling of the 1980s, only this time, instead of focusing on my privileged upbringing, I'll focus on how, why, and when I crossed the color line that second time. As I've explained, when I was in the fifth grade I became ashamed of my black friends and rejected them so that I could be part of my school's popular crowd. I would reject that popular crowd in time, and I would do it because I preferred the company of my black friends, instead.

Music was the lubricant of that transition back toward my truer self.

A lot of the most popular music from the late 70s was heavily influenced by the "black" genres of soul, and funk. Soul/funk groups who made the Pop charts in those years included: The Commodores; Ray Parker Jr. & Raydio; and Kool & The Gang. There were also groups that some music pundits called blue-eyed soul: Hall & Oates; The Bee Gees; KC & The Sunshine Band; and the Captain & Tennille.

In the sixth grade, as I came in contact with the older teenagers who attended my church, I learned that some of the coolest white high school kids in my town went beyond funk music from the pop charts and sought out what they considered to be more authentic funk music. They listened to artists like ConFunkShun; Cameo; Lakeside; the Bar-Kays; and the SOS Band.

Because I associated that music with the high-schoolers, I felt that if I had access to that more serious funk music, I could become a cooler person. I wanted to own that music by purchasing eight-track tapes of it, but the music stores in the mall didn't stock it. If I couldn't own it, I at least wanted to know all the words to the best songs, but I couldn't do that either because the local radio stations didn't play it.

I was disappointed to realize that all I could really manage was to memorize *what* I could, *when* I could, in the church parking lot. The rich, white, high school kids who went to my church would listen to music on their car stereos before and after Sunday School, so, each Sunday, I sat near their cars, on a curb and listened intently.

Some of the earliest songs I learned in the church parking lot were Kurtis Blow's *The Breaks*, the Sugar Hill Gang's *Rapper's Delight* and Grandmaster Flash and the Furious Five's *The Message*.

What I didn't understand at that time was that the kids who attended my church were just one clique of our town's cool white high school kids. There were other white cliques at the high school. One set listened to country & western music and spent their weekends at western dancehalls. Another set was into new wave and punk and spent their weekends attending small punk concerts and underground parties.

Within the popular crowd at my own school, the two primary queen bees each had older sisters who didn't listen to funk. One had high school sisters who listened to country music; the other had sisters who were in college and attended new wave and punk concerts. These differences in musical tastes led to a bit of tension in our popular group, but it wasn't enough to splinter us right away.

At the end of my eighth grade year, I tried out for, and made, the ninth grade cheerleading squad.

When it was time to start my ninth grade year, I was more than excited. As part of our school's programming for the first day of the school year, we cheerleaders had been organized into our school's ambassadorial regiment. We stood sentry in the halls, in full uniform, supposedly to help the underclassmen navigate. I checked into my first-period Biology class that morning and was thrilled to see Derrick, my grade school crush who'd moved to Atlanta after our fourth grade year, sitting at a lab table.

After greeting Derrick with a loud screech and flirtatiously ordering him to save me the seat next to his, I went back into the hall to continue my duties. I felt certain that Derrick would shower me with attention but would also understand that things were different now. Now that we were in junior high, blacks and whites did not mix socially. There was a racial hierarchy in our school that no one spoke about, but everyone understood. He could flirt with me, and I would enjoy the adoration, but his chances with me were nil because, as a white girl I was off limits and as a cheerleader, I was way out of his league.

During that first class, I noticed he'd written "Lerita" on his notebook several times and surrounded the name with hearts. When the bell rang to signal the end of class, Lerita was waiting by the door for him.

He forgot to tell me goodbye.

I only let it bother me for a short while. There were other black classmates who would give me the attention I wanted. Leaving biology class, I went through the halls singing "Alligator Woman" by Cameo and "The Message" by Grandmaster Flash and the Furious Five. I actually only knew bits and pieces of each chorus so I had to switch from one song to another to keep people from noticing how little I knew.

I pretended my singing was nonchalant but it was heavily contrived to attract attention. The bits and pieces I knew were sufficient that a few times that first day a black girl heard me singing and wheeled around with a shocked look, only to then praise me for knowing the song. I loved the attention.

One day, I got to school early and dropped my books and purse by my homeroom door. The teacher wasn't there yet and the halls were pretty much deserted. I ventured down the hall to see if I could find any other students. When I started back toward my homeroom, I saw a black girl pick up my purse and take off in the opposite direction. Rounding a corner, I heard a locker door close and saw her disappear down a flight of stairs. I opened a few lockers and found my purse stashed in one of them. I had my purse back.

When I told the story during carpool that afternoon one of the other cheerleader's mothers became outraged. She was adamant that a police report should be filed. I didn't see it as a big deal. The girl wasn't a criminal— she was a kid— and I had been silly to leave my purse sitting in the hall anyway.

Later that year, when a black girl was crowned Homecoming Queen, that same mother tried to launch an investigation that would revoke my black classmate's crown. Mrs. Johnston's claim was that the black girl's win was illegitimate because the black students had voted as a block.

A block.

In other words, the black kids had all voted for the only black candidate and managed to create a majority. Majority ruled for popularity contests like Homecoming Queen, except, I guess, when the majority is made up of black people.

Mrs. Johnston tried to recruit my mother to the cause of the "black block voting issue," but my mother told her that her campaign seemed a little racist. Mrs. Johnston insisted that it was not *her* who was racist. Couldn't my mother see that, if anything, black students were the racists? They had voted for the black candidate simply because she was black. Whites had voted for much more pure-of-heart reasons. Whites had voted based on the personalities of the candidates. That's the way it *should* be, Mrs. Johnston argued.

At the high school level, it was rumored, the vote counters had effectively put processes in place that ensured black and Mexican women couldn't win. That system was simply a policy that disregarded votes for non-white candidates and awarded the crown to the white girl with the highest number of votes. *But that was just a rumor, right?*

In the end, the school's administration team was not willing to hear Mrs. Johnston's pleas for white justice and the matter faded.

It was in that very environment that choosing new wave or country music over the likes of Michael Jackson and Prince became about much more than the cassette in your amazing new portable player known as a Sony Walkman.

The choice you made between those three types of music would dictate who your friends were, what you did on the weekends, and ultimately, your values.

I was already pretty much set on black music. I had noted that country music glorified alcohol, hunting, jingoism, and sometimes cheating. When I overheard a classmate making a racist remark it seemed they were always part of the group that listened to country music.

New wave and punk seemed to glorify opposition to authority and hard drugs. The punk scene, to the extent that I'd explored it, seemed to be about anger. But I wasn't angry. My parents hadn't done anything to me to make me dislike them or want to rebel against their rules. I loved my parents, even when I was getting in trouble for my terrible grades.

By counting out country music as well as new wave and punk, I arrived at black music by a process of elimination. Black music was still pretty wholesome. If you overlooked the cheating songs, most black music focused on love[55] and the lyrics were sweet and innocent.

Only recently I was singing the song "Cutie Pie," by the group *One Way*, to my daughter as if she were the girl the song was written about. That song came out in 1982 just as I was making my choice to stay with R&B. It stands today as a love song that I can sing to my daughter without having to change a single word of the lyrics.

---

[55] Of course they were actually full of double-entendres about sex, but all that flew over my head in those early years. I now long for double-entendres and far prefer them to the explicit lyrics popular today. I'm old, I know, and it shows when I make statements like this.

After choosing black music, I decided to become as expert as I could when it came to knowing artists and their music. I bought R&B fan magazines and read articles on Luther Vandross, Shalimar, The Gap Band, Barry White, Philip Bailey, Chaka Khan, and many others. I cut out pictures and used them in the collages I built for the cover of my see-thru view binder.

My clique was still completely white and I wouldn't have considered dating across color lines at that point, but in all my classes I seemed to be trying to find black girls to sit next to. Ann Morgan, Linda Payton, JoEddie Williams, Stephanie Caldwell, Sandra Washington...they were like magnetic fields pulling me in.

While other white girls whispered complaints about having to share curling irons with black girls after PE, I knew the slick residue from their hair was a beauty product and not a bodily secretion. When I heard white girls whispering their objections, I chided them for being *straight ignorant* and dismissively tossed them a towel.

In retrospect I see how this and other incidents were helping me make a slow, but certain, separation from whites I considered bigoted.

In the spring of that school year the high school basketball team won the state championship. My family had gone to all the games leading up to and including the finals.

When that championship game was over, the players came into the stands to celebrate with all their hometown fans. All the players hugged my mom, who was a substitute teacher at the high school. Then, my mom introduced the players to my dad. My sister hugged a few of the players as well.

I stood apart from my family, separated by several near-empty rows. I was jealous, for sure, but I also had this sense that the whole scene was disgusting. Most of the families that could afford to drive all over the state for the games were middle-class or upper-class and white.

Watching these bankers, car dealers, and other prominent white men chatting up the black players made my stomach churn. These men did not see blacks as equals and I knew it.

In the fall of 1983, I began my first year at the high school. By now the popular crowd in my class really had splintered, one or two went strongly into the new-wave-punk-music-expensive-drugs-meaningless-anarchy-graffiti lifestyle and several went the country-western-two-step-cotton-eyed-joe-drink-yourself–to-oblivion route.

Those of us leftover were gathered under the leadership of a half-German, half-Italian girl. Though the top popular group in each class had traditionally been WASPy, *times they were a changin'*.

Our new leader had decided that our group would include certain Mexicans. Namely, her Mexican boyfriend and the Mexican boyfriend of her Italian best friend. They'd been best friends since their parents freaked out over busing in the early 1970s and put them in Catholic school together. They'd bonded intensely over the fact that both of their parents hated Mexicans and forbade that they should ever date any.

Other Mexicans in our group included two Mexican girls who preferred to date black guys. Black guys weren't allowed in our group, but these two girls didn't care what our leader thought. This made them sort of group members, but sort of not, and their defiance attracted me a lot.

I looked up to them because they were so willing to ignore her attempts to control them. They were the only members of our group that could openly refuse to be manipulated by her and never suffer her retribution.

Our group listened to black music. DeBarge's "All This Love", Prince's "Purple Rain," and Michael Jackson's "Thriller" were hugely popular albums. Singles by Ashford & Simpson, Marvin Gaye, Stevie Wonder, New Edition, Chaka Khan and others, were the soundtrack for those years of high school.

I felt fairly satisfied within the group. At the beginning of that school year, I dated a Mexican guy from our crowd for a month or two. After he and I broke up, I began dating another Mexican guy, but only, again, for a short time. Our leader would often decide who should be dating whom and play a sort of do-it-or-else matchmaker. She'd arranged my second relationship, so both the guy and I were less than enthusiastic about our match-up.

In the late fall of that year I was starting to realize that our crowd was faster than I wanted to be. I drank with them nearly every weekend but that was the extent of my "drug" use. All the girls in my clique had lost their virginity but I had not. Some of them had smoked weed a time or two and several had even tried powdered cocaine. Cocaine was appearing more and more frequently at our weekend parties.

I was completely intimidated by their embrace of drugs and sex.

The popular crowds of the senior and junior classes were still exclusively WASP but several of the senior guys loved R&B and funk music. Near the end of football season that year, one of those seniors decided he wanted to throw the Mother of All House Parties. He invited black, white and Mexican kids to party together. We all liked the same music, he reasoned, so we would all enjoy a party where it was being played.

Most of the members of my clique were not invited, but I was, because I went to the same church as the host.

Since high school parties were generally kept secret from parents, no adults were able to warn of the calamities that would follow. No one said: *If you party together, some of you will end up dating each other.*

The party was talked about for weeks in advance and when it finally took place it was huge and the theme was toga. While I was there, one of the black basketball players asked me to follow him into the garage and I coyly went along. He kissed me and I was instantly in love. The next week at school I wanted us to be like any other couple. I wanted us to wait together in the commons before the morning bell and hold hands on the way to class.

As he stood with friends (all of them black guys) waiting for the morning bell, I came and stood beside him, believing that was exactly the place I belonged. Everyone in his clique went silent, confused by my presence. He jumped into the center of the circle to tell a funny story, complete with gestures and character voices. He stayed in the center until that first bell. Then he asked where my first class was, said goodbye, and took off in the opposite direction.

By the end of first period, he'd written me a note that said, "It seems like I am bringing you down in the eyes of your friends." He was breaking up with me and it had only been two-and-a-half days since his kiss had changed my life. I was appalled by the note. He seemed to be saying, "I am black, I am lesser. If you date me, you will be lesser, too." I wrote back a pleading letter in which I might as well have quoted from King's "I Have A Dream" speech because that note was so littered with high ideals about defying racism. Still, it did not sway him. He'd ended it and that was that.

I learned that another of the white girls in our group had been kissed at that party by another basketball player. She and I began spending more time together.

The Italian Queen Bee found out what had happened and started organizing secret relationships between the girls of our clique and the basketball team.

Within two weeks, there were six interracial couplings and everyone but me was dead-set on keeping the relationships a secret. Of course, I couldn't come out about *my* relationship because I didn't actually have a relationship – he'd completely cut me off with that note.

Our leader got busy playing matchmaker, trying to find me a new secret lover (even though I was still smitten with the first). One day after lunch, one of the girls in our group was discussing a disagreement she'd had with her secret lover. Our leader said, "Screw that! You're white, he's black. That means you make the decisions, not him. Just tell him how it's gonna be and let him know that *you* make the rules."

I was horrified when I heard her say that. The idea that within these relationships we would maintain a white supremacist hierarchy was shocking and deeply troubling. I returned to my afternoon classes unable to concentrate. I asked for a hall pass, found my mother where she was substituting that day, and told her I needed to go home because I was sick.

I'd thought the relationships were being kept secret because the teachers and administrators would have been against interracial dating. Our clique leader had made her bigotry plain and now I had to wonder about the motives of the other girls in our little Secret Lover Club.

Later, I learned that the basketball players were very interested in keeping the relationships a secret, too. They all had black girlfriends and didn't want to lose them. We were as much toys to them as they were to my friends. Once I became aware of that, I realized the object of my affection had only pretended to have been worried about *my* reputation. He'd only been looking out for himself.

No one was damaged more by these relationships than the black girlfriends. In the coming years, they would find that white women's increasing willingness to engage in secret relationships completely changed the economy of black relationships. White girls who wanted to keep secrets encouraged black men to be dishonest in their relationships with black women. And since these white women were nearly always more promiscuous than the black women, black women would have to contend with black men who suddenly saw no value in exclusive relationships during high school and college.

I became very depressed. I stopped hanging around with that clique. I had nowhere to go on the weekends but I wasn't terribly sad about that.

Summer came and went and now I was a junior.

In the mornings, instead of standing with my old clique, I stood with my sister, who was a senior. She stood with two black girls from her class named Joyce and Grace. Joyce and Grace had been best friends since childhood and they were so attuned to one another that they operated like a vaudeville comedy act. We laughed so hard each morning as we waited for first bell, it seemed like our cheeks hurt for the entire first period each day.

When I met Joyce's younger brother, I was smitten.

Ira was very shy and humble. He had never been to a high school party and wasn't interested in attending any. He was only interested in pleasing his parents and so he worked to keep them happy. He was a good student and a good athlete. He was already impressing the coaches as he'd been promoted, as a sophomore, to varsity teams for both football and basketball.

We began a phone romance and it sustained me through the fall and spring of my junior year. We met daily at school, just after lunch for about ten minutes in a busy hallway. Other than that we were never in the same physical space during the first eight months of our romance. He told me his parents would disapprove of him dating. My mother embraced the relationship as soon as it started because she had become worried about my weekend partying. She sensed that when I'd been going out to parties I'd also been drinking. When I started talking with Ira on the phone instead of going out on the weekends, she supported the relationship with a gusto I hadn't received for any previous romantic interests of mine.

That summer I worked as a lifeguard for the city. Ira and I came up with the plan that he would drive past whatever city swimming pool I was working at, and honk to say hello. He never stopped; just drove by and tapped the horn twice.

About a month after we started the lifeguard/honking routine, games began for his summer basketball league. He decided it would be okay for me to attend the games. His parents were warming to the idea that he was old enough to date, but they were still completely against him dating someone white.

Ira and I kissed for the first time early that summer and lost our virginities to one another the week before school was about to resume.

When the school year started back up I was a senior and he was a junior. We dated openly which meant we held hands in the hall, went to lunch off campus together, and waited together for the morning bell. Our school had a large, indoor, open area called the commons. It had a sort of grand staircase. Sophomore year I'd stood under the staircase, in the shadowy nook my clique preferred. Junior year, when standing with Grace and Joyce, we'd stood at the base of the stairs which was a pretty prominent place. It was as close as anyone had gotten to standing in the middle of the commons.

People stood along the railings on the second floor and they stood around the edges of the first floor. No one stood in the middle.

The grand staircase had a landing that was almost like a small stage halfway between the second floor and the ground floor. When dances were held in the commons the DJ would set up equipment on that landing.

Ira decided that we would stand on that landing while we waited for the first bell. So he, I, and his cousin, James, stood each morning as if we were on stage.

It was a bold decision. Ira was well aware that no one had ever made that their morning spot before but he had the kind of personality that managed to be both quiet and loud at the same time. Later that year, for instance, he'd be voted class favorite even though most people thought of him as "shy."

I decided that if Ira was going to lean up against a corner of railing on our stage, I was going to stand with my hip between his legs. This was an almost insanely bold move for an interracial couple, in Texas, in 1985.

The administrators at our school had always made interracial relationships their business. Of course, when white guys crossed the color line, principals were far more likely to look the other way. When white *girls* crossed the color line it was treated as a crisis. The female principal would pull the white girl from class and tell her she had to end the relationship if she wanted to avoid suspension. If suspension wasn't effective, she was told, her parents would be notified[56].

That year was a little different because we had two newbie white principals who had arrived from out of town. They wouldn't have known how interracial relationships had been handled in the past, and they must have been afraid to ask the other two principals: the white lady and the black guy.

One of them made a habit of approaching us on the platform and telling me my outfit was breaking the dress code. I would then have to leave school, go home, change clothes, and come back. After a while, I was dressing to avoid his attempts to intimidate me.

My mother was still everyone's favorite substitute teacher – students and staff alike. She had been that favorite for years. When teachers called in sick or had vacation days, the front office staff called a list of potential substitutes in order to line up coverage. My mom was the first person on the substitute teacher phone list and was often booked weeks in advance.

---

[56] I know how Principal Thornton had done it because the girls themselves told me their stories a few years later. This was after I'd become a little bit famous for shattering the color line at our high school. As silly as that sounds, about a year after I graduated, two girls came up to me in the mall, acting like I was some kind of local celebrity. They told me they both had black boyfriends and they wanted to thank me. They said, after what Ira and I did, it was like floodgates opening. "No one even cares anymore" they said. I knew they were mistaken and plenty of people were still against it, but I guess I was glad to get credit for moving our high school that small step forward.

We loved having her at school with us. On spirit days she always dressed up right alongside my sister and I. If we wore dresses made of silver garbage bags, she wore garbage bags, too. When we dressed up for 50s Day, Safari Day or Crazy Hair Day, her outfits were every bit as sharp as ours.

When the newbie white principals learned that she was my mother they called her in and told her that she needed to put a stop to my relationship with Ira. She was not pleased with me for flaunting the relationship but she was not going to let them tell her how to parent me.

She never got another call to substitute teach. That was a blow for her. She loved substitute teaching; it had become almost the core of her identity. I felt terrible that my choice to openly date across color lines had cost her so much but she told me not to cow to them. Before that, she'd been begging me to tone down the public displays of affection, but now she encouraged me to hold hands with Ira, and stand there on our little platform just as much as I wanted.

Later, at my mother's memorial service in December of 2013, one of her closest friends noted that, "She was a warrior, bigger than life! I know that probably sounds odd, but she stood up when it counted!"

It didn't sound odd to me. I knew her friend was thinking of the many times my mother politely informed people that what they were saying was racist. It happened quite often. It was Texas and it was the 1980's: a lot of white people would say openly racist things or tell racist jokes. My mother would ask them not to say those things in front of her or us.

I became close friends with Ira's cousin, Demetra, who was a sophomore. I went to her house nearly every day after I got off work. I loved the chaos of their extended family. Demetra's aunt lived next door to her mother and another aunt's back fence lined up to that. Sometimes in the span of a half hour we'd visit all three houses, forgoing all small talk on our way in and out of each residence.

The art of small talk, a skill required among the white families in our neighborhood and church, was something I dreaded and despised. The fact that Demetra's family had no use for it offered me great reprieve.

There were children everywhere, of every age. They all knew my name and were ready with hugs at the sight of me. I loved watching them interact with one another. I'd grown up among black and Mexican classmates who would say, "We're cousins," with a gravity that made no sense to me.

Once I was around Demetra and Ira's family and saw the interactions between cousins, I understood what my classmates had been trying to tell me. As cousins, their lives intersected and overlapped all the time. I saw my cousins every few years for three to five days straight. In Demetra's family, cousins could easily be closer than siblings.

I loved the buzz of weekday evenings at Demetra's when the family came together in a slow trickle. All the aunts worked long hours at tiring jobs. They picked up children and fast food and made their way toward the cul-de-sac, arriving just as the streetlights were flickering on.

In my house, these same evenings were full of tension. My father had been promoted to a management role that he didn't enjoy and this translated into his being easily peeved and generally averse to arriving home after a stressful day to see us happy and relaxed. For that reason, my mother encouraged us to keep a low profile. She spent her early evenings quietly busying herself in the kitchen because she knew that made him happier than seeing her sprawled out on the couch, watching television.

At Demetra's house, conversation was relaxed and laughter came easily. Everyone had a family nickname and knowing those nicknames made me feel lucky and loved.

At Demetra's, just sitting down on the couch meant wriggling into a niche between the throw pillows and one of her aunt's voluminous bodies. I liked the way it felt to sink in beside one of them. At my house, we did not touch one another.

I'd been suffering under a heavy sense that white, middle-class culture was full of unwritten rules and unforgiving approbations. I'd witnessed white women, mothers of friends, sniff about the phone ringing after 9 p.m. or overheard them as they excoriated the attire of an acquaintance. It seemed to me that every move I made among whites was under scrutiny. Poor souls like me who broke the white rules of propriety were never corrected openly and that left me with the ominous feeling that mistakes I didn't even know I had made were following me through life like a massive storm cloud.

Things were gloriously different when I was at Demetra's. I could drop by Demetra's house unannounced and no one cared. If I said I was coming by and then couldn't, no one held it against me. If, for some reason, someone had been counting on me and I'd failed them, they told me directly instead of criticizing me behind my back and leaving me unable to apologize or make it up to them.

How could I be so confident that they weren't talking about me behind my back? It was simple, really. When I was with them, they weren't spending that time talking bad about other people behind *their* backs.

That's what my family did. That's what other white families did.

Most of what I perceived as black values, norms and behaviors were actually *black working-class* values, norms and behaviors. I just didn't know enough at that time to see things clearly.

I started to believe that blacks did everything right and whites did everything wrong.

I believed that my father's best attributes were due to his having grown up poor. He worked hard, was ethical, and taught us not to worship money. My father was not materialistic, so I thought blacks would never be materialistic. I decided that, like my father, blacks had been forced to get by on so little, they knew that happiness didn't require a lot of material things.

My father was anti-racist because, as a poor Okie in California, many whites had looked down on him. He had used that experience to become a better person. I inferred that blacks would do the same. I believed they could never be racist, having felt the sting of discrimination themselves.

I romanticized the strength and nobility that I thought oppression brought forward in people. I came to believe that black people, just by virtue of being part of an oppressed group, were always good, righteous and humble.

Similarly, I thought blacks would never be elitist, use nepotism, cronyism, or be corrupt.

Within this paradigm of black worship, I was certain I wasn't a racist because – duh! – most white people in my Texas town seemed to dislike black people and I loved them. All of them. Even the ones I'd never met.

I wanted very little to do with white people. I didn't villainize whites completely – that's hard to do from the inside – but I would let out an exasperated "White people!?!" at key moments and that would win me a lot of approval from my black friends and even more acceptance from their parents and grandparents.

I was certain that my friendship was making Demetra's life better, as well as the lives of everyone in her family. Just by knowing me, they could feel better about racism. If, before I came around, they'd thought all white people hated them, they could now understand that they'd been wrong. Instead of worrying or feeling bad about themselves, my friendship would lift them up.

My Life as a *Good White Person*: The 1980s

Looking back on those days now, almost thirty years later, I hope my perspective is a little more accurate.

What I know today is that I reaped far greater rewards from those relationships than any of them did. Their closeness— that chaotic and high-spirited familial web was intoxicating for me – but I didn't deserve to enjoy that web.

The strong bonds of Demetra's extended family were hard won. They'd supported each other through thick and thin. Their connections to one another went beyond common ancestry. The web had been built through shared experiences, often those experiences included struggles to keep their children fed, avoid being fired, cope with the news of a grave diagnosis, or scrape enough money together for an emergency car repair. They were close because they had to be. They'd shared resources over and over again because they couldn't have made it if they hadn't.

This wasn't a movie. These struggles continued whether I was there to watch them unfold or not. The bonds that were reinforced because of those struggles traced back to root causes in racism.

Our town kept them working for the lowest possible wages because blacks in low wage positions made white lives more luxurious. When I enjoyed myself at Demetra's house, I was double-dipping.

Furthermore, I was disrupting bonds in the black community by having a relationship with a black man. My disruption hurt black women more than it hurt black men. And all the while I was patting myself on the back because I was so certain I was destroying the color line in a way that benefitted everyone.

Years later, because my teenage rebellion took place in the 1980s, in the South, I believed I'd paid some dues that other white women had not. Sometimes, in my own mind, it was as if I'd been beaten bloody on the Pettus bridge.

In the mid-nineties, when I was around the white wives and girlfriends of black professional athletes, I felt morally superior to them. The perky former professional cheerleader who'd grown up in California and dated just one black man (a rich, famous, football player), before marrying him and raising their children in a million-dollar house was not in my league. She had not suffered for her love of all things black.

Could she name the founding members of the Black Panther Party? Of course not. She had not given up *anything*. Every moment of their courtship had been a walk in the park. For her I had only a passing disdain. *Pshaww*...I would think...*Tourist*.

Going Pro

Ira and I were on-again off-again when a black football player from Texas A&M became interested in me. He'd graduated from our high school a few years before, and had heard that a cute white girl had crossed the color line, loud and proud. He actually knew a little more about me than that, because our families intersected in a number of ways.

He knew my mother as the fun substitute teacher. He knew my sister because they'd been at the high school together before he'd graduated. His mother had been my brother's teacher in elementary school. His father taught at the high school and knew both my mother and me. His sister and I were on the yearbook staff together.

One day, he and another Texas A&M football player showed up during my lunch hour asking about me. When I got back to campus a lot of people were abuzz about it. Ira heard about it and wanted us to get back together immediately.

How did I deserve the attention of someone who was on his way to play in the NFL? I was cute but I wasn't beautiful. I had no curves at all. I was a terrible student, unlike his sister, who worked hard and excelled at everything.

What made me worthy of his attention?

I was a white girl from a good family who was willing to date across color lines. That meant something to him. I knew that my whiteness was giving me extra points, and I should have felt bad about that, but I didn't. I reasoned that while I didn't believe my whiteness should count in my favor, if it did, then that was his problem, not mine. I thought of us as equals – he should too.

We began dating during the summer between my high school graduation and my first semester at Texas A&M.

As I previously noted, I got into Texas A&M as a legacy. I was a terrible student with no self-discipline. Before the first semester came to an end, I had dropped out.

In the spring, I got a job and spent most of my free time with my NFL-bound boyfriend. He was getting lots of attention from rich white men who wanted to serve as his agent and that meant rides in limousines and dinners out at expensive restaurants.

His family wasn't thrilled with my choices and I'm certain that he wouldn't have continued dating a black woman if she'd been a college drop-out. My whiteness evidently cancelled out the fact that I was on track to be a total loser.

By the time he was drafted into the NFL late that spring he'd already asked me to follow him to whatever city he ended up in. My mother protested and insisted that I could go to the new city but she would pay for me to get an apartment of my own.

In the new city, we fought a lot and I was unhappy. Whenever I thought he was cheating on me my first question was always, "Is she black or white?" If she was black I figured I may as well throw in the towel. I believed that black girls had it all, and that if he'd chosen a black girl I could never compete. If she was white then I could challenge her for his attention, even if she was beautiful and curvy.

I remember discussing this with my sister at the time and we both agreed: black girls had everything a black man could ever want, and we really didn't understand why they'd choose a white girl, but if they did, well, there we were. Later, I would hear it said that black men married white women because they were easier to cheat on.

In any event, he and I were fighting almost constantly so I broke it off and returned home to Texas around Christmas of that year. A few weeks after I'd arrived home, I realized I was pregnant.

I wasn't ready to be a mother. We couldn't get along anyway so I decided we had no business having a child together. I didn't anguish over the decision, I got an appointment for an abortion post-haste. I didn't think of the pregnancy as anything more than a microscopic fertilized egg so I had no qualms about having it surgically removed.

The Quest for Cheekbones

After the abortion, I wanted to get as far away from him, and our dysfunctional relationship as I could, so I took a nanny job in California. Even though our romance was over, I carried with me a self-image he had created for me. On several occasions during our relationship he'd told me exactly what drew him to me.

He said he liked it that I am tall, because he wanted tall children. He said my strong features (long nose and chin) meant I would be beautiful when other women's weak features shriveled with age. My small boobs would never sag. My intelligence would combine with his to create brilliant children.

He went on to point out how our children would benefit from hybrid vigor. Each of our weaknesses would be cancelled out by the other person's strengths.

He was intellectual and loved to debate topics and discuss ideas. He told me that the fact that I could hold my own in debates was another reason he wanted me to be the mother of his children.

Starting over in California, I carried his logic with me. For the rest of my single life, when I thought about dating, I always used the formula he'd presented. With any potential suitor the questions would pop into my head: What would our children look like? Would our strengths and weaknesses combine to make the kind of children I wanted?

With this attention to detail, I became more aware of the need to cancel out my long head, long nose, and prominent chin. I added to the list my thin lips and big ears. My skin doesn't tan to a rich bronze; instead I become the familiar terra cotta of the leathery, beer-swilling folks who hang out at the lake all summer. I would need someone with milk-chocolate or even semi-sweet chocolate to fix my terra cotta.

My body is boxy: My wide shoulders and broad pelvis practically invite fat to settle between them, promising a peaceful existence free from waistbands and cinch belts. Someone with narrow hips would hopefully cancel out my wide ones.

When I describe myself this way, many people get uncomfortable, misunderstanding my almost brutal assessment of myself as low self-esteem. I don't have low self-esteem, I'm just completely realistic about how I look. I decided the best gift I could possibly give my children (prior to their birth) was to realistically assess my strengths and weaknesses and try not to pass my least desirable traits on to them. To ensure them mildly-appealing, average looks, I felt I had to be very particular about what the phenotype of my children's father would need to be.

I decided that my ideal partner would have a short, round head. He would need to have great cheekbones, a short nose, and full lips. Small ears would be nice but big ears could be overlooked. He didn't have to be black, necessarily, but I imagined that he would be. My NFL guy fit the description, but we couldn't get along.

Introversion, ADHD, and Malcolm X

A lot of things happened while I nannied in California: I figured out I'm an introvert; I learned how to overcome my ADHD somewhat; and I read the *Autobiography of Malcolm X*.

Once I got settled in with my host family in California I swore off men. I'd decided that during my nanny-time I would focus on improving myself and not worry about having a relationship. That was a fairly easy decision to arrive at because I had no way of meeting people my own age and I couldn't imagine having a male friend come over to my host family's house. I didn't attempt to make any female friends and not having any didn't bother me. A few times I went several weeks straight without ever stepping outside. I realized I was either a troll who should be living under a bridge, or I was an introvert. I settled on introvert.

It was also during my time as a nanny that I discovered exercise and coffee. Those two things calmed me and gave me a newfound ability to focus.

Because so many of my hours were spent sitting around while the kids played, I started reading a lot. I'd never read for leisure, but now I wanted to.

I loved basketball as a spectator sport so one of the first books I checked out from the local Sherman Oaks branch library was Wilt Chamberlain's autobiography. In that book he talked about meeting the young Lew Alcindor. That made me want to read Alcindor's biography. I found that book easily, listed under the author name Abdul-Jabbar. Abdul-Jabbar's book talked about Malcolm X and put a new biography on my list of books to check out.

It took me a long time to track down Malcolm X's biography because it was filed under the author name of Malcolm Little. The librarian at that small local branch had never heard of him.

Reading Malcolm X's story, in 1988, had a significant impact on me. It was hard to digest the idea that while I worshipped Malcolm X, he would have thought little of me. After feeling sad for a while, I bucked up and told myself that I was dedicated enough to the cause of black rights that even if Malcolm X had shunned me, I would have forged ahead as a *Good White Person.*

I decided that when I did start dating again, I would not date American black men because marrying one was harmful to the black community. The point was made in the book that every educated, accomplished black man who marries a white woman, reduces the pool of black men available to educated, accomplished black women. I reasoned that if I truly loved black America, I could not be part of its continued disintegration. It was as if I'd made a promise to the spirit of Malcolm X.

I took that promise seriously, yet Malcolm X was now the prototype for the man I wanted to marry. He was intellectual, didn't care about money, and was dedicated to racial justice. He also didn't worship white people and that was something I very much admired because I thought our society probably made it hard for blacks not to be brainwashed into admiring whites.

The paradox of Malcolm X as my ideal mate and the vow I'd made not to date black men was obviously problematic. Additionally, there was that genetic profile I had decided would be necessary to create the children I wanted. Since I wasn't dating at the time, it seemed like a problem I could resolve at a later date.

THE 1990S

The nineties have been called the Dawn of the Information Age. The decade certainly was a digital decade for me. I began using computers in the late eighties, took my first computer programming class in 1991, and by 1997 I had transitioned into a job that relied heavily on my knowledge of technology.

My family had a home computer at a time when that was still a rare thing. This became a tremendous advantage for me. I was not only comfortable using one but I had endless hours to push my skills to new levels out of pure curiosity. By the time I had transitioned to a technology job with high pay, William still hadn't so much as turned a computer on.

As the Information Age developed, people began talking about the Digital Divide: Those with access to computers, those without access, and the wide chasm of opportunity between them. In many ways, I and my future husband, were emblematic of that divide.

Leah's Black Dad in the 1990s

Leah's dad, William, spent the entire decade going in and out of jail. He was twenty-six when they began, and thirty six when they ended. He was addicted to alcohol and, because of his felony record, was cut off from any and all forms of assistance. He could not get food stamps, housing assistance, grants for school or any other program designed to help a person get back on their feet.

Very few jobs were open to him. He joined labor pools each weekday morning and hoped for jobs that were either mentally stimulating or at least not physically exhausting.

Upon release from prison, William would often work for a time and chant his intent to stay straight to anyone who would listen. After one prison stint, he was able to get a waiver and attend a vocational business school for half a semester before falling prey to the temptation of alcohol, failing a number of urine tests, and getting sent back to prison for violating his parole. Such behavior often resulted in a new felony charge of "escape."

Whenever William was released from any of his prison stays, he always lacked a stable place to live. His mother's home was not really an option. The problems she'd had with her feet became problems with her legs. Doctors had amputated both of her legs and she was confined to a wheelchair. Financially, she was barely getting by on her disability payments and did not have any extra money to help her son get back on his feet. Additionally, her extra room was already being used by Tammy and *her* children.

Colorado law requires a minimum one-year mandatory parole for many offenses; other offenses require up to five years of parole. The idea of keeping watch over convicts after their release seemed like a solid policy to me back when I was an outsider looking in.

Later, when I witnessed the system from the inside, as the wife of an alcoholic felon, I saw how unfair the system is for those with unstable lives. Coming out of jail with few prospects to make a life for oneself is depressing. For an alcoholic, the temptation to begin drinking again is hard to overcome.

Missed appointments, failing to stay employed, testing positive for alcohol use, missing curfew—all of these things are within stumbling distance for someone without a place to live. If a person on parole fails a urine test or misses an appointment, they often become scared and begin to procrastinate making things right. Soon enough, they are several months delinquent and they decide not to report at all. A warrant is issued and they'll be under arrest the first time they're stopped on the street because the police decide to do a stop and frisk.

When on parole or probation, a person must pay an administrative fee of around fifty dollars a month. Additionally, they must pay nine dollars for each urine test. If they are assigned to classes for substance abuse, anger management, parenting or any number of other focus areas, they must pay fees for those classes as well. As another condition of parole, parolees often have to perform community service. The cost of enrolling in community service programs in Colorado, currently, is $100.

Those who go to halfway houses are charged nineteen dollars a day in rent, making a parolee's attempts to stay straight even more precarious. Many get behind in rent fees and decide not to return to the halfway house, thus putting themselves on even less stable footing.

Shelter life for William was untenable. He was never guaranteed a bed in the shelters and if he didn't get a good night's sleep, he would likely miss work the next day. If he got fired, it was all downhill from there.

Leah's White Mom in the 1990s

After California, I went to Phoenix, Arizona and found a job as the live-in aid to a quadriplegic man. After a few months with him, I decided to enroll in a computer class at the local community college.

I tried really hard. I read over the syllabus a half-dozen times. I followed assignments to the letter and turned them in early. I checked and double-checked with the instructor to make sure I was meeting her expectations and standards.

I got an A.

An A.

An A!!!!

I was so proud of myself. It was the first time in my life I'd ever cared what grade I got in a class. But it was more than that. I really wanted to be in college, and I didn't *just* want to make good grades; I wanted to *learn*. I wanted to soak up everything: every topic, every idea, every question and every answer.

I did so well at the community college, that I decided it was time to give a four-year university setting another try. I applied to Arizona State University and was accepted. I felt amazingly happy and completely in control of my life for the first time ever.

My enthusiasm was short lived though, because it turned out the out-of-state tuition was prohibitively expensive. I called my mom in Texas, sobbing through the phone.

My father had just accepted a job in Fort Collins, Colorado as an endowed chair professor. My mother said, "Why don't you just meet us in Colorado? You can live at home while you go to school at CSU."

I was grateful beyond comprehension. There I was, a twenty-two year old who had disappointed my parents too many times to count and yet, I had been invited to "come home" and go to college on their dime, no questions asked, no penance assigned.

I left Arizona and moved to Colorado. On the first day of school, I mounted my bike to ride over to campus and found that tears were streaming down my face. *How lucky was I to have this second chance when so many people don't even get that first chance?*

That gratefulness has stayed with me even today. I did not deserve what amounted to their grant of a "full-ride scholarship." But they had the money and the extra bedroom so they made it happen. This time around, with my ADHD under control, I was a stellar student and graduated Magna Cum Laude.

I started CSU as an Anthropology major but after about a year and a half came to understand that I wanted to create educational videos aimed at lower income populations. I thought I could create videos that bridged the cultural gaps and motivated poor black and brown children to learn[57], and therefore love learning.

My dad had a friend who owned an educational video production company, so I was offered a summer internship. My parents gave me money to make the trip from Colorado to Texas and they covered my expenses so that I could have the internship on my résumé.

The fact that cronyism got me the job was something I didn't fully recognize at the time. Throughout high school and college I'd heard whites say, "It's not *what* you know, it's *who* you know." I found that saying repugnant. Even if the world worked that way, it was not how the world *should* work. I wanted no part of a system that rewarded relationships over skills.

---

[57] Ironically I thought black and brown children had motivation issues, but not white kids, even though for most of my life I had been the poster child for a lack of motivation.

Figure 35: Leaving for graduate school in Arizona, I pretended I was going to take my niece, Payton, with me. I left Colorado in the reliable car my parents purchased for me. When the car pictured here broke down later that semester, they told me to sell the car and keep the cash. They then purchased another car for me and had it delivered to Arizona.

Yet, here I was, taking the internship. My repugnance had become nothing more than lip service when I learned of my dad's friend's business. I didn't recognize it as cronyism at the time, instead, I considered it a "lucky" coincidence.

Needless to say, my husband could not have benefited in a similar fashion. His parents had networks, but the people in their networks were equally strapped and had to save their measly favors for their own extended families. William also didn't have parents who could have helped him avoid student loans or given him a place to live during college that would have been conducive to learning.

My parents provided me with a car so that I could get back and forth to campus. I worked during college, but the money was mine to spend on whatever I wanted.

Just prior to my graduation in 1993, I received a job offer from the educational video company at which I'd had the internship.

At my graduation ceremony, as we all waited in caps and gowns, someone yelled out for everyone who had a job to hold up their hand. I was one of very few with my hand up because there was a slight recession at that time. I was very proud of my accomplishment and certainly didn't mention that I was being hired by one of my father's close colleagues. What's worse, is that I wasn't hiding it, I simply didn't recognize it for what it was. I was immensely proud that my work during the internship had earned me the job offer.

It was only in writing this book that I have come to terms with what actually happened. I got an internship because of *who* I knew (not *what* I knew). Stating the facts out loud, over a decade later, was challenging for me. After I'd forced myself to state it openly four times: to my father, my

Figure 36: On the job, after graduate school, with my DOD security credentials.

mother, my husband and my sister, I was finally able to really own what had happened.

I had been good at that job, but someone else, who didn't have the same connection could have been just as good, or perhaps better at it than me. That "someone else," however many thousands of "someone elses" there were, didn't get the chance to compete with me for the job, because their father did not know the owner of the company.

Many of my fellow graduates who didn't have jobs lined up, but who did have wealthy parents, simply stayed in school to get their masters degrees. Their parents could afford to keep them in school while they waited for better economic conditions. A masters looked far better on a resume than eight months working as a barista at Starbucks or as a cashier at Walmart. Working hard was the kind of thing someone who didn't know better might do to make it through the recession. You know, someone who wasn't from a rich family or was the first in their family to go to college.

I worked making educational videos for a year then I decided I wanted to create educational software, instead. I researched graduate schools, made a list of my top three and, somewhat ironically, chose Arizona State. While in my master's program, all my jobs were awarded to me through my professor's networks.

I graduated from my master's program with a 4.0 GPA and spent another semester there, working toward my PhD.

Then, not feeling certain the PhD program was right for me, I left school, moved to Washington, DC, and worked for a company there.

My job in DC required me to have Department of Defense (DOD) clearance, something I would not have been awarded if I'd ever had a felony. Luckily, I had a perfectly clean criminal record.

The War on Drugs in the 1990s

Reagan's presidency ended in 1988. His vice president, George H.W. Bush, succeeded him and was president until 1992. Bush left nearly all of Reagan's policies and programs intact, including the racist ones.

In the early '90s I'd heard people claim that the government was pumping drugs into the inner city hoping blacks would annihilate themselves. Like most people, I thought it sounded pretty far-fetched. Turns out, it wasn't far-fetched at all.

In 1996, a journalist for the *San Jose Mercury News* named Gary Webb wrote a series of articles with the title, "Dark Alliance." In those articles he detailed evidence he'd found that proved a link between the selling of crack in the US and the funding of a guerilla army in Nicaragua. This guerrilla army was called the *Contras*.

From the 1930s until 1979[58], the country had been ruled by the Somoza family. During the time they were in power, the Somozas became very rich and made sure their family members and friends got very rich as well.

Most other Nicaraguans were very poor; unable to stay fed, find clean water, or get medical care. Any Nicaraguan who protested the Somoza family's policies, or the wealth the family continued to amass, was tortured or killed by Nicaragua's military, the National Guard.

In 1979 though, an anti-Somoza group called the Sandinistas managed to run the current Somoza ruler and his friends out of the country. Once the Sandinistas were in power they set up a number of programs hoping to make things better for the country's poor. The new government started literacy and education programs, promoted equality for women, improved housing, and worked to make basic necessities more affordable.

The US government had supported the Somoza regime for decades and in return the Somozas did anything the US government told them to do. When the new government came to power they were adamant that being loyal to the US had been the root of many of the country's problems. The US had looked the other way as the common people of Nicaragua starved, or were tortured and murdered by Somoza's military. Under the new government the poor of Nicaragua would be more important than the rich of the United States.

Many of the formerly rich Nicaraguans fled to the US. They didn't

---

[58] During the 13 years Somoza family members were not president during that time, the family still controlled the government through their close ties to the National Guard.

like being in the US, where they had to get jobs to support themselves. They wanted their Nicaraguan houses, cars, servants, and bank accounts back and they began pressuring the US government to support them in their attempts to regain power there. These formerly rich and well-connected Nicaraguans worked to set up a new guerilla army and they called that army the Contras.

The Reagan administration tried to get Congress to approve sending money to the Contras. Congress voted against it and the public was led to believe that the US would leave the new Sandinista government alone.

Instead, the Reagan administration decided they would have the CIA send money to the Contras, anyway. A Marine lieutenant colonel named Oliver North was put in charge of a program that both raised money and then worked with the CIA to funnel the money to the Contras. North worked out several schemes. One involved selling arms to Iran but another involved allowing the formerly-rich Nicaraguan exiles to make a lot of money off the US drug trade. The exiles did this by flooding the cities with crack cocaine.

North and his cohorts got the Drug Enforcement Administration (DEA) involved as well. The DEA agreed not to investigate or prosecute the Nicaraguans who were bringing drugs into the US as long as they passed their profits along to the Contras.

Gary Webb later published his findings in a book that expanded his earlier articles, including more citations and background notes. His book, *Dark Alliance: The CIA, the Contras, and the Crack Cocaine Explosion*, details how the Reagan administration, North, the CIA, and the DEA were involved in drug smuggling.

Webb's book reads like a spy novel. He tells the story of how he received the first lead and almost dismissed it completely. Then he tells of conversations he had with a number of journalists who warned him that the US government would make him pay if he tried to expose the program.

Sure enough, shortly after the series began running in the California newspaper, a massive smear campaign was launched against him. He believed it was orchestrated by the CIA.

US Congresswoman Maxine Waters (who represents South Central Los Angeles) stood beside Gary Webb and his controversial findings. She also followed up, visiting Nicaragua and interviewing key figures. Later, she questioned the Contra leadership during investigative hearings. When Webb completed the book, he asked Waters to write the forward.

In that forward, Waters states:

> The time I spent investigating the allegations of the "Dark Alliance" [newspaper article] series led me to the undeniable conclusion that the CIA, DEA, DIA, and FBI knew about the drug trafficking in South Central Los Angeles. They were either part of the trafficking or turned a blind eye to it, in an effort to fund the Contra war.
>
> The saddest part of these revelations is the wrecked lives and lost possibilities of so many people who got caught up in selling drugs, went to prison, ended up addicted or dead, or walking zombies from drugs.

The smear campaign against Webb led to his being fired from his job at the *Mercury News*. When he began looking for another job he found himself unable to get work and unable to support his family financially. Waters goes on to say:

> It may take time, but I am convinced that history is going to record that Gary Webb wrote the truth. The editors of the San Jose Mercury News did not have the strength to withstand the attacks so they abandoned Gary Webb, despite their knowledge that Gary was working on further documentation to substantiate the allegations of the series. We all owe Gary Webb a debt of gratitude for his brave work.

Webb may have believed that Waters' prediction about his vindication would come when the book was released nationally and had a chance to reach a broader audience. That vindication did not come quickly enough. Webb was never able to rejoin the journalism community, even though he'd been an award winning journalist, earning even a Pulitzer Prize for his work, prior to the *Dark Alliance* articles and book.

In 2004, he committed suicide.

Since his death various newspapers have revisited Webb's reporting on the CIA/Contra/crack connection and his ill treatment by so many organizations and individuals. In nearly every case, those efforts to revisit the scandal have resulted in apologies and regrets for the way Webb's reporting was smeared and his career was destroyed. And it's not just news organizations that have come to support those facts. Even the CIA has admitted the role it played.

In *The New Jim Crow*, Michelle Alexander states:

> The CIA admitted in 1998 that guerilla armies it actively supported in Nicaragua were smuggling illegal drugs into the United States—drugs that were making their way onto the streets of inner-city black neighborhoods in the form of crack cocaine. The CIA also admitted that, in the midst of the War on Drugs, it blocked law enforcement efforts to investigate illegal drug networks that were helping to fund its covert war in Nicaragua.

It gets worse.

At the same time the Nicaraguans were pumping the drugs into the cities, Reagan's War on Drugs policies were sending in SWAT teams with battering rams to knock down the doors to people's homes, and police were rounding up two-bit corner hustlers, emptying their pockets and confiscating any cash they had on them[59] before handcuffing them and putting them in the back of a patrol car.

Television shows at that time[60] led us to believe that the War on Drugs was all about arresting the low-level street dealers and turning them against each other, having them fall like dominoes as the police and prosecutors walked the convictions up to higher and higher levels within the drug distribution ring.

According to Alexander, the reality was nothing like that. Local police departments cared very little about getting the higher-level dealers

---

[59] I can't help but be reminded of "the lease" when I hear of the confiscations of property without due process that are legal and lucrative under War on Drug policies

[60] Shows like Law and Order never show the police or prosecutors getting the wrong person or piling up tons of very weak charges so people have little choice but to accept a plea deal even when they aren't guilty. Law and Order make heroes out of prosecuting attorneys and there are never any characters wrongly accused. It's a great show and I love it, but it's not anywhere close to reality and since reading Alexander's book I've started to wonder whether I do harm when I tune in to old episodes.

convicted. Alexander details how police departments were rewarded based on the number of arrests they made. It was much more cost effective to round up street dealers and rack up arrest numbers than it was to work through a long chain of witnesses hoping to get to some dealer at a higher level.

Police departments got cash rewards based on the numbers only. There was no sliding scale wherein major players in the drug game brought better payoffs.

Likewise, it was much more cost effective for District Attorney's (DA) offices to deal with street-level dealers. These corner hustlers didn't have any money to fight the charges against them.

Furthermore, one rule of the streets (according to my husband) was that if someone was arrested and came back from jail quickly, they must have agreed to become an informant. Therefore, these street-level dealers knew it was better to accept a plea deal and a few years in prison than to push for a trial and possibly be released for lack of evidence or some other technicality.

Mandatory sentences were extreme. DA's offices could mention the length of the mandatory sentence that would result from a guilty verdict, and defendants would quickly and wholeheartedly agree to any plea deal the DA decided to offer. The jailing of scores of street dealers pleased the general public.

Conversely, if police departments wanted the higher-level dealers, they had to set aside money for investigative units. Those units cost money but did not make a lot of arrests. Once enough evidence had been collected to arrest the high-level dealers, there were serious costs to the DA's offices if the case went to trial. These local kingpins had the money and the attorneys to go to trial and win. On top of that, according to Webb, the local kingpins in Los Angeles were Nicaraguans—untouchable for prosecution.

In some political climates, a DA's office might ask police to pursue higher level drug dealers—but in the nineties, high conviction numbers were far more impressive to the public.

There were also abuses where police were allowed to confiscate any possessions thought to have been bought with drug money. The police departments could sell the property and keep the cash. Any lawmaker should have been able to predict the level of corruption and abuse such a policy would encourage in local law enforcement organizations, yet they passed these bills just the same. These confiscation laws looked good in the newspapers and helped suburban citizens feel better.

The details of how the property confiscation programs worked (and were abused) can be read about in *The New Jim Crow* by Michelle Alexander. When you read about the outrageous antics of the police in justifying confiscation, you truly won't know whether to laugh or cry.

In 1984, the Corrections Corporation of America (CCA) was awarded a contract to take over a prison in Tennessee. This was the first privatized prison and Reagan's friends celebrated. The public was assured that private companies would be able to save taxpayer money because they would run prisons like businesses and would discover efficiencies and cost savings that would make prisons run like well-oiled machines.

Once prisons became private, prison owners and investors would benefit from locking up as many people as possible and keeping them there indefinitely.

Privately run prisons have shown themselves to be disastrous. It's almost as if "the lease" has been re-instituted. The business efficiencies these prisons came up with ended up being bright ideas like not running the air conditioning in the summer and putting four men in a cell designed for two.

In 1991, Bill Clinton ran his campaign for president by declaring that he would be tough on crime.

Alexander notes:

> Once elected, Clinton endorsed the idea of a federal "three strikes and you're out" law, which he advocated in his 1994 State of the Union address to enthusiastic applause on both sides of the aisle.

> He signed the Personal Responsibility and Work Opportunity Reconciliation Act, which...imposed...a lifetime ban on eligibility for welfare and food stamps for anyone convicted of a felony drug offense— including simple possession of marijuana.

> *Clinton also made it easier for federally assisted public housing projects to exclude anyone with a criminal history—an extraordinarily harsh step in the midst of a drug war aimed at racial and ethnic minorities.*

These laws would have disastrous and long-lasting ramifications for William. But of course, he was not alone. They would also be devastating for anyone who had been caught in the "justice" system, which, in his world, meant just about everyone.

Alexander makes a compelling case that this was the plan all along. By arresting scores of black men using stop and frisk, charging them with everything but stealing the kitchen sink, forcing them to take plea deals that would mark them as felons, and then passing laws that prohibit felons from participating in aid programs that would help them get back on their feet, they have turned blacks into second-class citizens.

This system is why my brother-in-law can get a job as a dishwasher in a restaurant and be praised endlessly by management for his work habits, his reliability, his ingenuity, and his attitude, but can be legally denied the chance to move up and become a waiter. The restaurant owner doesn't have to say it's because he's black, because he can say, "Our policy is to limit those with a criminal record to positions in the food preparation and clean-up areas."

In 2015, there's no racism needed to keep my black brother-in-law from ever being anything other than a dishwasher.

Crime Drops in the Early 1990s

Crime rates began to drop in the early 1990s. Levitt and Dubner write about that drop in their book *Freakonomics,* and their findings about the possible causes for the decline are fascinating.

Regardless of the cause (there were many theories) the crack wars were trickling out. Crack and crime were not over for William though. He would soon be fully addicted to crack and that addiction would haunt him for another two decades. The only upside to the crime rate decline for him was that he was much less likely to die in a drive-by.

Levitt and Dubner note that crack devastated the black community as it dominated inner-city life through the late 1980s and the first few years of the 1990s:

> *The gap between black and white children widened. The number of blacks sent to prison tripled. Crack was so dramatically destructive that if its effect is averaged for all black Americans, not just crack users and their families, you will see that group's postwar progress was not only stopped cold but was often knocked as much as ten years backward. Black Americans were hurt more by crack cocaine than by any other single cause since Jim Crow.*

Housing Changes in the 1990s

Remember how the back door of the ghetto opened just a little at the end of the 1980s? Well, that slow trickle became a surge in black home ownership by 1995.

A few years after that, economists and others wanted to know what factors had fueled the surge. I found two separate studies that both concluded this surge could only be attributed to a lessening of discriminatory practices. These researchers looked at all the factors they usually look at for changes in home ownership levels; like changes in credit availability, the loosening of banking regulations, and the aging of the population (Baby Boomers), etc.

After they systematically ruled out the usual suspects, the only cause left un-denied were the recent legal and policy efforts aimed at reducing housing discrimination.

Writing in 1998, one team of researchers[61] had this to say:

> *[T]he significant gap between white and black homeownership rates has been the cause of much concern to policymakers and others who fear some or all of this gap could be attributable to racial discrimination by real estate agents or lenders. In this context, the especially rapid increase in black homeownership rates since 1995 is encouraging and could be interpreted as evidence that increased attention to the CRA, Fair Lending Act, and other laws are having beneficial effects on blacks' access to housing and credit.*

---

[61] Lewis M. Segal and Daniel G. Sullivan, two members of the Federal Reserve Bank of Chicago, released their study results in their article, "Trends in homeownership: Race, demographics, and income"

In the Denver area, black families were moving from inner-city Denver to eastern suburbs like Aurora. Certainly, there were some black families who lived outside of inner-city Denver before the 1990s—but every one of those families would have told a story more or less extraordinary.

What made the 1990s so special was that black families moving into middle-class, traditionally white neighborhoods could, for the first time in America's history, be ordinary. Each black family purchasing a home could be just as ordinary as any white family doing the same.

As black families moved into the eastern suburbs, those whites who were alarmed moved to the western suburbs of Denver.

I've heard elitist whites refer to Aurora as the "armpit of Denver." They say they'd much rather live in the western suburbs like Wheatridge. One man told me he liked "White"-ridge much better than "Saudi Aurora." He told me he'd left Aurora in the 1990s when all the blacks were moving in.

"Oh my goodness!" I said, "Thank you so much!"

He looked at me, confused.

"I live in Aurora and none of my neighbors are bigots! I'm so glad you moved. Wow. I can't thank you enough, really!"

According to the US Census Bureau statistics, as of the 2010 Census, Aurora was 15% black and Wheatridge was 0% black. However, the same source shows that Aurora has a lower percentage of families with incomes below the poverty level and has a higher median income than Wheatridge. To each his own, I guess.

Yes, in the 1990s, unlike during the mid-century blockbusting, a certain kind of white family fled and a certain kind of white family stayed. Whites welcoming of diversity stuck around and they helped make Aurora the great city it is today.

Our Aurora neighbors are white, black, Mexican, American Indian, Moroccan, Japanese, Nepali, and Ghanaian. We interact with Ethiopians and Sikhs daily. My daughter attends school with children from across this same spectrum. Among us are some American black families who escaped the inner cities in the 1990s, moved to various suburbs, and put their children into the local, stable, middle-class schools. Many are doing quite well for themselves. For some, the dominoes in their children's lives immediately started falling along a much different path thanks to their move.

When good whites stay and bigoted whites leave, white flight can be a very good thing.

Hart & Risley's Meaningful Differences

Neither William nor I was raising children in the 1990s. We were both in our twenties and both a decade-and-a-half away from becoming parents. What stands out about childrearing practices in the 1990s is the fact that Betty Hart and Todd R. Risley released the first edition of the landmark book, *Meaningful Differences in the Everyday Experience of Young American Children.*

I've opted to give a short overview of their work in this chapter on the 1990s and consider the implications of their research on the way William and I were both raised, as well as the implications for the things we would someday fight about, when we began to raise a child together.

Among their key findings was the phenomenon of parents subconsciously raising their children in a way that prepares their children for the jobs they will have when they grow up; assuming the children follow in their parent's footsteps.

Other findings included:

1) Depending on social class, parents speak to, and with, their children in very different ways.

2) The mode and frequency of conversation parents use emulates the job and/or workplace experiences (or expectations) of the parents.

3) When a parent consciously uses the mode and frequency of a different social class, their children move easily within the "new" social class.

Hart & Risley studied professional families, families where parents worked hourly jobs, and impoverished families – specifically, families that were signed up for Aid to Families with Dependent Children (AFDC).

They found no racial differences in techniques, only class differences.

The key thing professional parents did to prepare their children for professional careers was to talk *with* their children about anything and everything. The hourly-wage parents talked *to/at* their children and did so far less than the professional parents, but more than the AFDC parents. The AFDC parents talked to their children least of all.

Hart & Risley noted that the topics of conversation didn't matter, only the fact that the conversations were taking place. That seemed completely counterintuitive to me so I paid special attention to their explanation of why that was the case. As it turns out, when people make an effort to "talk a lot" they naturally have to get somewhat creative in order to find enough topics to keep the conversation going.

The more you talk with your child, the more you use a wider variety of words, ask more questions, talk about the future and the past, as well as the actual, the possible, and the impossible. In order to keep a child's attention you will almost certainly have to use more encouragement and praise. You will sometimes have to go out of your way to make topics interesting. When you work to interest a child in talking and listening, you will in turn be generating in them an interest in learning. When you praise your child, you will be building the love of learning as well as the sense of self-worth and value.

Professional parents praised their children twice as often as they corrected them and, as Hart & Risley put it, professional parents "tried to be nice" when they told their children they were incorrect.

Professional parents are also the most responsive to their children. When the child of a professional parent tries to get their mom or dad's attention, professional parents are, by far, the most likely to respond immediately.

In other words, when the child says "Mommy?" the professional parent responds with, "What?" or "Huh?" or "Yes?" much more often than do hourly-wage workers or AFDC parents.

Professional parents are more likely to convey to their children that they believe their children are good people who do good things.

Hourly-wage parents and AFDC parents often convey messages to their children that they are a burden and that they have an evil nature that they must be forced to surrender.

The oft-repeated career advice goes: *Dress for the job you want, not for the job you have.* A similar mantra could be applied to class-based ambitions. In other words, if you work on a factory assembly line but you want your child to become a doctor, you will have to raise them as if they will be a doctor, and not a factory worker. Oh, and by the way, you need to start that program when they are less than a year old. Luckily, conversation is free.

Hart & Risley observed that when AFDC or hourly-wage parents used the techniques of the professional parents, their children developed higher IQs and excelled in school.

In fact, their work proves that social mobility has less to do with insisting to your children that they will go to college and more to do with how you cultivate their language and thinking skills through everyday conversation.

Hart & Risley's book was intended for sociologists, social workers and policy makers. The book wasn't something mothers were expected to find and read when looking for direct advice.

When Hart & Risley's findings were translated into direct advice for mothers, the instructions were simple: don't let them watch too much television, try to make every day experiences teachable moments, use more praise than correction, be responsive, and be nice.

But culturally, all mothers don't read childcare books and all mothers don't believe doctors, psychologists and sociologists know better than they do when it comes to raising children.

In fact, middle-class parents respond to changes in childrearing advice with an alarming speed whereas working class and the chronically poor are opposed to change and slow to adapt to new techniques.

Working class parents, especially black working-class parents, are often much more suspicious of new trends and approaches partially because the books are associated with doctors. Author Harriet A. Washington, lays out the full justification for black peoples' wariness of the American medical establishment in her book *Medical Apartheid*. While some white doctors have tried to claim blacks have some genetically innate foolishness that engenders a fear of medicine, Washington says:

> *Historically, African Americans have been subjected to exploitative, abusive, involuntary experimentation at a rate far higher than other ethnic groups. Thus, although the heightened African American wariness of medical research and institutions reflects a situational hypervigilance, it is neither a baseless fear of harm nor a fear of imaginary harms.*

Unfortunately, black wariness of the medical establishment can end up hampering a black mother's ability to make use of the latest research on childrearing techniques. When that happens, their children can enter school needlessly disadvantaged.

The Wheat Land in the 1990s

During the 1990s, my mom's nephew was running the family farm. Under the guidance of my uncle, and with my mother's approval, the land was enrolled into something called the Conservation Reserve Program. The CRP is run by a sub-department of the United States Department of Agriculture (USDA) called the Farm Services Administration (FSA).

According to fsa.usda.gov: "The long-term goal of the [CRP] is to re-establish valuable land cover to help improve water quality, prevent soil erosion, and reduce loss of wildlife habitat."

Once my mom's land was enrolled in the program, the government began paying her *not* to grow crops on the land. The amount they gave her was less than what she would make in a great farming year and more than she'd make in a really bad year, so all in all, no work for a guaranteed paycheck was a pretty good deal.

A few years after the contract was signed, it dawned on my mother that she shouldn't be paying 2/3 of proceeds to her nephew anymore. Two-thirds made perfect sense when he was working hard farming the land, but two-thirds of the money was way too much when the land was in the CRP program. After all, during CRP contract years, there was very little work that needed to be done.

The government was paying roughly $48,000 a year for her land to sit fallow. My mom thought she should get $32,000 a year instead of $16,000.

She wrestled with her frustration for years, not wanting to divide the family by bringing up her feelings. She knew if she broached the subject with her nephew, her brother would get angry at her, and no doubt remain so, for the rest of his days. She accepted a loss of $16,000 a year in the interest of family harmony.

My Life as a *Good White Person*: The 1990s

When I started back to college, it was 1991, and a wave of black pride was cresting in popular culture. I had seen blacks on BET wearing leather medallions with the outline of the African continent on them. I bought five from a guy I saw wearing one at a Denny's. He was skeptical of me, but my money was green so he shrugged it off. I mailed four of them off to black friends back in Texas and I kept one for myself – not to wear, but to look at, and wish I could.

On campus at Colorado State I met with open rejection from blacks for the first time in my life. The color line in college was starting to be crossed pretty casually by white girls. It seemed to me that black girls had zero interest in making friends with white girls, especially if the only thing they had in common was that they were both at a party with the basketball and football players.

Black girls were successful in letting the black guys on our campus know that they expected shows of solidarity on a regular basis. When black girls were around, black guys would pretend not to know white girls, even if they had been sleeping with them for months.

I was jealous of the way the black guys seemed to have such respect and warm feelings toward these black girls, but I understood it just the same. When the black guys and black girls were all together in one place they presented a united front. White girls who showed up at parties that were predominantly black almost seemed to suffer vertigo. *Why weren't the black guys falling all over them? What should they do or say without all that adoration? Who were they supposed to talk to now?*

Those white girls would leave the black parties bewildered, only to receive booty calls from the same guys a few hours later. The net effect, unfortunately, was that black guys could cheat more easily because the black and white girls never communicated.

I only ended up making one black friend in college. She was a middle-class black girl named Sue and we worked together at the student television station. When a fraternity on campus held a Jamaican-themed party and dressed in blackface, Sue and I went after them. She was the investigative reporter and I was her cameraperson.

It was a good thing we had the station in common because if she'd been seen with me around campus I know it would have hurt her standing among the other black students. I am blessed that we reconnected years later and she is my friend today.

Even though I yearned to take classes like *African-American History* or *Race and Society* I felt certain that I would not be welcome in those classes. I opted instead to focus on all of humankind and all of human history by majoring in Anthropology.

The problem is that while I sat in Anthropology classes, I missed the opportunity to learn about institutional racism, the social justice movement and the burgeoning study of whiteness. I also missed the opportunity to be introduced to the names of authors who would inform so many other white people and allow them to surpass me in becoming personally post-racial, even as I felt like I was among the few whites who could claim true post-racial enlightenment.

I avoided serious relationships with American black men by dating brown-skinned men of other heritages. My first boyfriend in college was a dark-skinned Jew. He looked Arab and I was excited because I thought he was of Palestinian descent. A week before meeting him, I'd read an article in *Time* magazine about how the Palestinians were like the black people of Israel in the way they were treated. I was slightly disappointed to learn he was Jewish (the evil oppressors of the downtrodden Palestinians), but then heartened by the fact that in the US, he was still disliked by many white supremacists because he was a Jew. His very Jewish nose made him something of a target for bigots. I was anxious to prove I could love him, and his nose, and help him come to love his nose.

Now, if this sort of thinking seems pretty twisted, understand that I only see these things clearly in retrospect, and I wholeheartedly agree that my thinking was twisted.

It is also in retrospect that I realize that the two most important criteria I had in mind when selecting a boyfriend post-1990 were: (1) they had to have dark skin and (2) their people had to have some history of oppression. As I've mentioned before, my interest in the oppressed was based on the fact that I believed oppressed people were (and would remain) humble and good-hearted. I also thought they would not be materialistic, would not be elitist snobs, and would never develop one of those revolting senses of entitlement I always seemed to find in white guys.

We had a great relationship for a little over a year and were even taking steps toward marriage. What ended things for me was the fact that his mother's circle of friends encouraged and rewarded Jewish insularity. That was both understandable and heartbreaking for me. I knew that I would always be on the outside of every holiday and my children would be considered outsiders as well.

Through the remainder of college I would date a Somali, an Indian from Tamil Nadu and a Colombian. The Somali was a great guy but had grown up in the palace of the ruler and could hardly be thought of as oppressed. The Tamil guy had oppression going for him, but was very materialistic. The Colombian turned out to be an elitist.

As for my friendships with blacks, rather than put up with rejection from American-born blacks on campus, I opted instead to turn my attention to the African community.

I had been learning how to say the phrase, "I love you" in different languages since the late 1980s and I knew about fifty languages by that time. I would strike up conversations with any Africans I saw around the student center. I would ask them about their country, their tribal language, and their experiences in the US so far. The friendships grew easily from there.

After college in Northern Colorado, I was off to Texas to work for a year, then to Arizona for graduate school. In both Texas and Arizona I avoided long-term relationships. After graduate school I went to work in

Washington DC.

Accomplished blacks were everywhere I looked in Northern Virginia and the District. As part of my job in Washington, I interacted with powerful, intelligent, black women who held high positions in an array of federal agencies. In my Texas town, black men in suits were always on their way to church and their suits were in the loudest colors they could find. Not so in Washington DC. During my commute on the Metro every day, I saw black men in low-key suits on their way to work just like everyone else.

All my life I'd been declaring that blacks and whites were equals, but it wasn't until I worked with, and saw, so many blacks of accomplishment and power in Washington that I knew it in my bones. Once I knew it in my bones, I suddenly realized that all the years before, when I had declared it, I'd been hoping it was true, and worried that it was not.

Curiously, when I let go of that burden I stopped feeling rage toward people who displayed the Confederate flag. Since I had nothing to fear about the capabilities of blacks, I now had nothing to fear about the whites who were bigots and racists. For the first time in my life, I could clearly see that the message the "rebel" was sending was about themselves; not about black people.

Without realizing the implications of getting over my deep-seated fears that blacks were inferior, I also seem to have decided that all blacks everywhere were now able to achieve whatever they wanted. In DC, it looked to me like racism had ceased to hold black people back. They no longer needed me to save them, or protect them from mean white people, or help them with their self-esteem by smiling and making small talk with them. Now I could enjoy their friendship, companionship, and the artifacts of their culture, free of guilt.

I knew a former NFL player who was living and working in Washington D.C. He was divorced so I felt comfortable with the idea of us dating. I didn't want to get married and had decided I liked being an aunt with a high-powered career much more than I longed to be a stay-at-home mom who (as Hilary Clinton infamously joked) baked cookies and stood by her man. By dating him, I wasn't harming the black community in any way I could think of. Besides that, the black community wasn't hurting anymore (at least not that I could see).

The 1990s Come to a Close

In 1999, I decided I wanted to return to the Denver area. I applied to employers in Denver using the internet. I did phone interviews and even flew out to Denver for face-to-face meetings with potential employers. Because I had disposable income and no dependents, I had the flexibility to negotiate the best position and salary for myself. I was able to secure a great job working in computer consulting.

A few years before, I'd begun to move away from educational software and toward more technical work as a database developer. I became fixated on my salary because I saw it as a measure of how much I was valued by my employers. Denver had a new business park called The Denver Tech Center. I accepted a position with a consulting company that was headquartered there.

I anticipated a new life in Denver that would be every bit as slick and shiny as the glass-plated office towers of DTC.

THE NEW MILLENNIUM AUGHTIES

Figure 37: From 2000 to 2005, I worked and I traveled. The first picture is of me, my niece, and my mom in Paris at the Sacré Cœur. The middle picture is of me at Stonehenge in England. The last picture is of me in Australia, in front of the opera house.

When I arrived back in Denver, poverty and oppression were the furthest things from my mind.

The apartment complex I moved into was mostly white, as far as I could tell. Then again, everything in Colorado is mostly white. I chose my apartment based on its location in relation to my preferred commuter route.

The Somali I'd dated in college was on my radar. He and I had tried numerous times to date seriously, but somehow it never worked out. It wouldn't work this time either but we gave it a go, for a while anyway.

I enjoyed my job. It was challenging and the days flew by. I spent the weekends with my niece and nephew, often picking them up Friday afternoon and dropping them back at their parent's on Sunday evening. Their presence in my life kept me from feeling lonely. I took them to museums and cultural events. I bought them supplies for art and science projects and we had a great time painting, sculpting, whittling, and blowing things up. I tried to expose them to older forms of black music like big band, bebop and cool jazz. I taught them about MLK and Rosa, but also Malcolm, Angela Davis, and the Panthers. Because they are half black I wanted to make sure they would be exposed to the history and culture that would fill them with pride and teach them about the indomitable strength and resilience of the Freedpeople who were their ancestors..

Having this self-appointed mandate when it came to my niece and nephew kept me busy and made me believe that by making a difference in their lives, I was making a difference in the world.

CandyLand

I'd arranged my life in Denver to suit my needs as a young professional. I didn't have any contact with poor blacks and I lived my life as if they didn't exist. Then again, I lived as if no one anywhere was hungry or cold. I was, as I had so often accused others of doing, living in CandyLand.

Some middle-class people only leave CandyLand when a big news story features a tornado or tsunami. They go online from their corporate desk-job cubicles, navigate to the Red Cross website, and type in their debit card numbers.

Others leave it for a few moments around Christmas and Thanksgiving when they participate in a toy drive or the serving of some communal meal for the homeless.

I'd spent a good portion of my life stubbornly refusing to go to CandyLand and somehow, in the year 2000, I'd woken up there anyway.

How acceptable is it live in CandyLand? How much harm is there in being oblivious to the truth that there are people suffering, sometimes within a rock's throw of one's home or workplace?

Furthermore, is it worse to be oblivious or is it worse to be a well-meaning, ham-handed, do-gooder who occasionally, in trying to make things better, says something patronizing to a successful middle-class person whose ethnicity happens to match the target population of a given charity?

In other words, for me, whose favorite population of oppressed people had always been American blacks, was it okay that when I'd been so attentive and engaged, I occasionally stepped on toes, offered advice that no one asked for or wanted, or treated someone in charge as if they were my assistant[62]?

Of course, my goal was, and always has been, to be neither oblivious nor obnoxious, but in the early 2000s there's no question I was oblivious.

In any event, when the complexion of my apartments started to change, I slowly came out of my CandyLand coma.

About a year after I'd moved back to Colorado, the leasing office of my apartment complex seemed to be welcoming more and more low-income families, probably by taking advantage of government-sponsored affordable housing programs.

I got to know some of the middle-school girls who moved into nearby apartments. Most of them were black and all of their families were on assistance.

These girls adored me and I felt the same way about them. I started doing a sort of wholesome, home-grown, glamour photo session thing for them. I reasoned that if a girl had pictures of herself in which she looked very confident and ready to take on the world, it might change the way she moved through life. She might carry that picture of herself in her head when she interacted with people. If she looked at that version of herself every day before leaving home, it might give her a confidence in her own right to an empowered life.

I did various photo shoots of the girls together and apart. I would deliver the prints to them: They would beam and rush home. Shortly thereafter, I would often get an invitation to meet their mothers.

The mothers would compliment me on my photography and thank me for the prints. Some would ask if they owed me money and I would

---

[62] I would swear I never did that last example, but how can I know for sure?

assure them the pictures were completely free.

And just like that, it was back, that old itch they'd scratched for me. It was the approval of black women; and it felt magical. Like so many other events in my past, it is only in retrospect that I understand how important it was to me that black *women*, especially black *mothers*, approve of me and offer me something resembling friendship.

When they thanked me, they looked me in the eye and I got to imagine that they genuinely liked me, whether it was true or not.

Every evening when I got home from work, the girls would come to see me. I told them to bring their homework and I had my very own Girl's Club. I didn't interact with their mothers a lot, but I always had their mothers in mind. I imagined those mothers, slogging their way home from thankless jobs, exhausted and worried about their daughters, but having too little energy left to give.

Then, (in my imagination) they would remember that their daughters were at my apartment and they would smile half a smile, knowing that I was working to lighten their loads by giving what *I* could of *my* time to their daughters' development.

Recession

When the dotcom bubble burst, I got laid off, and my mother suggested I move back to Fort Collins and live with her and my dad. It meant leaving my Girl's Club behind. My options were limited, so as much as I hated to do it, the Girl's Club was no more.

I lived with my parents—managing to avoid debt and continuing to look for a well-paying job instead of being forced by circumstances to take a lower-wage substitute. My parents had a large custom home. While I lived with them, I had a bedroom and bathroom to myself in the fully-finished basement. I also had an office area with a computer and a high-speed Internet connection. Obviously, while there, I had no bills: no rent, no utilities, no cable. I was welcome to eat their food and use their toilet paper. I didn't have to use up any unemployment benefits, which I might need in later years when I was no longer single and childless and no longer found it easy to pack up and move home. I had a nice, reliable car so I could go out for interviews as needed.

When I found a job in consulting again, about six months later, I thought back to the Girl's Club I'd had to leave behind and decided that I was going to live in downtown Denver, in a mixed-race, mixed-income neighborhood; one that had lots of children.

I wanted to start a new Girls Club and I was determined to start one in an area that had what I considered to be authentic people. To me, authentic people were people who'd grown up in challenging environments. Poverty was challenging. High crime neighborhoods were challenging. The predictability and conformity of the suburbs were not challenging.

Though I was already an adult, I thought my character would also be improved by the chaos of inner-city life. I was convinced that, out in the suburbs, people tried to buy their personalities through their choice of consumer goods. In my estimation, they all ended up with same one: mass manufactured and purchased at a big box retailer. Conversely, I believed that in the city, especially in the poorest sections, people earned their individuality by overcoming "real" problems.

The idea of being out in the suburbs, where CandyLand might lull me to sleep again, was no longer an option.

City Life

As a renter downtown, I made friends with neighbors of Mexican descent who accepted me as a *Good White Person* after I told the right stories and shared my exasperation with bigoted and/or ignorant whites.

I loved being downtown. I loved the horrible parking, the quirky plumbing, and the zoning catastrophes. I loved that nothing could be taken for granted the way it was in the suburbs.

One night, I was awoken by singing. There was a homeless man sitting in the bus shed across the street, singing as loud as he could, at two in the morning. I pleaded with him from my second floor window, but he would not stop. I went downstairs and across the street. I learned his name was Gary, just like my father's, and I convinced him to let the rest of us get a little more sleep before our alarms went off.

Situations like this invigorated me, but they did something more: They convinced me that I was more interesting than any of my white, suburban-raised coworkers, especially those who had slept peacefully through the previous night.

I had stories to tell now: City stories.

I've heard it said, though I can't remember where or when, that the kids who grew up swaddled in the comfort and convenience of the mid-century suburbs ended up with a deep need to orchestrate for themselves a period, or periods, of contrived suffering. Of course, contrived suffering was exactly what I was looking for in the city proper.

I'd actually been looking for it my whole life. When my car broke down and I refused to call triple A, it was because I wanted the struggle of changing a tire myself. If I could have done it in a blizzard, instead of on a balmy May afternoon, I would have been elated by the extra challenge the weather presented.

Back when I was 19 and a college dropout, I'd slept in my soft-top Jeep Cherokee for a week, convincing myself that I was homeless, even though I could have called my mother at any time and she would have fixed everything.

One night in Kansas City, a police officer referred me to a women's' shelter because I told him I had no place to go. The intake process took far longer than I would have imagined such a thing would need to. As the counselor prattled on, and I was presented with one form after another to read and sign, I began to fall asleep in my chair. I was supposed to start a new job at dawn after having been out of work for almost three months. When the officer had given me the address I'd lit up at the idea of being to empathize with other women who'd stayed in shelters. It no longer seemed like such a great experience to court. Dawn was creeping ever closer, and I was still being read pages of rules. When I was finally assigned a room, I was thrilled to see that my roommate was a black woman with two small children who were fast asleep on the bottom mattress of a bunk bed. I imagined how she and I were destined to bond in the morning and over the coming days. I climbed the ladder to the top bunk as quietly as I could. The ceiling was too low for the bed and I had to scoot myself sideways to center myself. The mattress had a plastic cover, presumably in case of small children who might pee themselves during the night. Every shift I made in search of some kind of comfort resulted in loud crackling noises. Still restless after laying there for twenty minutes, I crept back down the ladder, grabbed my Ann Taylor suit from where I'd hung it on a nearby hook and left the shelter to rent a hotel room.

I had moved from DC to KC on a shoestring and I had no other place to go, well, unless I was willing to put a hotel room on a credit card, which evidently, I had decided, I was. Even as I turned the key and collapsed onto the hotel room bed I castigated myself for not being tough enough to stay at the shelter for more than a few hours.

Whenever I managed to create a life-test for myself and then chose the easy, comfortable, or convenient way out, it only increased the extent to which I felt unworthy and inauthentic.

But what did I hope to gain out of building friendships with women I had almost nothing in common with? Whenever I'd known people who'd suffered, I'd mined their experiences, begging them to re-tell their most painful memories and I'd imagined that I was offering them some sort of free therapy. I thought of this as a compassionate act, but was it? Looking back on it now, I'm just not sure.

I spent a night on skid row in Arizona and got to know two homeless women. They both had jobs but were not looking for shelter. They taught me that, for them, a sleeping bag and a fifth of whiskey each day was far more desirable than a mortgage. I carried their words back to my 9-to-5 crowd triumphantly. I knew *actual* homeless people so I felt I could speak authoritatively anytime I found myself in any conversation about the homeless.

I spied a Holocaust serial number tattoo on the arm of a friend's mother and sat rapt as she detailed teenage years in a concentration camp. Her son, daughter-in-law, and most of the people at their synagogue had heard it all before and I'd seen them shut her down anytime she seemed to begin recalling that time in her life. I encouraged her to open up to me instead. Then of course, I believed I became a more fascinating person whenever I related *her* concentration camp experiences.

I acted as a sounding board for the anger of a mother, diagnosed with cancer, who railed at the injustice of her disease, believing that having given up her youth to Mao's Great Leap Forward, she deserved much better. *Oh Dear. What did Mao's policies force you to give up? What were the horrible things neighbors did to neighbors out of fear during that time period?*

To have met these women, and held them in private conversation, felt like a blessing beyond belief to me. But were my intentions coming from the right place or was I just some sort of voyeur of pain? I saw my exchanges with these women as something we all benefitted from, but were they really?

When I wasn't putting myself into situations that I could use to test my mettle, or appropriating the suffering of those I met and came to know, I was on the lookout for books and movies about human suffering.

So it was that in 2004, I was living downtown, and driving to an office in DTC each day. Just a few weeks after moving in, I would recount the story of Gary, the singing homeless man. *Oh my goodness, this guy kept me up half the night and I am sooooo tired. I could barely make espresso this morning.*

So many whites grew up in the suburbs yet only some of us came to feel burdened with the belief that we needed to pay some kind of penance for it. The non-cursed go to college, get jobs in offices, get married to other suburban progeny, and buy their own shiny houses in the suburbs. In some ways, I envied them, because they accepted themselves and didn't feel the guilt that myself and others did.

To spot someone who, like me, feels at least some need to suffer in order to become interesting and authentic, just look at any gentrifier. Especially look at those who are among the first wave in any neighborhood. Some gentrifiers claim that it's the architecture of the homes or the walkable neighborhoods that draw us to old city neighborhoods but the truth is, we imagine somehow that renovating a hundred-year old house is akin to fleeing the Khmer Rouge.

Don't get me wrong, walkable neighborhoods are great but just moving into an older neighborhood while dressed as if you are living in the 1940s, (driving up the rent prices and property taxes) is not the same as appreciating the city planning principals of New Urbanism.

Gentrifiers like me do what we do because we are terrified that we might embrace a life that turns out to be the same empty, aching, consumerism our parents accepted as "The American Dream." I was certain that if I married someone middle-class and white I would be just moments away from selling my soul in exchange for convenient parking.

As I rode the light rail to and from various downtown locations (you know, because *when you live downtown, the light rail is just so much more convenient than a car!*) I would look out the windows and imagine myself living in different houses and apartment complexes I passed along the way. Over time I began riding the green line to its terminus for no other reason than to play out the fantasy of living where it went. Dismounting at the green line's last stop I would scan the crowd and proudly make the mental note that I was one of very few whites. I would then re-board and take the train back to my own neighborhood. After just a few trips I knew I wanted the Downing and 30th station to be *my* station.

I was certain that when that neighborhood became mine, the final stage in the moulting of my plastic suburban shell would begin.

Homeownership

In May of 2005, I purchased a house three blocks from the end of the green line. I was actually recruited by a mortgage broker who thought he'd convinced me to browse the suburbs with him. At that time, there was a frenzy of activity going on around home purchases. Mortgage brokers sought out people who were renting and practically begged them to buy a house.

Lawsuits have now revealed that black and brown people were disproportionally victimized by the frenzy. They were damaged by predatory mortgage brokers who gave them subprime loans when they qualified for prime loans.

In 2013, I got letters in the mail informing me I was part of a class-action lawsuit. The mortgage broker who pursued me and carried out a re-financing of my home, without me even realizing what had taken place, seems to have been part of an aggressive and ethically flexible operation. The lawyers wanted to know if my income had been inflated on the paperwork. Evidently, the way they got the best commissions was to get big, big loans for people like me, whether my collateral and salary were good enough to secure the amount, or not.

Those who did not experience the buying or refinancing of a home during this period seem to imagine that we all put our signatures on documents knowing full well we couldn't afford our houses or our re-fi terms. That's a ridiculous notion. What could we have possibly thought we would gain from such recklessness?

Many people seem satisfied to sit on high ground and judge without understanding that their experiences may have been far from universal. Maybe they had bankers and brokers who worked under tight regulatory constraints. I've heard friends say that *their* brokers explained things in depth and were careful to craft solid deals for them because those brokers' jobs depended on the servicing of the loan.

Conversely, during the frenzy, no one's job seemed at risk due to

Figure 38: My little house in downtown Denver. The house was just outside of Five Points, a neighborhood made infamous during the crack wars.

reckless lending. Even after the dust settled, few of them were held to account. They walked away with fat pockets, full of commissions and bonuses. Borrowers like me walked away from foreclosed houses and toward life with terrible credit.

But wait, back before the foreclosure, and the plummeting of my credit score, I was a super-excited new resident of a neighborhood called Cole.

In 2005 the neighborhood of Cole was, by far, the most recalcitrant to gentrification in Denver. It was the place the homeless and the addicted had been consciously corralled in deference to the other, more rapidly gentrifying neighborhoods. The police were complicit in this herding northward.

After I purchased, a real estate broker came poking around.

"We're trying to brand Cole and Clayton as 'NoDo,' for *North of Downtown*," a woman with big helmety hair and pancake makeup told me, "Some brokers are still .calling this area 'NoGo', but I'm super-excited about your purchase. If a young, single, career woman feels safe here, I'm certain this neighborhood is ripe."

I tried to explain to her that she was mistaken. My purchase was not indicative that the neighborhood was ripe. I wasn't trying to lead a reverse block-bust where I, as pioneer, led to an invasion of whites.

Using me as a bellwether would lead her astray for sure. I was someone who *wanted* to be around poor black and brown people. Our neighborhood was supposed to be for them, their children, and me. Within just a few months of my arrival, three houses on my block had "For Sale" signs in their yards.

When it came to discussing my home, I was proud that it was not in a chi-chi, fully-gentrified downtown neighborhood. When I revealed that I lived in a neighborhood called Cole, people's faces would often go blank because they didn't know where Cole was.

"Where is that in relation to City Park?" they might feebly offer.

"Nowhere close," I would say, my reverse snobbery seeping out through the tone of my voice, "Cole is just across Downing from Five Points."

Proximity to Five Points sent a coded message about just how hard-core I was. After that, I would volunteer more info, telling them about Cole's racial, ethnic, economic, and age diversity. Then I'd let them know that I wasn't a bit concerned about my property value doubling or tripling.

My block did end up attracting young white couples and singles, but I am proud to say all of them ended up frustrated with the neighborhood because their property values did not improve. The neighborhood wasn't ripe. The servers, alcoholics and crackheads stayed. The gentrifiers that couldn't take it, sold their homes and lost money in the course of doing so.

Sadly, these gentrifiers passed on a chance to get to know the locals. One, instead of extending himself to make their acquaintance, gave them all nicknames based on their appearance and wrote a blog about them and their "antics" for the endless entertainment of his frat brothers. Oh how I rejoiced when he finally sold, accepting tens of thousands in losses.

In moving to Cole part of the life I envisioned for myself involved creating an even more beneficial Girl's Club than the one I'd built in my suburban apartment complex. I saw myself becoming the neighbor lady who all the kids knew they could count on for help with homework projects, life advice, and, from time to time, money. I figured my presence and my encouraging words would also benefit them because they could know that *some* white people are good.

I began to get the reputation I'd been hoping for, and kids from the neighborhood visited me often.

It worked really well for a while, but soon I would be side-tracked by pregnancy and marriage.

Leah Tyler's Parents Meet

William introduced himself to me one day as I pulled weeds in my front yard. He began pitching his landscaping services but I held up a palm and stopped him short. "You are like the thousandth person to tell me they do yard work!"

He smiled. "Yeah, but I'm not like all these other cats out here. I don't be procrastinatin'"

Now, I was smiling. "Well, as long as you don't *procrastinate*, I guess

I'll *have* to keep you in mind."

As he continued down the street I thought about how strange he seemed. He wore glasses and he'd used the word *procrastinate*. I'd rejected him, claiming that he was one among way too many but he'd managed to set himself apart.

When my husband and I met that day, we'd both been blessed with fairly sharp minds and yet our lives had turned out so very differently. We'd both been lackluster students who didn't pay attention in class and didn't care much about school.

By the time I'd decided to get serious about my future, I was just a twenty-two-year-old college dropout who had to convince my parents that *this time* things would be different. My parents had paid for my college the first time around and when I asked to go back again, they'd just written another check.

Conversely, when my husband was twenty-two, he had a felony record and a very spotty work history. He was estranged from his father, and his mother had long since been on disability. He was a college dropout just as I was, but since he'd used federal financial aid during his first attempt, he wasn't allowed to try again until he paid off some portion of his tuition from the first go round. He was also required to put a seven year gap between his last felony and his application date.

Jim Crow had been outlawed when he was a toddler, but he was still suffering its effects because his parents were not educated and wealthy the way mine were. Even though Bill had worked hard and earned the credentials that should have given him opportunities, discrimination had kept doors closed to him. Bill's inability to support his family had devastating effects on his children.

After Bill was gone, forced segregation kept Diane and the children in a neighborhood so stripped of opportunities and resources that to grow up there meant daily lessons in dashed hopes, disappointments and abject injustices. While he would try to forget those things and forge ahead, I was running around collecting stories of hardship from others as if they were trinkets for my charm bracelet.

He was a thief, to be sure, but so was I. My thieving was ethically worse because I had grandparents sending me money in the mail just about every month. What he'd done out of a need to survive, I'd done on a lark in an attempt to prove that I was smarter than the adults who designed store security systems and supervised those stores.

The school-to-prison pipeline and the War on Drugs had all but ensured William would be channeled into the system sooner or later. And if all that weren't enough, he'd become addicted to crack, in many ways due to the willful negligence of our federal government.

Getting to Know William the Non-Procrastinator

About five steps from my front door I had a wooden fence with a gate. The gate swung open onto the sidewalk and walking three steps toward the curb would put you at the bus stop bench.

The bus stop provided cover for drug transactions and because of that, just across my fence there was always a beehive of activity. It would be another month before I realized all the people I'd befriended were involved in the drug trade in some capacity.

My house was on a corner lot. If you walked along the side of my house you would soon be peering into my backyard. The backyard was fairly large. There was an old aluminum shed situated there; its door missing such that it wasn't fit to store anything.

William had come by again to remind me of his offer to help with the lawn. He kept volunteering the information that he was not homeless, even though I'd never asked. He kept reminding me that he had an apartment in one of the western suburbs. I could only infer that he was trying to impress me by appearing to be more stable than he actually was.

One day I was walking in my backyard and I saw the edge of a backpack inside the shed. I reached in and picked it up. Under the bag was a neatly folded sleeping bag. I held the backpack high and pulled at various zippers looking for something that would identify the owner.

"Um, Miss Kristl?" It was William. He was outside the fence, a few feet away. He told me that he'd been staying overnight a few doors down at Ms. Roper's house. He explained to me that he kept his stuff in my shed during the day and he wanted to know if that was okay with me.

"Ohhhhh, Ms. Roper's House?" I said, wiggling my eyebrows suggestively.

"No, Miss Kristl, it's not like that. I just stay there sometimes to protect her and her daughter. I sleep on their couch." He asked again about storing the backpack there during the day and I said it was fine.

A few days later I ran into Ms. Roper, "So, I didn't realize you and William had a thing."

"What do you mean?" Ms. Roper said.

"I mean, you know," I said, again using my eyebrows to suggest romance.

"Uh-uhn," Ms. Roper scowled, "I've let him stay on the couch a few times but only when the weather was bad."

"Oh," I said, "I'm sorry, I didn't mean to be in your business."

I went back to William but didn't let on that I'd talked to Ms. Roper.

"You know," I said, "If you *ever* need to sleep in the shed, I don't have a problem with that."

He thanked me and said there was a possibility that someday, he might take advantage of the offer. I'd only owned the house for a few weeks at that point and still had my old apartment a few miles away. One night I decided it was time for me to sleep over at my new house. I hadn't moved my bed over yet but I had a couch there, so I laid down for a few minutes.

Hours later, I woke up feeling cold.

I knew I had a blanket in my car. Could I feel safe going outside at two in the morning in my new neighborhood? My walls were thin and all was quiet outside. It didn't seem scary to me at all.

I unlocked the front door and went out. As I made my way across the yard, William came out of the shed and asked if I was okay. He looked so sweet and innocent, his face puffy with sleep.

I mentioned that this was my first time staying overnight and he assured me that I didn't have to worry about anyone giving me any trouble because he was there for me and he would protect me. My heart fluttered. I drew the blanket close to my chest and cut the conversation short, rushing inside.

On June 7th, I turned 37 years old. Roughly twelve years prior, I'd decided in a split-second that I didn't ever want to have children. Now, in a similarly singular moment, I reversed my decision.

I was in the shower getting ready to go meet family for my birthday dinner and I started crying. *What if I do want children?* as I poured shampoo into my cupped hand became, *Oh my god, I want children!* before I could get all the conditioner rinsed out.

When I got out of the shower, I sent a text message to the Jewish guy I'd dated when I first started back to college. He was the only person I'd ever considered marrying so he seemed a natural choice. I asked him if he'd be willing to donate sperm. He didn't take the inquiry seriously. He messaged me back, calling me "nutty as ever." I shot back with my own LOL. *Of course I'd been kidding!*

That night at dinner I told my sister, "I've decided I want kids." She laughed uncomfortably. "I pinged [Jewish Guy] and asked if he would donate sperm." She laughed again, but this time with a little bit of an eyebrow twist.

My change of heart had the potential to be a big problem, at least from a public relations perspective. I was thirty seven and I wasn't in a serious relationship. I knew my family was going to do all kinds of amateur psycho-analysis on me when they heard that I was suddenly pursuing motherhood, and I hated that. When the gossip trickled its way back to me there would be all kinds of crazy diagnoses and talk of intervention. I wasn't going to be able to explain why I'd changed my mind so suddenly because I didn't really understand it myself.

Rather than make an announcement and accept the drama that would no doubt follow, I figured my best bet was to try to find a sperm donor and, when the time seemed right say, "Oh, by the way, I accidently got pregnant and I'm keeping it so...let's all try to make the best of it."

As long as they didn't know about it until the second trimester, there would be no pressure to terminate.

I started going through a mental catalog of past boyfriends, friends, co-workers and acquaintances trying to think of a suitable sperm donor.

At night I had dreams about those various potential donors. It seemed like every dream ended up like a sit-com, with comedic misunderstandings and missteps.

One day William came by on his bike and called out to me across the fence. He had two yogurts and asked me if I wanted one. The thought flashed through my mind that perhaps he'd found them while dumpster diving. I accepted the yogurt and the plastic spoon he offered with it. It was really kind of him to offer me food. Most people in the neighborhood would never have thought to treat me as an equal (no matter how hard I tried to create that persona). I knew they saw me as a rich white woman, who could never need something they had, and that hurt me. We stood on the sidewalk enjoying the yogurts together. I complimented him on his great nutritional choice.

"Yogurt is very, very good for you," I said.

He nodded.

"It has some bacteria in it that gets in your intestines and helps you fight disease," I said, "Eating a healthy diet can help with addiction."

He nodded again.

After a few silent spoonfuls I said, "Are you a crackhead?"

"No, I'm not a crackhead," he said, "But I'm not going to lie. I *serve* crack."

When I told him I didn't understand what "serving crack" meant, he explained that a server acts as a middle-man between users and dealers. He told me that he was very popular and well-respected as a server. A lot of dealers and users trusted him because he was very careful not to attract police attention and he made sure that the customers got their money's worth. As we wrapped up our conversation he said, "I just didn't want to lie to you."

And I said, "I appreciate that."

The following week William knocked on my front door.

"Uh Miss Kristl, if it's not too much trouble, could I borrow a trash bag?"

"Borrow one?" I said, laughing and recalling a junior high joke about borrowed paper, "What are you gonna do? Bring it *back*?"

He looked confused, and a little hurt, by my question.

"Yeah?"

An hour later, he returned the trash bag. He had used it to rake leaves for an older woman who lived a few doors up the block. He filled the bag several times and emptied it into the alley dumpster, then returned the nearly perfect and neatly folded bag to me.

"Thanks Miss Kristl," he said.

"No problem *Mr.* William - anytime *Mr.* William," I replied.

A few days after that, I was trying to get a caulking gun to work and I walked over to the ice cream shop where the crack addicts and servers stood when they got chased away from the bus stop. I came up carrying the caulk gun and William offered to return home with me and use a nail to get the gun started. Afterwards we stood at the fence line and chatted a while about the neighborhood.

He stood outside my fence leaning back onto it and I stood next to him, inside the fence, leaning forward. It was a slow, quiet chat about nothing on a cool summer evening. I felt peaceful and I thought about how much I enjoyed his company.

A twinkle of desire rose up and it startled me. I quickly excused myself and walked into the house, cradling the caulk.

A few days later, when William told me he'd purchased a children's tent and wanted to know if he could set it up in my backyard and live in it, I told him that if we could agree to some ground rules, I didn't have a problem with it. For starters, I told him, no drugs in my yard, because I'd heard that the police could confiscate my property if he used it as some sort of drug operation home base. Also, I didn't want a lot of people coming and going so I told him that as well. He agreed but asked if he might have a "female" over.

"Of course, if there's someone you're seeing, you can have her over," I said. This time it was not a flicker, or a twinkle, or a flutter: I felt a full-on surge of jealousy. If he'd paid close enough attention he'd have noticed that just after I forced out the words "of" and "course" there was a split-second during which my forced smile and clenched jaw caused my eye to twitch.

MENACE

On July 3rd, 2005 when I arrived at my front gate after work, someone at the bus stop told me that William had been arrested the night before.

"Oh," I said, "For what?"

"Possession."

"Oh..." I said again, "what does that mean?"

"It means five to seven."

A third time, "Oh."

I was secretly relieved. I was sad for him, but I was relieved for me. I didn't need to complicate my life by following through on any of the weird thoughts or crazy feelings I'd been having.

I told my niece and nephew that he'd been arrested. They were sad for him, too. We all thought he was a genuinely good guy. I half-joked to my niece and nephew that the police should let *us* make out a list of all the people they should lock up and another list of those they should leave alone. Even though William was a crack server I thought he was better for the neighborhood than quite a few other people who hung out at the bus stop.

I went into the backyard to check on his tent. Inside I found a woman I'd never met before who told me William had just gone to the store and would be right back. I came back a half hour later and she said the same thing. I asked her to leave and she did. I quickly disassembled the tent and hung it on the clothesline along with his single set of spare clothes. I found a key, two bolts and a coaxial cable coupler. I pocketed those things, and then I took the bones of the tent inside the house and laid them among my tools.

The next morning the tent's shell was gone. I considered it possible it had been used to help someone stay warm or dry, or both and that made me feel just a little better about the fact that I'd been stupid enough to leave it out.

On August 13th I was in my yard when I saw William ride up on his bike. I ran over to him and threw my arms around his neck. He told me all about his arrest and the time he'd been gone. He'd been serving crack when someone tried to jack him by pushing him out of a moving car. He'd decided to go over to a house where he suspected he'd find the jack crew partying. He took a 2x4 with him. The police spotted him walking along with the 2x4 across his shoulders and put him up against a car. The report they filed later said the 2x4 constituted "menacing." They searched his pockets and found a rock of crack cocaine.

After six weeks, the judge released him on a personal recognizance bond. This meant he was free to go based on his promise that he would come back for court appearances.

He'd lost his glasses in the scuffle, so as we stood talking he squinted to look over my shoulder, checking where his tent had once stood.

"I know people came over and looted my stuff as soon as they heard I was arrested, but not you, Miss Kristl, I know you saved whatever they didn't take."

I looked at him sheepishly, "I messed up," I said, "I hung it up to dry and someone took it."

William looked disappointed then forced a brightened expression, "That's okay. It wasn't your fault. People 'round here's scandalous."

"How about this?" I said, "I can either get you a new tent, or I can give you enough money to get *yourself* a new tent. Or I could take you around to some thrift stores to see if we can find one. If we can find one cheap enough, I'll be able to give you some cash as well."

During our ride that day, William said he'd spent a lot of time thinking about his life while he'd been locked up. He had decided he wanted to give up serving and get a real job so that he could get an apartment. He said he was getting too old for hustling.

My heart leapt. What fun it would be to teach him about nutrition and help him find a job! I would be there as he rejoined society as a contributing citizen!! I was imagining him, *my project*, in a film-like montage, complete with a soaring score when he interrupted my thoughts, pointing out an ATM.

Over the next few hours, we laid out the broad strokes of our joint project: Operation William The Non-Procrastinator Goes Straight.

Not only had he lost his glasses, he had also lost his wallet the night he was arrested. He had a voucher to see an eye doctor but he'd been told the doctor was booked six months to a year in advance. He also needed to get a replacement drivers license and social security card before he could look for work. We agreed that, for starters, my role would be limited to giving him rides and paying paperwork fees.

We made a great team. I showed him how I used my computer to find licensing office locations, hours, and best times to visit. He was humble and grateful for every moment I spent helping him get the things he needed.

One evening, we were watching television and a commentator mentioned Langston Hughes. William asked me if I was familiar with the poet. I said that, in fact, I knew one of his poems by heart. William asked me to recite it, so I did.

The poem I recited for him is called *Harlem*, though many people know it as *A Dream Deferred*. When I finished reciting it, William told me that he, too, knew one of Hughes's poems by heart. He then recited for me *The Negro Mother*, which is much longer than the poem I'd recited for him.

He told me that when he was fifteen, he was scheduled to be released from a group home just days before Mother's Day. He decided to learn the poem so that he could recite it for his mother as a gift. Now, almost thirty years later, he'd been able to recite it for me.

I was in awe.

I asked him to be my sperm donor. He explained to me that he would love to, but that he was sterile. I asked him if he'd been formally diagnosed. He said he had not, but that all his life he'd tried to have children with various girlfriends and they claimed to get pregnant but no child ever came.

I decided that his belief in his sterility gave me additional cover. I could get pregnant and then tell my family, "I thought he was sterile and now it's too late! I'm having a baby."

In retrospect, I don't know why I thought a cover story was so important. When it came to our relationship, I ended up openly defying every bit of guidance and advice my mother had ever tried to impart regarding the kind of partner she envisioned for me.

Twenty days after he agreed to act as my sperm donor, I was pregnant.

Two months after that, my mother visited me unannounced and seemed to have some sort of extrasensory perception that I was knocked up. She guessed it, I confirmed it, and the family exploded with disapproval. There was a fevered attempt to persuade me to terminate the pregnancy.

The next time I visited my sister's house, my mixed-race nephew started singing a popular song, paraphrasing, "We know Kristl ain't a gold digger, cuz she's messin' with a broke n****a."

Figure 39: Leah Tyler's parents, a few months after meeting.

THE BROKEN DOWN LIMOUSINE

Oprah Winfrey is quoted as having said, "Lots of people want to ride with you in the limo, but what you want is someone who will take the bus with you when the limo breaks down." Though Oprah was most likely using the limo as analogy for fame, her words spoke to me when I first read the quote because I so disdain people who can't meet hardship with ingenuity, perseverance and a sunny disposition.

When I'd dated the NFL player from DC, we'd taken a vacation in England. I'd awoken early in our London hotel room and mapped out a plan that had us taking the Tube[63] from one tourist attraction to another. When we first set out, his mood was pleasant, but by mid-day he was whining about any and everything. His lamentations centered on how much walking he was being subjected to.

"Princess," I had said, "How can you run six miles a day on a treadmill at the gym but you can't walk two or three miles over the course of a day? Take a cab back to the hotel if you're so exhausted. There's no point in you ruining *my* experience of London."

In spite of that regrettable trip, I'd still been seeing that delicate flower of a man, long-distance of course, when I'd purchased my house.

He visited me about a week after the sale was finalized. I took him to see it and excitedly described my plans for each room. The expression on his face brought back my worst memories of London.

As I'd made arrangements to buy the house, I hadn't stopped to consider the impact it would have on my relationships with family, friends, and Delicate Flower. By the end of his visit that weekend, I knew he wasn't going to be joining me on my renovation journey.

A few weeks later, when I decided I wanted children, I'd quickly dismissed him as a potential sperm donor. His forehead had the same Neanderthal quality as my own. It wouldn't be fair to pass that trait down, multiplied by two, to an innocent child. Besides that, Delicate Flower was clearly a limousine-only type of guy and I was looking for a genetic sequence that spelled out grit.

When it came to my house – that thing no one seemed to love except me – William was immune to shock. Before he officially moved in, I leveled with him about the plumbing.

"If I need to go to the bathroom, I line a bucket with a trash bag, go in that, then tie the bag off and set it to the side. Later, when I'm out, I put the

---

[63] London's subway system is nicknamed "the Tube."

bag in a public trash container," I said, looking him in the eye and waiting to see if he blinked.

He didn't.

While it may seem obvious that someone living in a tent would see moving indoors as an upgrade, it still made me really, really happy that I didn't have a toilet and he wanted to live there with me anyway.

Growing up, it seemed like people on TV and in movies would always be talking about how, when they were young and first fell in love, they were also very poor. That was a very romantic notion to me. I'd always wanted to start a relationship under distressed conditions and build to something greater, together.

I understand now that the house was just another contrivance for me. I had created the conditions under which to suffer. But even recognizing that I'd deliberately stacked the deck against myself, I was pooping in a bucket and that's real, every time. It made me happy that he didn't think he was too good to poop in a bucket right alongside me.

CRACK AND MARRIAGE

As I tried to manage a full-time job and a pregnancy, William was trying to get his menacing and possession charges taken care of. He was addicted to crack but I wouldn't know that until I set up a hidden camera in the house and captured photos of him hitting the pipe.

When I'd first learned of his addiction there were a number of factors that made me believe I could help him overcome it.

First, I'd been addicted to food for two decades when I started taking anxiety meds and the anxiety meds cured me of my binge/purge cycles. I was hopeful that perhaps some anti-anxiety medication might help him like it had me.

Second, I grew up with parents who drank about one evening a year, and even then, they never got drunk. I had no experience with substance abuse.

Third, the American Medical Association classifies alcohol and drug addictions as diseases of the brain and I happen to agree with them. Even though the AMA decided the issue back in the 1950s, there are still lots of people who continue to judge addicts as if it's entirely a matter of self-discipline. I concede that self-discipline can be brought to bear in positive ways but I also recognize that addiction is complex in nature and I am convinced it is predominately biochemical. Kicking him out for disease of addiction seemed as cruel to me as kicking him out for cancer

Fourth, I'd read up on the research surrounding the quest for a cocaine vaccine. There are scientists pursuing this and other addiction vaccines and I'd read articles that projected they'd be ready within the decade.

Finally, I was well versed in the science of human behavior as it related to rewards and punishments. When I was in graduate school I taught an undergraduate course on learning psychology. The first module of that course covered Skinnerian behaviorism. I know my behaviorism backwards and forwards. If, in the course of trying to help him, I started creeping toward co-dependency, I felt confident that I had the training to recognize it and thwart it.

He'd gone back to court for an appearance in front of the same judge who'd granted him the PR bond. The judge preferred not to put him in jail and told him that if he got a job and stayed out of trouble he would eventually dismiss the case. That was more than fair and William began excitedly looking for a job. He'd go to labor pools and get work, sometimes even a whole week of work, but as soon as he got a paycheck he'd relapse.

When he relapsed he'd often binge on alcohol and crack for 72 hours straight. When his body was mad enough about not being allowed to sleep and began to scream louder than his crack cravings he'd wander home, shimmy sideways down the fence line that divided the three foot space between my house and the Villanuevas and begin tapping lightly on my bedroom window. He'd quietly say my name as he tapped, calibrating the volume of his voice carefully with each new attempt. He knew that if he woke Baldomero and Juana I would be angry. Their bedroom window was right across from mine so finding the volume that would wake me and not them was tricky.

Coming down off a crack binge, he would always ricochet into a deep depression. I'd agree to let him come in the house, telling him we were only going to talk for a few minutes. He would tell me he had nothing to live for, daring me to tell him he did. He'd sit down, cradle his forehead in his hands and beg my forgiveness. As he spoke, his tears would speckle the wooden floor beneath his hidden face.

The judge gave him several chances to prove he was on the right track so just before each appearance he'd freak out and beg me to forge a paystub for him. I refused each time telling him that jail time would be a good place to go get his head together.

"Malcolm X used his time in prison to turn his life around," I told him, "You need to decide whether you want to just be a sperm donor or a father. I can make it without you, but I would love to be a family."

After a fourth appearance and no believable paperwork, the judge sentenced him to a year in prison.

My belly was just beginning to show when I watched him leave the courtroom in handcuffs. Four months would pass before I would see him again.

That day, after they ushered him from the courtroom in handcuffs, they locked him up in the Denver City Jail. Within twenty-four hours he was transferred to the Denver County Jail. Next, he was moved to a sort of clearing-house facility for some psychological and IQ tests. While he was there, I was not allowed to visit because I had no legal standing. If we'd been married, I would have had visitation rights.

Our letters kept crossing in the mail and I relied on the other crack servers to explain the ins and outs of the prison system to me as I waited week after week to finally get a phone call.

When the call finally came, I asked him to marry me. I claimed it was just so Leah could be told we were married when she was born, but I really missed him and I wanted us to be a family.

I learned that in Denver, if you want, you can solemnize your own marriage. That's what they called it if we wanted it to be just me and him, making whatever promises we wanted to make to one another, without any other person being involved. I took off work one afternoon to go get the paperwork and when he called that night, I told him, "Okay, I'm signing it right now."

Then, I put it in the mail, addressed to the prison, complete with his inmate number after his name. Once he had it in his hands, he called me on the phone and announced to me that he was now signing that same piece of paper.

He signed it on April 10th so that became our wedding anniversary.

PRISON

When I was finally allowed to go for a visit, I didn't know what to expect. He had four-hour visitation slots available on Saturdays and Sundays. As I drove the hundred or so miles to the prison he was housed in, I wondered if we'd have anything at all to talk about. It suddenly seemed obvious that we barely knew each other.

After waiting almost two hours and almost being turned away for having dressed too sexy (which I found baffling given how bloated with pregnancy I was), I was finally sitting in a room that looked like a junior high school cafeteria, waiting for him to walk through the door.

When he'd gone away, he was a muscular, chocolate-brown man who looked kind of beatnik cool in his glasses and goatee. Now, four months later, he walked into the visitation room and it was clear he'd been eating well. His skin was pale and he was wearing prison-issue glasses: the most moronic looking glasses I had ever seen. He looked like a fat, yellow, Roger from *What's Happening*.

That's not to say he wasn't equally shocked. I was a whale of a pregnant woman, and I'd dyed my hair black.

For the first ten minutes or so I felt like I was a thirteen year-old on a first date with her crush. I couldn't look him in the eye without feeling a self-conscious urge to giggle. I knew if I allowed myself to smile I'd overdo it and end up exposing my gums. Better to examine my cuticles with scientific intensity than to risk the eye contact that might turn me into Mr. Ed.

He asked if I wanted to play chess. I told him I didn't know how. He asked about Scrabble and I agreed to play him, thinking my large vocabulary would give me a decided advantage. I figured I'd have to go easy on him. He ended up beating me by just a few points, but it wasn't because I threw the game. It had been he who was kind enough not to run up the score on me.

Each week, our visits were a mix of talking and playing board games. He tried to teach me chess but I proved pretty hopeless at it. He also tried to teach me to be better at Scrabble, but I will never be as good as he is.

While William was locked up, my mother hired a plumber to fix up the bathroom and kitchen of my house. The very real challenges of pregnancy allowed me to let down my guard and accept her help.

When he was awarded a parole hearing in the first week of June, I waddled all over town gathering up letters of reference and past pay stubs. Every place I contacted there were people who chose to tell me what a wonderful person he was and, in addition to providing glowing reference letters, asked me to send along greetings and best wishes.

On the day of his parole hearing, as I waited for him to arrive from his cell, I was seated next to a young white couple. The man was in prison clothing and asked me if I was there for William. I confirmed that I was.

"He is the nicest guy I've ever met in my life," the white guy told me. "Back in 2003, I was paroled to a half-way house where he was already living. My first day there, he took me under his wing. He took me around to all the different places so I could get some job interview clothes and my bus pass. He took me to the job boards and coached me on how to get a job – you know – how to talk and act in an interview, that kind of stuff."

"Thanks for telling me that," I said, "I think he's pretty great, too."

We met with the parole board guy via a television screen. He asked William some questions and told him he'd read over the reference letters and was impressed. He then directed his attention toward me. He told me he'd received the four-page typed letter I'd written asking that William be granted the early release.

We left the room without knowing the outcome. We hugged goodbye and I drove home to Denver. That night, William called me on the phone with the news that he'd been granted early parole. On June 15, 2006, I picked him up in southern Colorado and drove him back to Denver. Leah would be born two weeks after that.

The Most Important, Impossible Time

By the time I married William, I thought I'd spent enough time around working class black people that we wouldn't have any cultural conflicts. As it turned out, aside from the issues related to his addiction, all of our disagreements centered on what each of us believed were the best techniques for raising children.

I was completely blindsided when, at twelve days old, he accused me of spoiling her. I guess I'd assumed he would defer to me as a woman when it came to parenting. When that didn't seem to sway him, I thought my mother's input would be something he would listen to, since she'd raised four kids and he had raised none. Next, I tried citing child rearing books and research studies.

I was super lucky that Leah turned out to be an amazingly cheerful baby. She almost never cried. Because of that I was able to convince him that we could take a short vacation from worrying about spoiling her.

By the time she was around seven months she knew how to

Figure 40: Leah Tyler and her parents, right around the time she learned to walk.

communicate with us using sign language and that kept her smiling and happy just that much longer. From that time until about nine months old she had a couple of those bouncy things she could sit in that had toys built into the surface that she loved to spend a good deal of time in. They had moving parts; things that rattled and honked, tiny doors to open and shut, and buttons that triggered happy little songs.

Throughout each day we could move her from one play area to the next and she would smile, coo, and actively engage with toys, us, and the cat.

Then, she learned to walk.

Oh. My. Freaking. *Hey little girl!! Get back here!!!*

Suddenly, she was into absolutely everything. She became an exploration machine and she was relentless. She understood "no" but only in the present tense. She didn't understand logic or consequences so my if-then-else commands meant nothing to her.

One night I actually dreamt that we built a rubber room, tossed in a trunk's worth of plastic toys and locked the door. In my dream, I kept track of her via a webcam I could watch from my desk at work.

In the dream, my mom and sisters were telling me I was a bad mother. I was trying to convince them that the rubber room was simply a substitute for my presence because my husband was unwilling to parent her according to my wishes. My wishes, of course, aligned with the latest research. Research he had no respect for.

They were clucking their tongues and saying, "Now will you admit that all of this is mistake?"

In the dream, when they said that, they meant the house, the pregnancy, and the marriage. They wanted me to say that Leah was a mistake.

It wasn't hard to decipher the meaning of my dream. Hart & Risley's findings make it clear that during those months of Leah's life, her primary caregiver was supposed to be talking to her almost constantly while also letting her explore any, and everything. That wasn't happening during the day when my husband was in charge of her. Instead, when he cared for her, all she heard from him was "stop," "no," "don't touch that," "give me that," and "get away from there."

I was able to give her the full-on chatter-fest only in the evening hours, after I got off work but I felt intensely guilty that she was only being properly stimulated a few hours a day.

Typical weekday evenings went something like this:

Arriving home around 5:45pm, I enter our apartment with a big, loud, falsetto, "Leah? Leah? Hi Sugar! Can momma have a hug?"

Leah toddles over, I crouch down and she stands stock still while I hug her for a second. I pick her up and try to cover her in kisses. After the third or fourth kiss, she is squirming against my arms, wanting her freedom back. I set her on the floor. She points at the kitchen and grunts.

"What's in the kitchen? Are you hungry?"

She shakes her head, "No," and points again.

I look over at my husband. He's at the desk, staring toward the computer screen. We exchange unenthusiastic hellos.

I've arranged the computer desk perpendicular to the wall. From where he sits, he can see the entire living room including the front door and the door to the kitchen. I've set it up this way so that either of us can use the computer while also keeping track of her. Even with this clever setup, he manages to lose track of her way too often.

I follow her to the kitchen. As I pass him, I look back over my shoulder and see a casino slots game on the screen. I hate when he plays that game. All he has to do is tap the spacebar. He claims it relaxes him.

Leah grunts a third time, waving me further toward the kitchen. I follow her to the refrigerator. She makes the hand sign for juice.

"Where is her sippy cup?" I call out.

He says something in reply but I can't make it out.

"What?" I call back.

"I. Don't. Know," he yells, separating each word for me.

I look in the cupboard. Nothing.

He was supposed to get some new ones and he did, but the ones he got were from Family Dollar and I'm too scared they might have BPA. He says if I want to be that particular I have to go get them myself. I say *fine*, but I haven't had time yet.

I begin loudly shifting things around; opening and closing cabinets, pulling drawers open and banging them shut again. Then I move back to the living room and make lots of looking around noises in there as well.

Finally I say, "Do you think you might be able to help me look for it?"

He gets up from the computer with a loud sigh and starts making his own searching noises. I am on all fours looking under the couch when I hear a hollow plastic pop. He has forcefully placed something on the coffee table next to my hips. I raise my head and turn to see it.

I say, "Thanks," but I don't mean thanks, I mean, *Now, was that so hard, Jackass?*

I return to the kitchen. Leah has opened the doors to the area under the sink and is peering inside. *Dammit*, I think, *I keep forgetting to get some of those kid-proof latches.*

I want to pull her back, slam the doors and say "No!" but I know that's not the super-mom way to handle the situation.

I remind myself I'm committed to enabling her safe exploration. Yes, there are chemicals under the sink but just opening those doors isn't going to force toxic chemicals down her throat. Even if she ate a scoop of dishwashing powder, I doubt it would do anything more than make her sick.

In any event, I've already lost precious chattering time with her while I searched for the sippy cup so I'm anxious to get to the business of it.

I watch her pull out a package of multi-colored sponges and tear off the clear plastic packaging that had been holding them all together.

"Ooooh. Look at the sponges. Those are pretty colors. I like all those colors. Are you gonna open them so we can see them all? Look at that! You opened those so fast! You like the pink one? Look Pink. Orange. Green. Yellow. One. Two. Three. Four. Say 'one.' Can you say 'one'? Wuh. Wuh. Wuhn?"

I pick up two sponges and clap them together. She picks up the other two and does the same. I take the soft side and run it across her forearm. "Smooth," I say, smiling.

Then I flip it over, "Rough!" I say, scowling.

She loses interest in the sponges and looks toward a can of Comet. I say, "Okay, let's put the sponges back where we found them," and she happily helps me place the sponges in a stack, back under the sink.

"Good Job!" I say, "Good job cleaning up!"

Next she grabs the Comet. It hasn't been opened yet so she's not in any danger. She lifts the cylinder, shaking it and sees that nothing comes out. She spots the sticker that covers the holes and tries to loosen it.

"No you don't. You can't take the sticker off. There are chemicals in there and chemicals can hurt the baby."

We repeat the cycle of her shaking it, then reaching for the sticker three or four times. Finally, she drops the Comet and takes off, intending to leave the kitchen.

"Hey little girl, get back here! You need to put the Comet away."

She comes back and I tell her again to put the Comet back under the sink. She does. I tell her to close the doors to the cabinet. She does.

I take a deep breath and blow out my entire lung capacity's worth of air. This is hard work. I haven't even had a chance to put my purse away or take off my jacket.

I am hungry and I've just realized I've been needing to use the bathroom since I left work almost an hour ago.

She walks back to the living room, over to the desk, strains to reach up onto it and grabs the computer mouse. He grabs it, too, pulling it back. She screams. He slaps her hand. She releases the mouse and toddles over to me, wailing.

I pick her up, sit down on the couch with her, envelope her as much as I can and rock back and forth. She quickly regains her curiosity and scrambles off my lap. She toddles over to the TV.

He yells across the room. "Stop!"

She hits the right button to turn it off.

"Do NOT TOUCH THE TV!" he yells while raising the remote and turning the television back on. He's got it tuned to a horror movie.

She goes for the button again.

He yells at her again.

I scoop her up intending to take her with me into the bedroom. I grab one of her toys as I pass the toy box. It's one of those half-red half-blue balls that has the different shaped holes and the yellow pieces you have to match to the holes. She doesn't really get it yet but part of this "concerted cultivation" approach requires that you challenge your kid to do things they can't.

I set her on the bed, pull on the yellow handle things and the yellow pieces tumble out. I watch her push a star-shaped piece as hard as she can over the round hole.

This is not fair.

I hate him.

Hours later, after Leah has gone to sleep. I go into the living room.

Tap. Tap. Tap. He's still hitting the spacebar on the casino game.

"Can we talk?" I ask.

"About what?" he says.

"About Leah."

"What about her?" He gets up from the computer and walks down the short hallway into the bathroom.

I follow him. Standing in the hall while he pees, I say, "I just think." I sigh, "So, I read this book called *Meaningful Differences*."

"If you need a book to tell you how to raise our kid, she's gonna be running this house by age three."

I sigh again, "Can I tell you what my mom would recommend we do with her at this age?"

"Sure, go ahead." He flushes the toilet and pushes past me.

I watch him pass, staring daggers that he clearly doesn't feel. He enters the bedroom, lays down on the bed and turns onto his side. His back is facing me as I stand in the doorway.

"Okay, fuck you." I say.

"Why's it gotta be fuck me?" His lower body is still facing away from me but he turns his head toward the ceiling as if showing me his wrinkled brow will cow me.

"Because I feel like you don't care whether Leah reaches her full potential or not."

"Full potential?"

"Yes."

"Full potential?" He turns to lay flat on his back, his eyes remain on the ceiling and his expression is flat.

"The person she becomes depends on how we treat her. Her personality will be shaped by the negativity of you telling her no, no, no, all the time. This is a time in her life— in her development— when she should be allowed to explore. This is a time when she is either rewarded or punished for being curious and creative. My mom would say that if she starts messing with something we don't want her messing with, we should turn her attention toward something else instead. We should distract her with something we don't mind her messing with."

I pause, giving him time to respond. He turns back on his side as if he's finished listening.

"I know it's hard work. It's *very* hard work. The easiest way to do it is to just stay busy all day with housework and engage her in whatever you happen to be doing. It also takes reams of patience but luckily this stage only lasts about six months. Once she starts to learn about consequences, it becomes less stressful. During this time we should reserve the word 'No' for as few situations as possible."

"Reserve the word *no*? She *needs* to be told no. No means no."

"Holy lord," I say, rolling my eyes.

"What?" He's looking me in the eye now and suppressing a smile.

"Did you just use an anti-date-rape slogan and pass it off as a childrearing mantra?"

He smiles. I smile.

"Maybe?" he offers.

I laugh, remembering that I actually do love him.

"Honey, I know you're bored being here all day. I couldn't be the stay-at-home partner. It's a really, really difficult job when she's at this stage. You're not happy here. I know that. We have to figure out how to make sure all *three* of us are happy. You aren't interested in being the kind of primary caregiver Leah needs right now."

"She's *one*. What does she need besides food, naps and diaper changes?"

"Like I've said a few times now, she needs to be in an environment where she can explore freely. Frankly, that environment is probably daycare."

"You're saying she's better off in daycare than with her parents?"

"No, I'm saying she's better off in daycare than she is with *you*."

"Oh, so it's like that?"

We both laugh.

"You just want to raise her the white way," he says.

"What is the *white* way?"

"Where you spoil her and let her disrespect you in public."

"Yeah, you know what? I've seen all the black comedians talk about the differences between black parents and white parents."

"So then you know it's *true*."

"No. I don't know it's true. I know that there are some out-of-control white kids in the world. Some."

"And you want to raise Leah to *be* one of those kids."

"No. I don't. I want to raise her to be smart and happy and curious."

"She's gonna run you. She's gonna run you like all those other little white kids run their white parents."

"Okay. Since you seem to wanna go there, let's talk about black parents."

"Let's go there."

"Let's"

"Okay."

I look to the ceiling and lick my lips. I close my eyes, gathering my thoughts, worrying that I will say something I regret. I'm going to say *something* because I've sat silent too many times over the years while black people talked about how crucial it is to whip your kids.

My husband loves to strike up conversations in the grocery store, doctor's office, wherever. It all starts when my husband spots a white parent giving their kid a command. He focuses on the kid, waiting for the kid's response, almost seeming to hope the kid won't comply. If there's anything at all to notice in the kid's reaction time, facial expression, tone of voice – anything – he'll get the attention of a nearby black person, then he'll point to the white kid and say, "What that kid needs is a good old-fashioned ass-whoopin." Then, the two of them will happily commiserate over their own childhood beatings. Those incidents have pushed me to my breaking point.

Still, I want to make sure I express just what I feel I need to say, nothing more and nothing less. I remind myself that I'm fighting for my child.

"Go ahead," he says.

"I'm getting it right in my head."

"You don't have to arrange it. Just lay it out there."

"No. I have a lot of anger behind this so I need to get the words just right."

"Anger?"

"Yeah."

"At who? At me?"

"Some of it is at you. Some of it's at Steve Harvey, Bernie Mac, and whoever the hell else does that same stupid comedy routine about how great it is to beat your kids all the time."

"That's not what those comedy routines are about."

"Well what are they about, then?"

"They're about how white kids disrespect their parents."

"Yeah, I know. I get it. It's actually funny. The comedians are funny. White kids make their parents look bad in public. Black kids do too, but when they do it, hurray! they get wailed on. Go mom! You really rocked it as a parent! You sure showed that five-year-old how big and bad you are."

"Well, white people let their kids run crazy, that's why they grow up to shoot up malls and schools."

"Seriously, you don't have to explain it. I get the joke. The joke itself is funny. Ya'll are right about what white parents are doing wrong, you just fail when you claim that you know how to do it better. Y'all suck too. Just in a different way."

"How do we suck?"

"You beat your kids. You're negative all the time. You don't pay any attention to 'em unless it's to tell 'em to stop doing something. It's constantly *no, stop doing that,* and *shut-up.*"

"Yeah, and they don't disrespect their parents in public."

"Wrong. We *know* that black kids do, in fact, act a fool, they just get beat for it. So it really isn't about the kids, it's about the parents. It's about whether the parent's reaction is approved of by all the other parents who happen to be there as a witness. So, it's like a fancy church hat. It's like a fashion show. It has nothing to do with the kid. It's basically, *Look at me! I beat my kid! Do you like it? Don't I look pretty?*"

"A kid *has* to learn to be respectful."

"Is that how kids learn to be respectful? I think that's just how they learn to get beat. And they learn that the less they do, like, of anything, the less likely they are to get beat. So they learn to be scared to move."

"Scared to move? Move where?"

I take a deep breath and blow it out loud, for effect. I sit down on the bed, one leg tucked under me and the other on the floor. I put my hand on his hip. He looks me in the eye suspiciously.

"When I was in college, I learned about this experiment with dogs. They put a dog in this two-part chamber. The dog could jump over the barrier to avoid an electric shock that came from the floor beneath it. I can't remember if the researchers would ring a buzzer or turn a light on, but there was some way they fixed it so that some dogs were given a warning signal but others were not.

The dogs that got the signal just before the shock figured out how to avoid being shocked – they jumped over to the other side right before it happened. And they were happy dogs. They had pep in their step, you know? They were energetic and productive.

Then there were these other dogs. They never knew when they were gonna get shocked, so even though the shocks hurt them, there was nothing they could do about it. These dogs became really screwed up. They would just lay there and take it. Even if the chamber was opened, they didn't bother leaving. They just laid there.

So now the researchers decided to close up the chamber again and start giving the screwed up dogs the warning signal before the shock. The researchers thought the messed up dogs would learn to jump over the middle just as fast as the other dogs had, but they didn't. At least not right away. Those dogs continued to accept being shocked. They were miserable and all they did was play casino slots on the computer all the time..."

He looks at me suspiciously.

I bug my eyes at him.

He does a slow motion fake slap movement accompanied by a slap sound-effect. The "slap" lands gently on my cheek.

I grab his wrist, smiling. "What?" I say, "I was just checking to make sure you were listening."

We play-fight for a few seconds. That culminates in his trapping both my hands. He holds them long enough that we share a look that acknowledges his victory. He drops my hands and says, "You're just making too much out of it. They're not saying you should beat your kids all the time."

"I know they're not and you know what? That's probably the worst part of all. Steve Harvey doesn't beat his kids. He *talks* about beating his kids. I guarantee you Steve Harvey has talked about whooping his kids thirty times more often than he's actually done it. And that's why the comedy routines are so poisonous. Here you have this middle-class guy talking about how he raises his kids different than white folks, cuz *white folks is crazy*. Yeah, alright. But you've got parents in the audience: horrible parents, abusive parents, lazy, self-centered parents who are thinking – Yeah that's right! We're excellent parents! We beat the shit out of our kids! Our kids don't disrespect us without getting their ass beat."

"You don't know that."

"I have *seen* it. Over and over and over. Working-class and welfare-class parents and their horrible ideas about how to parent. And my heart has broken for those kids, over and over and over."

"What? You saw this on TV?"

"No. I've been around a lot of black people in my life believe it or not."

"Like who?"

"Like people you don't know."

"Where?"

"Everywhere. Oh my god. You can see this kind of parenting

anywhere. The bus. WalMart. The park. It's everywhere."

"Well, it's not just black people."

"You're right, it's not. But abusive white parents don't have cheerleaders who make public speeches that talk about how great it is that we all beat our kids."

"Yes you do."

I search my brain for a minute, trying to figure out what he's talking about. Then it hits me. Right, that *Spare the Rod* kook.

"So let me rephrase this then, *I didn't marry* a religious fanatic who's a fan of the *Spare the Rod* book, and who uses that book to bully me into beating our daughter. Instead, I married a black guy, who, when he defends his lazy parenting, sounds suspiciously like a *Kings Of Comedy* routine. I'm talking about black people's terrible parenting that they're so proud of because you're sitting here endorsing it."

"Kings of Comedy, I gotta pull that up on YouTube."

"And I know it's our fault, white people's fault, because my ancestors beat the shit out of your ancestors. We're the ones who taught your people this technique for treating people like shit. This telling your kids *do what I say, don't ask questions, don't try to negotiate, shut up, don't expect me to praise you, don't expect to be entertained or catered to. You Don't Matter.*"

"Who said that?"

"That's the message of slavery and Jim Crow. But today we have a situation of too many poor black parents conveying that message to their children. In fact, it's a chicken egg thing. The research pretty much shows that it's not that welfare causes shitty parenting it's that shitty parenting causes welfare dependency. And it *is* from Jim Crow. Researchers have already proven that parents treat their kids just like they're treated, as adults, in their work environment.

Well, black people's work environment was Jim Crow! But some blacks in each generation adapted differently. Some secretly developed middle-class values but pretended to be dumb and sycophantic until they could find a way out or around. Because once you adopt middle-class values you do this thing called 'concerted cultivation' on your kids and you raise them in a positive way but also you helicopter them and push them to succeed.

If you start when they're one year old they'll have a higher IQ and do well in school and then, in that very middle-class way, you'll support them while they go through college and even for years after that you'll keep pushing them and supporting them.

And finally, *Voila!* no more cycle of poverty. But it's only been one or two generations since Jim Crow ended and it's not like things changed magically overnight and racism vanished –"

"Racism vanished?"

"No. I said it's *not like* racism vanished overnight, so the majority of blacks haven't had time to figure out the middle-class system. Well actually, blacks that haven't figured out the middle-class value system have more kids so they become the majority of blacks over and over. And these poverty-class parents keep raising their kids in anticipation that they will be mules and because they raise them that way, they turn out not to be fit for anything other than working in low-level, low-wage labor jobs. They don't have the verbal skills to negotiate what they want or need. They only know hitting so they use violence to resolve conflict. That includes their on-the-job needs. They end up quitting instead of negotiating better working conditions. It's a big ugly mess."

"Blaming the victim"

"No!" I say, shaking my head, "Oh no. Did I do that? Wow. Maybe I did."

I stare at the wall in silence. Remorseful.

I turn my back toward the headboard and lay down next to him, digging my shoulder into his so that he scoots over to make room for me.

Now, we're both staring at the ceiling.

"Pretend I never said any of that…because I know it's not their fault. So, wait, I stand by part of it. Okay – what are the facts and what part is my theorizing? Fact. Blacks *do* brag about hitting their kids. Fact. Working class and poverty class blacks do definitely pop their kids a lot in public. And for reasons middle-class people do not approve of. But I'm not saying it's their fault. *That* would be blaming the victims. I'm blaming white supremacy for the whole thing. Well, except the Steve Harvey stuff. That's on him. That's on y'all.

"We whites created the ghettos and *we* locked people into them. We sucked out all the resources and forced you to develop a whole different culture. It's only when the ghetto world bumps up against Whitey world that we get all freaked out about the rules you were forced to live by. Middle-class people, black and white, don't like the way poor blacks act sometimes but we created the system in which those behaviors were survivalist.

"People adapt to survive in whatever conditions they find themselves in. Poor mothers are tired and stressed. Unlike me because I have good, legal drugs that allow me to be endlessly upbeat. I can be patient with Leah because I have so much less stress in my life, in addition to the meds.

"Did you know that like, *every* white woman in the suburbs is on some version of these same SSRI drugs? It's not just me. It's *all* of us. *All* the white ladies, we are all on anti-anxiety meds."

I turn to look at him. He subconsciously registers my head movement and nods his head slowly in response, his eyelids eclipsing half of each iris.

I turn back to the ceiling, "So, that's the reason I have this endless patience with Leah. I have this wonderful prescription! I don't snap at her because she doesn't try my nerves...

...All my nerves are swimming in feel-good serotonin. Then, I have more hours I can spend with her, even after work, because I have a car and I get home from work quicker that way...I do our laundry at home -- less stress, more time with Leah...I use the car to get groceries -- less stress, more time with Leah...I have more cash because I have a nice salary -- less stress, more time with Leah...I have a great job for a number of reasons that trace back to my whiteness. ...College taught me how to read research results so I'm not intimidated by the statistics in these studies on childrearing...I'm not wary of doctors, and psychologists, and medicine. No one in my family ever had surgery performed on them without pain killers just because some doctor wanted to view their internal organs and considered them so much less than human that he felt entitled to do whatever he pleased with their bodies."

I look over at my husband again, suddenly worried because I know he hates hearing about terrible things white people have done to blacks.

His eyes are closed; face fully slackened. His chest rises and falls in the slow rhythm of sleep.

The Good Wife

When William relapsed that first time after getting clean in prison, my mother wanted that to be the last we saw of him, but I was excited that he'd made it as long as he had.

For me, each day he was on the wagon, he bought forgiveness for each day he was not. Ever the optimist, I imagined a life where he relapsed for just one 72-hour binge every few years. Maybe we'd go along like that at first and then later, the relapses might happen just once a decade or not at all.

So even as my mom campaigned for an unceremonious heave-ho, I was steadfast and certain that our life with his addiction was completely manageable.

I'd dated men who cheated on me with other women. The pain of being cheated on was so much worse than a husband with an addiction. A mistress named Crack didn't have the power to hurt me the way the other mistresses had.

One thing was clear to me after that first post-prison relapse: We had to leave the inner city and move out to the suburbs. I'd fought so long to escape the suburbs, you'd think I would've put up more of a fight, but I wanted what I thought was best for him

Once we began looking for an apartment outside of the inner city, I quickly discovered that we would be refused tenancy in most apartment complexes because of his felon status. The exact same places that had once posted signs saying, "No blacks" now turned away felons.

We would be forced to either lie on applications or accept living in areas that were high risk for an addict.

We chose to lie.

We kept up payments on the house while renting an apartment. The insurance on the house skyrocketed because no one was living there.

Thieves broke in and stole our copper piping. They left the valve open on the water line in the crawl space, and we had a $7,000 water bill before the water company showed up to turn it off. The water caused a mudslide that took out the water heater, furnace, and air-conditioning.

When he relapsed a second time he skipped an appointment with his parole officer so he could avoid giving a urine sample. The parole officer agreed to reschedule, but William skipped that one, too. I confronted him and he admitted he'd been smoking crack again. He was certain that the next time he showed up for a parole appointment he'd be arrested. He was scared and he begged me not to give up on him.

I told him that I had to protect Leah and give her a stable home and *that* might mean he couldn't live with us until he got himself back on track, but I would never give up on him. I tried to reassure him that he might be offered another chance.

He decided not to share in my optimism. Instead, he was determined to go out with his pipe blazing. Since he was sure he'd have to go back to prison, he went on a binge; remaining out of touch with both me and his parole officer for almost a week. His parole violation led the DA to charge him with a new felony charge of "escape."

Shortly after he turned himself in, we learned he'd been hit with "the Bitch."

The term "the bitch" was short for "habitual." William was charged under the habitual criminal law— Colorado's version of a three strikes law.

Being charged with the habitual criminal offense meant, if he were found guilty of escape, he would get an automatic mandatory sentence of forty years.

Forty years in prison for not coming home to our apartment or calling his parole officer for a week. Forty years for a man who (excepting his actions after his sister's death, while he was still a juvenile) had never committed a violent crime and whose primary problem was his addiction.

People who are convicted of murder get significantly less punitive sentences. The habitual criminal and three strike laws were a direct result of the War on Drugs.

The district attorney for our county was well known for her outright abuse of the habitual criminal law. She charged just about everyone she could with The Bitch and used the leverage to get nearly every person arrested to take plea deals. She touted her "conviction" numbers so that she'd be seen as tough on crime. The fact that she was locking people up for minor offenses, many related to minor drug possession and parole violations was never successfully publicized. She drove up the costs of incarceration by jailing non-violent offenders for decades.

From where William sat in the county jail he told me some terribly tragic stories. Have you heard the one about the mother who was offered twelve years on a plea bargain for a bounced rent check and took it because the mandatory sentence would have amounted to a life sentence? How about the one about the guy who was caught with three joints in his car and charged with intent to distribute? That poor guy chose to accept sixteen years when faced with The Bitch. Just a few years later Colorado legalized his crime, but he, no doubt, is still in there with many years left to serve.

News from the Arapahoe County Jail was a string of terrible tragedies carried out by a woman who swore publicly that she was doing God's work.

At about $25K per year, per inmate, her decisions seemed insane to me, but voters re-elected her based on the statistics they never really understood.

With my husband now needing a lawyer, and understanding that we could never live in the neighborhood again, we decided to walk away from the house and the mortgage loan. My credit rating was trash anyway so walking away made sense.

Our lawyer advised that if we could bail him out, it would give us leverage against the DA. I was able to post my husband's bail (and kiss seven thousand dollars goodbye forever) as soon as my tax return arrived.

Alphabet Soup: SNAP, WIC, CRP

The names of federal programs almost always get shortened to acronyms or initializations. Keeping them straight can be challenging.

What used to be called food stamps is now called SNAP:

Supplemental Nutrition Assistance Program. There's also WIC: Women, Infants and Children; a different food program that focuses on pre-natal, infant, and early childhood nutrition. And let's not forget CRP: the Conservation Reserve Program.

These three programs are all related to food. SNAP and WIC provide money for use in food purchases that its beneficiaries then consume as meals and snacks. The CRP is related to the nation's food supply in a less direct way. All three of them involve government agencies providing benefits to its citizens. These benefits cost money, so, they cost the taxpayer money.

Having land in the CRP is a choice.

What the CRP comes down to, for a lot of farmer-landowners, is whether they'd rather bust their butt and make the most money possible off the land, or do almost nothing and make a guaranteed pre-agreed amount.

Choosing between working and not working is a benefit reserved for the CRP people. SNAP and WIC recipients still have to work. They work for wages and then use SNAP and WIC to purchase food so they can ensure that their children have enough to eat. So why is it that SNAP and WIC recipients are demonized, and CRP recipients are not?

The same way our society decided we value soil conservation, we decided that we wanted every citizen to get proper nutrition during their formative infant and toddler years, and furthermore, we decided we didn't want them going to bed hungry during their grade school years.

Programs were developed. Programs were implemented. Sometimes we saw that parts were broken and we tweaked something here or there and made the programs more efficient. But when CRP problems and solutions were discussed, there was always an understanding that the *system* was the problem, not the *people*.

If, for example, the land was found not to benefit from the years it lay fallow, the program organizers might say, "We did a study and found that the program will be more beneficial if we require scientifically proven methods X, Y and Z."

Curiously, when problems arise with programs designed to help the poor it's almost a forgone conclusion that the *people* are the problem; not the *system's* design.

"The program should end because the welfare types are liars and cheats," they say. "Food-stamp recipients are lazy, immoral, and gaming the system. The only way to fix things is to drop the program altogether. When these broken people's children have suffered enough, they will finally get off the couch and go get a job! What? They already have jobs? Well then, they'll get a second job! Huh? Some of them already have second jobs? Well. They'll do something different… I guess."

If the general public knew about the CRP program, I wonder how they would react. Would they shrug it off? Or launch a petition to end it?

Would you be likely to find small groups in local diners discussing those "lazy CRP farmers and landowners"? Would we hear people pointing out how the CRP families are going to end up with deplorable work ethics and teach their own children that staying on CRP is a perfectly reasonable (and honest!?!) way to make a living? Would Anti-CRP groups form that could find a way to blame the soil depletion itself on the lack of morality in the CRP families?

If the CRP was benefitting black people, I think that's exactly what we'd see.

As Paul Kivel writes in *Uprooting Racism*, when a government program involves giving money to black and brown people, we (society) set up a vast network of white workers to oversee them and make sure they use their benefits in ways we (whites in power) deem appropriate. We then give the white workers (not always white, but certainly predominately white) the power to use various carrots and sticks in an effort to bring the black and brown people into line with the behaviors we want them to express. In other words, the benefits will only continue to flow if they jump through all the hoops we set up.

Historically, when we have found problems with programs that aid the poor, our solutions have tended to be hiring more white people to carry out additional oversight activities.

If we solved CRP problems in an analogous fashion, we'd have to hire a bunch of black and brown people to save the degenerate, almost-exclusively white, CRP families.

A veritable army of black and brown people would go out, visiting the CRP farmers in their summer homes, insisting that they report regularly on how they are spending their time and money by filling out various forms. These government overseers would enroll the farmers' family members in classes taught by black and brown people with titles like, "How to Teach Your Children About Work Ethic When You Don't Actually Work," and "Ending the Cycle of Government Dependence." The farmers' and landowners' children could be given coloring books that show people going to work so that the CRP children would understand that our society operates fluidly only because of all the people who have jobs.

To Hit Or Not to Hit: Round Two

After innumerable discussions, I convinced William that we had to let Leah negotiate with us because having those negotiation skills would be critical for her in getting the things she needed or wanted in life. I counted that as a small victory for what I'd come to believe was my far superior understanding of the best childrearing techniques.

After agreeing that negotiation was a skill we both wanted her to develop, we also agreed that negotiation had a time and a place. We'd need to teach her that there were going to be situations when we would be willing to negotiate with her, but there would also be times when we would expect her to respond to a command immediately and without question.

I was planning to continue with the threat of time out. Leah knew that when I began to count to five that was my signal to her that we were no longer negotiating.

What, I asked him, was going to be his system for signaling command mode? And what would be waiting on the other side of a command if she didn't fall in line?

He didn't need a signal, he said, and of course whipping would be the punishment.

I sighed loudly to show my exasperation, "Don't you understand?

Without some sort of signal to let her know negotiation mode is ending, you won't have the control you need."

"I'll just say her name in a serious tone."

"That's it? You think she's always going to be able to recognize a tone change?"

"Yeah."

"Good luck with that."

"It'll work. Watch."

"Well, beating in the mall, here we come."

"If she needs one, that's what she'll get."

"She'll never *need* one, I guess you'll just enjoy doing it so you can show off for all the other black people. Then, they can congratulate you on being a stellar father. How does that work? Do you try to get them as close to death as possible without killing them?"

"What?

"How do you decide how badly you should beat them each time? How about this? I'll tell you about some beatings I've witnessed and you tell me if you think they sound like solid parenting. Okay?" He nods, almost imperceptibly.

"I once saw a black mother, the older sister of my friend, beat her kindergarten-age daughter because the girl had gone to stay with her grandmother overnight and came back with her hair looking a little crazy.

"Little Ebony's real offense was that she'd let a white lady see her looking 'ugly.' My friend explained to me that it was Ebony's responsibility to appeal to her grandmother, aunt, or another adult to make sure her hair was done after she woke up that morning. By allowing herself to look ugly she'd brought shame to her mother and was therefore punished.

"Is that something you would condone? Is that a good reason to beat our daughter? Because her hair looks crazy?" I asked.

"No," he said, but his faced showed no judgment, and I really wanted to see disapproval. I searched his eyes but they were blank. He was unwilling to judge the mother in my story.

"Okay, here's another one. I once saw a mother beat her child in the center of a living room where I, along with her several aunts, a few uncles, and her grandmother were looking on. Her offense? Her cousin had taken her glasses from her and was refusing to give them back. Most of the kids were outside playing. We adults were inside talking and eating. She came in the house crying and reported it to her mother. Her mother stood up, grabbed a belt, and much to my surprise, grabbed this crying girl by her upper arm and started hitting her all over her backside.

The explanation I heard later was that the girl was beaten because she had shown weakness. In her mother's eyes, she should have retrieved her own glasses, not run to an adult to ask for justice. The parents of the boy who had taken the glasses just sat there. They didn't call their son in and demand that he return the glasses. He wasn't expected to apologize to her. He, evidently, had shown strength and was rewarded by having his actions completely ignored. So, again I ask you, dear husband, is this the kind of parenting you see in our future?"

Again, all he had to offer was, "No."

We stayed in that in-between place for a long time. He gave lots of lip service to the claim that whippings were necessary; but he wasn't carrying them out. Instead, he simply avoided situations where he thought she would defy him.

A decade before, when my niece was still very small, my mother and I had once commiserated over the fact that we both found it much easier to be stern with a child than to listen while someone else was being stern. I was betting that if he was third party to a whipping, he'd regret that he'd ever encouraged me to whip her.

Leah was almost four years old and we were living in an apartment that had tile floors and stucco walls. In other words, we lived in an echo chamber.

I had sent Leah to her room for misbehaving and she was dramatically wailing about it. I joined him in the master bedroom and he began his usual criticism of my methods.

The portals to the master bedroom and her bedroom were at right angles to one another. From where he lay on the bed watching television, he could not see into her room. From where she stood wailing, she could not see into ours.

"Fine," I finally said, "You're right. If I whipped her a lot she would be a much better kid. In fact, I should use that as my first resort. She is a horrible child and it's all my fault. I don't know what I was thinking. All those times I gave her warnings. I should have just smacked her. Why did I waste so much breath explaining rules to her? I cannot believe I didn't see this clearly until now. Thank you so much."

My husband had a skeptical look, unsure of my sincerity. I got up and walked out of our room and into hers.

Then, I took Leah's little arm and I shouted, "Dammit, Leah! I'm sick and tired of your crying!"

Leah's eyes widened and she began crying louder.

I kept hold of her arm and started slapping my leg to simulate a whipping.

"When I tell <smack>

you to do <smack> something

you do it <smack>

you do not<smack>

ask me <smack>

shit <smack>

about <smack>

shit <smack>

you do <smack>

as I say!!<smack>

<breathing heavily>

Now you stay in here until *I say* you can come out!

<whisper and hug> I love you baby, and I'm so sorry."

Leah had reacted to my words as if I'd actually been beating her. She'd never seen me yell like that, and it echoed so much it was three times louder than I was actually yelling. It was terrifying for her. My whispered renunciation gave her no comfort at all.

I walked back into the master bedroom and sat on the edge of the bed. Looking off into the distance, I said, "Damn that felt good... I've never felt so powerful. The look in her eyes was so...great. It was so...rewarding.

<chuckling> She sure knows who's boss now!"

Then, I lay back onto the bed and put my hands behind my head. I crossed my legs at the ankles and tapped the air with one foot. I stared at the ceiling smiling while our daughter continued to wail.

My husband looked over at me but I did not look back at him. I continued smiling toward the ceiling.

He got up and went into Leah's room. I could hear him trying to soothe her. His voice was a muffled baritone. Her cries took on a rhythm such that I knew he was rocking her on his lap. Slowly, the wails became sobs and then quieted completely. She'd cried herself to sleep in his arms.

Never again has he claimed that I should whip, hit, pop, slap, pinch, shove or even nudge her.

A Member of the Felon Caste

In the first few years we were together, it seemed like everywhere we drove throughout the city and out across the various suburbs, William would say, "Oh! I applied for a job there."

And early on, I would brightly inquire, "Yeah? What happened?"

He would always reply, in a matter-of-fact tone, "They never called me back."

He kept saying it: "Oh! I applied for a job there."

But I stopped asking what the outcome had been. I know my sadness can't have compared to his very real dejection each time he was ignored, but I felt sad nonetheless.

As the years wore on, I saw it for myself. Even very low-level jobs were just not available to him. By law, he had to check that box that said he'd been convicted of a felony. Potential employers saw the check mark, and they didn't even consider calling.

When he was growing up, his mother used to say, "Don't do the crime if you can't do the time." He took that admonition to heart. When he got arrested, he always took the plea deal. He'd known what he was getting himself into, and he took pride in owning up to his guilt and serving his sentence. What he didn't realize was that a sizable portion of society really doesn't believe in the value of time served. Many believe that felons should be stripped of their rights forever. The adage should be: *Don't do the crime if you can't accept being cut off from all manner of opportunities for the rest of your life. Don't do the crime if you can't accept being marginalized into a permanent underclass forever.*

As Michelle Alexander explains in her book, *The New Jim Crow*, my husband's experience as a member of the permanent underclass is not at all accidental:

> *What has changed since the collapse of Jim Crow has less to do with the basic structure of our society than with the language we use to justify it. In the era of colorblindness, it is no longer socially permissible to use race, explicitly, as a justification for discrimination, exclusion, and social contempt. So we don't. Rather than rely on race, we use our criminal justice system to label people of color "criminal" and then engage in all of the practices we supposedly left behind.*
>
> *Today it is perfectly legal to discriminate against criminals in nearly all the ways that it was once legal to discriminate against African Americans. Once you are labeled a felon, the old forms of discrimination, employment discrimination, housing discrimination, denial of the right to vote, denial of educational opportunity, denial of food stamps and other public benefits and exclusions from jury service --- are suddenly legal.*
>
> *As a criminal, you have scarcely more rights, and arguably less respect, than a black man living in Alabama at the height of Jim Crow. We have not ended racial caste in America; we have merely redesigned it.*

THE NEW MILLENNIUM TEENS

On the first day of 2010 we clanked our glasses of water, water, and apple juice together and I offered up the toast: "To the twenty-teens being an amazing decade for the Tyler family!"

Leah was three years old, William was still out on bond for his escape/habitual charges, and I was still convinced I could cure him.

The DA put him in a drug court program as she tried to avoid taking his case to trial. The staff of that program regularly tested him using urinalysis. Under their watch he racked up some impressively long stretches of sobriety. Sometimes I was so awed by his performance in the program I began to believe he was cured.

But he wasn't, and as soon as I let my guard down I would provide him with some tiny temptation that proved too great for him to resist.

Just the Four Of Us

If he was already weak for some reason, a ten dollar bill loose in my purse, or some item from Target that he could pair with my receipt and return for cash were enough to break him.

I almost never clued in to a relapse until I called his phone and realized he'd turned it off. After so many attempts over so many years, I was defeated. We were a family of four: Father, Mother, Daughter and Addiction.

Contemplating his relapses I still refused to consider divorce. Instead, I always threw myself into redesigning our family's processes to close loopholes and improve contingency plans. As night fell though, I would lay next to Leah, watching her sleep, entertaining the idea that if I couldn't keep him safe, maybe forty years in prison could. This would mean that he would likely die in prison and Leah would only know him through prison visits.

Under those circumstances, she would spend her entire life answering questions about her father, not knowing when it was okay to tell the truth and when she was better off lying. She would struggle to decide when she felt safe to open up and when it was better to just change the subject.

I didn't doubt that she would continue to love her father but I worried that she would someday wonder why his love for her hadn't been enough—why it hadn't given him the power to overcome his demons. And as she grew older I felt certain that she would resent our trips to the prison to visit him. I was sure that every time we sent regrets about a birthday party or weekend activity she couldn't attend, she would complain to me that if she didn't have to go see Daddy; and get patted down by officers; and play Scrabble and Chess for hours while eating Chili Pie from a vending machine; her life would be so much better.

I also entertained the alternative idea that if we won in court William might choose to return to his life on the streets of inner-city Denver, no doubt serving crack and sleeping in alleys. He wouldn't be likely to live another ten years under those circumstances.

I started hoping he would die.

Death has a way of making everything possible again. If William died who could say how close he might have been to overcoming his addiction? Once he was dead we could write our own tidy ending and we could believe whatever served us best.

Then, as Leah grew older she would only have my recollections filtered through my highest hopes for him. Her photo albums and videos from the first years of her life could be extrapolated into the wonderful life together that would seem so inevitable had he not met that untimely death.

He would forever be the smiling face holding her, swaddled, in the first moments after her birth. He would continue as the character sleeping mouth-agape and disheveled next to her infant onesied body.

He would be the guy in our home videos who hugged her, and teased her. The guy who told her how perfect she was, and reminded her that she was the brightest light to ever shine in his life.

If he could just disappear early enough, while she was still young enough to forget the details, he could be preserved forever and always in the photos and videos I would so carefully curate.

I Inherit Some Wheat Land

In 2011, my mother passed her land down to my siblings and I.

"I own land," I would repeat in disbelief, then as a joke between me and myself I'd say, "I'm a farmer."

It had never occurred to me that I'd own part of the land, though it should have, I guess. Each of us was given the option to sell our portion to the others. All of us declined.

My mother had decided to pass it to us sooner rather than later because she wanted us to raise the questions on the contract that provided her with just one-third of the CRP money.

My mother's brother had passed in 2005 but she still couldn't bring herself to discuss it with her sister-in-law, the widow of her brother, and a woman who'd been a part of her family since before she was even born.

We began negotiations with my cousin shortly after the land had officially passed from my mother's hands. In 2011, there were two years left on the contract that supplied my cousin with two-thirds of the CRP money. My cousin did not agree with us that the deal was unfair. He believed he deserved the full two-thirds even though we'd learned that across Whitman County most farmers were splitting the money from the CRP the way we wanted it split.

We offered our cousin a deal. If he would give us a fifty-fifty split for 2011 and 2012, when the contract came up for renewal in 2013, we'd still hire him as our land's caretaker. He would then begin getting only one-third, but one-third was far better than zero. He opted to continue taking his two-thirds for the remaining two years on the contract.

It was sad to see Otto and Leah's living descendants go our separate ways, but in 2013, that's exactly what we did. We try to maintain social relationships with that branch of our family even while acknowledging that from a business perspective, we are no longer tied together by Ai's land.

I did some fairly rudimentary math, and I think I now own about two percent of Ai's land. The money I got in 2013, right around the 150th anniversary of the Emancipation Proclamation, was about $4,000.

My Other Government Money

The wheat money isn't my only source of government money. In fact, you could justifiably call me a Welfare Queen because I've deposited money earmarked for Medicare, Medicaid, TANF, SNAP, WIC and many other programs right into my bank account.

It was all legal, too.

There is great irony in the idea that when I met my husband I was relatively affluent, yet a lot of my money had come from programs designed to help people like him, his parents, siblings, neighbors, etc. People who remained poor, while I got "rich."

I was encouraged along the path because I am an underrepresented minority: a woman who went to work for other women.

When affirmative action was instituted in federal programs, one of the stipulations was that government agencies should try to award some of their contracts to minority-owned businesses. Remember that the word "minority" has to do with the amount of power held by certain groups, not the size of those groups. Women of all colors are a minority because we are under-represented in positions of power, just as black and brown men are.

I don't know the actual rules of the government contracting system, I just know that when a woman-of-any-color-owned (or black-man-owned, or brown-man-owned) business bids on a government contract, the agency personnel are really happy to see the representatives of these minority-owned businesses because they "need" to give a contract or two each year to minority-owned companies.

Now, it might seem like this policy would open up a lot of opportunities for fraud but there are checks within the system. Primarily what guards against fraud and abuse is that those happy government agency workers actually need the work to get done and they need it done right. They can't just award the contract to *any* minority-owned organization that stumbles through the door. The minority-owned business actually has to prove they have the expertise and track record to meet the agency's needs.

The policy allows smaller, often younger, companies to compete with huge companies like, for instance, Halliburton, Arthur Anderson, KPMG, and the like. The policy seems to have put a dent in the good ole' boy network of government contracting. Then again, maybe the policy's effect is miniscule and only feels significant to me because that government money funnels right into my bank account, via my paycheck.

I have worked for three separate companies that were woman owned and most of the work I did for those companies was computer consulting for federal and state agencies.

While all three companies I worked for held high standards for hard work, proper billing, and quality products, only two of the three were actually woman-run.

One of the organizations had a woman who acted strictly as a figurehead. One evening at a small informal dinner I sat next to the purported owner and asked her to tell me the story of how she started the company. She replied, "Oh it's not really my company. It's [her husband's name]'s company. I go to some meetings here and there but I don't make any important decisions."

I was really disappointed to find out she was a rich, white welfare cheat. I left the company shortly after that dinner.

I've seen this kind of fraud carried out by another rich, white, welfare cheat who tried to pass his company off as a black-owned business. I knew a black NFL football player who was recruited by a white, Floridian businessman to be a partner in a company bidding to build low-income housing. The NFL guy had not studied business in college and had no role in the operation of the company, nor was he interested in learning it.

I was very angered when I learned of the arrangement. A mutual friend asked me where the harm was if, after all, our NFL friend made money for a few "appearances." My feeling was that a more qualified black man, one who actually built and ran a company should win the contract instead. Perhaps *that* black man would be more likely to practice affirmative action in *his* hiring and promotions, thus potentially creating the kind of economic justice the program was designed to promote. I was relieved to learn that my friend's company did not win the contract they had come together to bid on, so they decided to dissolve the arrangement shortly thereafter.

One of the two legitimately woman-owned companies I worked for hired and promoted other women but almost no ethnic minorities. The other company hired few women and no ethnic minorities. I wish minority-owned companies had to prove that they also maintained some percentage of minority workers in their ranks as well, because underneath that top position, there are still twice to three times as many white men in the ranks than everything else put together.

When a minority-owned company gets preferential treatment but then passes the benefits on to non-minority workers, all those non-minority workers are, in my estimation, welfare cheats.

When people protest "big government" they often cite programs designed to keep the working poor afloat and the chronically unemployed from starving or freezing to death. No one would ever look at me and blame me for the amount of money taken out of their paycheck each month, but maybe they should.

Anti-government protestors might loathe my husband for the years he ate food bought with his mother's food stamps or for the years he was in prison and racked up room and board costs. They'd waste a lot of energy hating him while I, as a middle class white person, can walk right past a demonstration, into an office building, stop by the break room for free coffee, and settle into my cozy cubicle. Then, for eight hours a day I will sit, typing, and reaping substantial financial gains as I move data around for state TANF, WIC and SNAP or HUD's Section 8 programs, or HRSAs Medicare and Medicaid.

My computer work should make these programs cost less over time so eventually the money paid to me will hopefully result in less money needed by the program overall. I am proud of the work I do and I hope that my work removes red tape from the lives of both the agency personnel and the aid recipients.

Still, if someone wants call out all the Welfare Queens, they shouldn't overlook me because they won't be able to balance the tax books they protest without taking my salary (and those of thousands like me) into account.

Government Money in Private Pockets

I know a middle-class person who, during the worst days of the housing bust, bought up houses in the inner-city and did very little work on them. He accepts Section 8 tenants. Section 8 is a program run by HUD that helps low-income families find affordable places to live. Residents pay 30% of their adjusted income and the government pays the owner the rest of each month's rent.

Without this program, my slumlord acquaintance might have to charge far less in rent just to get a tenant to move in. Instead, he gets full "market" price for his property and he gets a guaranteed rent payment every month. Rather than keep his properties up to HUD standards, he simply bribes the HUD official in charge of his inspections. Two white guys, a couple of welfare cheats, playing the system.

When I lived in downtown Denver, the local grocery store owner had to put up with a lot of theft. It was still worth it for him to operate in a low income neighborhood though, because the rent was very low, and SNAP cards paid inflated prices for his sparse and unreliable selection. He seemed to stock his shelves based on whatever he could get a good deal on someplace else. Another example of free market capitalism? Yeah, right.

I have a friend of Mexican descent who runs a lube shop. He was awarded a city contract for the lube and filter maintenance of the city fleet. That contract was so lucrative he was able to open a second, and then a third location. His contract bid was pulled to the top of the pile because of affirmative action rules that require ethnic and gender diversity to be considered when awarding contracts.

To acknowledge the role the program played in helping him secure the contract says nothing about his shops' abilities to do the work well. Again, the program is designed to make up for the fact that rich whites have networks full of powerful friends. You know, in case the contract would have otherwise been awarded not based on *what* each bidder knew, but *who*. Astonishingly, this friend complains about government regulations and taxes and claims his business would be far better off without them.

I know a small business owner who complains about government regulations and taxes incessantly. He claims that the government is not doing enough to support his attempts to live the American dream. Yet, when the recession was full bore just a few short years ago, he was clearing $120,000 a year in profits, and those profits were realized even after he'd paid the $60,000 to himself as yearly salary.

His take and bake pizza store was thriving because his primary product qualified as a SNAP purchase. He purchased the franchise using a loan his parents gave him, interest free, and now the government was essentially purchasing his product for the proletariat.

Many businesses saw drastically reduced revenues during the recession, but not this guy. His profits flowed so freely he built a brand-new custom home. I suppose when he parks his luxury car in the garage of his huge custom home one can still hear him whining about the federal government's dastardly deeds and loudly proclaiming his amazing personal bootstraps story.

Pull Hard on Those Bootstraps Y'all

Chris Raab, in his book *Invisible Capital: How Unseen Forces Shape Entrepreneurial Opportunity*, has shown us that upper-classes and middle-class advantages continue to accrue as we learn other vital lessons from parents, extended family, and friends. Raab explains how a stockbroker's children will have an advantage if they want to start trading stocks.

Likewise, the children of a dry-cleaner will have an advantage if they attempt to open a dry-cleaning location.

From *Invisible Capital*:

> Take Donald Trump, perhaps one of the best-known businessmen in modern times. In *Trump 101*, "The Donald," as he is popularly known, tells readers they can succeed if they "tough it out," "listen to your gut," and "take chances."
>
> What he doesn't tell them is that they will have a better chance to succeed in the real estate business if real estate is the family business, if they work in the family business before venturing out on their own, if they have access to the right connections in that world, and if they know how to look, talk, and act once they start operating in that world.
>
> Success comes easier if you start with capital—not just cold, hard cash, but a kind of hidden capital most people don't even know they have. Donald Trump spent his first five years in business working with his father, Fred Trump. He learned the art of the deal from his dad. He learned from his father the elements of success that few books can teach you—from what jokes to tell to where he would have the most success with different types of people (in the office, at a restaurant, or on the golf course).
>
> The young Donald could get his calls answered just by saying he was Fred Trump's son. That's invisible capital.

Raab notes:

> You and I have invisible capital of all kinds. Our cultural background, occupation, age, gender, educational training, and sexuality give us entree to some social groups—and may make it more difficult for us to enter others. Where you went to school, whether your parents were in business, what neighborhood you lived in as a child—all these factors can either propel you further or hold you back.

Raab positions his book as a practical manual for entrepreneurs. The book's goal is to help entrepreneurs see the advantages they start with and likewise recognize the ones they lack. I'm sure the book would be a godsend if I wanted to be an entrepreneur, but I don't.

What attracts me to the book, instead, are the implications of "invisible capital" for current racial disparity. As we've denied blacks the right to build businesses or go to certain schools or live in certain neighborhoods, we have simultaneously affected their ability to develop the invisible capital that would propel them along certain paths they might desire.

This is why Leah's generation still does not have equal opportunity. It's why Leah's children's generation might not either. Will Leah's grandchildren be born into an America where race *doesn't* predict income and education nine times out of ten? That will depend on how we go forward from this sesquicentennial.

We, as white people, have to stop talking about what's wrong with black people and start talking about what's wrong with us. We whites have to admit (to ourselves, our children, and each other) that many of us accept cash gifts from our parents; we inherit property from our parents; we are accepted into college based on our legacy status; we get job and business opportunities through cronyism; our personal networks from white churches give us access to a vast supply of resources; when we encounter the police we are treated with respect and often given warnings or other "passes" for our illegal behavior; when we get into real trouble with the police, our parents pay for lawyers and we get the charges dropped so we don't have to join the felon caste; we ask for and get special treatment wherever we go because we've been trained to be bold enough to ask for it and we think it's our birthright anyway; and somehow, someway, we manage to accept all of those gifts, while still giving ourselves credit for all that "hard work" we did to get wherever we are.

Playdates of Immeasurable Healing

When I was six years old and in my first week of first grade there was a black girl in my class named Sheila who used to taunt me: *White patty, white patty you don't shine, you got bumps on your booty like Frankenstein.*

By the second week of school I had convinced her to be my best friend. From that year forward, I never stopped craving the approval of black women. There had been a time when I had also sought the approval of black men, but after decades during which their approval came too cheaply and turned out to be too transient, I stopping putting any value on it.

All through elementary, middle school, junior high and high school being a *Good White Person* was as simple as showing up. But then, from the 1990s through the 2K-Teens, everything I did in an attempt to convince black women to be my friend seemed to backfire. My attempts either came off as lame, ignorant, overzealous, or desperate.

I resorted to worshipping black women from afar. I immersed myself in the literary works of Toni Morrison, Alice Walker and Maya Angelou. I loved Terri McMillan before and throughout *Waiting to Exhale*.

If my favorite books by black women were converted to movies, I was in line at the theater on opening night. Alone in a dark theater I could be Nettie, Shug Avery or even Sophia. Later, I was the Savannah that was there for Bernie, and, on second viewing, the Bernie that was there for Savannah. No one could deny me those experiences, as long the house lights were still down.

Even though I'd made that promise to myself that I would not harm the black community by stealing one of its men, I'd never found a way to reconcile that promise against my obsession with everything the black community created and enjoyed, together, without me.

Then, one day, in the poorest part of town, it hit me. I'd promised not to steal one of their best and brightest. I'd never promised not to get all Svengali on an adorable, good-hearted, crack-addicted felon.

So, quicker than you can say snowflake-flossy-top-miss-ann, I became a black woman. Well, I had one growing inside me anyway, and until that umbilical cord was cut, I was her and she was me.

As she grew older I told her how, when we were still one person, I'd caressed my distended belly, dreamt of hair that reached for heavens and formed a halo around her full-featured face. I'd begged the universe for her brown skin and ebony eyes. The universe had delivered her to me.

Sometimes, when we were together in the grocery store I would see a black woman look at me, look at her, then look at me again. Some of them would grant me that extra half-second of eye contact and I heard harpsichord. Others granted me the tiniest hint of an approving smile and that was Handel's Messiah Hallelujah chorus.

But then, if Husband's head was right and he came along to the grocery store, I got death stares. The better he looked, the worse I was treated. No one understood that I'd wanted to make the community better by making him better. I hadn't stolen him. I had done a solid for his mother who wasn't around anymore to help him herself.

I grew bitter.

You can reject me if you want, I reasoned, but my daughter needs to learn to be a *strong black woman* so screw you.

Screw you. *I know what's in my heart.*

Screw you. *You can't challenge my hood pass.*

Screw you. *I am the mother of a black woman. I will not sit down and I will not shut up.*

After all that yelling I was a sniveling, whimpering puddle on the floor.

"Why do you care?" my husband asked.

"I don't know," I said, "But I do. I do."

Leah started school. I saw black mothers there, picking up their black daughters and I scanned my brain for the right thing to say. Should I reference a black movie? A song? A television show? How can I let them know that I'm not like all the other white moms? How will they understand that I am white-mom-with-an-asterisk?

I was all out of energy and I wasn't sure I wanted the friendships because they came with too much pain. Sometimes I'd fret so much, remembering how royally I'd screwed things up in the past, that I'd decide it wasn't worth the effort. *Those bitches are never satisfied. Nothing is ever going to be good enough for them. I don't care whether they like me or not.*

With nothing left to lose, I said, "Playdate?" to Noelle. And she said, "Yes."

Then, I said, "Playdate?" to Zarinah and she said, "Sure."

I said "Playdate?" to Ilishia and she said, "Great."

And I was better because of their compassion; compassion they don't even realize they extended to me.

Paying the Wheat Money Forward

When we received the first wheat money check in 2011, we spent it all on ourselves; our home, our bills, our delights.

By the time we were due for the next one, in 2012, I started looking for ways to give some of it away. There were two black families living in our old neighborhood that I wanted to give money to, for very specific reasons. With both families I explained where the money came from and that I felt the money was mine because of racism. I asked them to do me the favor of taking the money because I didn't know of any other way to deal with the guilt.

Giving a portion of our wheat money away in 2012 gave me a measure of peace, but I knew it wasn't enough. It wasn't enough money and it wasn't enough peace.

In the years since I moved to Cole, I have seen my middle-class mixed-race niece and nephew get high school jobs, go to college, work at internships, make college friends and date other college students.

They are half-black and, perhaps in spite of that, are well on their way to middle-class lives.

The children I know from Cole are not. There were two young men – best friends— tall, good looking kids who should have had the world on a string. When I lived across the street from them I was constantly haranguing them about getting after-school jobs. I told them that the earlier they started working, the earlier they'd learn what sorts of work they enjoyed doing and which sorts they preferred to leave to others. I taught them about references, résumés and two-week notices. I invited them to imagine how great it would be to have money in their pockets, and they agreed it was fun to ponder.

They found jobs. Dishwashing jobs. My niece and nephew hadn't been expected to accept dishwashing jobs, they'd had options.

In any event, these boys didn't complain, they worked to get money and the money was enough to keep them interested.

But, it wasn't long before those jobs went away. Since Cole was still a ghetto, the restaurant had been yet another attempt to appeal to young, white professionals who worked downtown. That attempt didn't pan out. The restaurant closed down for lack of business.

Those young men started looking for new jobs, and they asked me for guidance. I realized how naïve I'd been in thinking their high school work experiences would be like mine. They didn't have my network. They didn't live in resource rich areas. Their mothers' couldn't drive them to and from work each day the way mine had because their mothers were busy at their own jobs.

They finished high school and went to college. They found college alienating and lonely, just as I had. They lacked the self-discipline to push through that loneliness, just as I had.

They dropped out of college, just as I had.

They broke the law, just as I had.

They got caught, just as I had.

They went to jail.

Hmmm.

After I'd followed my NFL boyfriend to the big city, I'd gotten caught shoplifting and was given a citation. I didn't go to jail, I just had to make a court appearance. If I'd been charged with a felony, my mother would have thrown large sums of money into keeping me from having a felony record.

These guys parents didn't have the money to negotiate them out of a felony record. These promising young black men got their felon labels and became second class citizens.

Life was bad.

They were ashamed and frustrated.

It was hard to go looking for a job knowing people would judge you once they knew you were a felon.

But then, they each fell in love with a beautiful girl, and it wasn't so bad anymore.

Life became tolerable again.

Their girlfriends got pregnant, just as I had.

Their girlfriends gave birth to beautiful baby girls.

Hmmmmm.

I hadn't done that. I didn't want to complicate my life. It was so much easier to go back to college without that extra complication.

Later, I found that not being a parent made it much easier to get my master's degree as well.

Today, both these young men want to go back to school and they, just as I once did, want to get the right training so they qualify for higher-skilled jobs. They need more money if they want to take care of their daughters properly.

But, unlike me, who had parents who happily wrote tuition checks, they can't, because they have student loans in default from the first time they went.

They can make payments to get back in good standing but the primary reason they want to go back to school is because they never seem to have enough money to make ends meet. They are in a catch-22 that none of the government staff assigned to regulate their lives can help them overcome.

Remember that when I buckled down and went back to school my parents welcomed me home. Their mothers can't do the same because they have landlords who check and double-check occupancy rates. They aren't on their mother's lease agreements and can't get on them.

One of these young ladies has been in foster care since the age of eleven. Her mother, like my husband, has struggled with crack for as long as she can remember. She started making adult decisions when she was still a preteen. When she gets depressed and anxious, as so many people today do[64], the Medicare folks tell her they aren't allowed to prescribe SSRIs. Instead, they prescribe her anti-psychotic, bipolar meds. These meds make her feel crazy. She decides it's better to struggle through than to take the bipolar meds.

Today, she juggles the role of mother and wife in addition to working

---

[64] Personally, I think it's all the food additives in processed food that are making all of us crazy. Check out the book "Excitotoxins: The Taste that Kills" by Dr. Russell L. Blaylock for more information along those lines.

and going to school. She does all of this without the use of a car. Then, she and her felon-class husband try to pool enough money to pay their bills. They never have enough to make ends meet. Ever. Yet, they still wake up the next day and start the grind all over again.

I've never been anywhere close to that amazing, yet I'm the one who's supposed to prattle on about my bootstraps.

Who should they turn to for help when they can't pay the light bill? When will *their* wheat money checks come?

As it turns out, of course, we've committed to sharing the wheat money in support of their schooling and other training they might decide will help them be better parents and better people.

The crazy thing is, it doesn't feel like an act of charity—it feels exactly like the things my parents did for me when I was their age and the things I'm sure we'll do for Leah, when she is their age.

Vignettes for Your Consideration

When I was dating across color lines, in Texas, in the 1980s, white guys would justify their opposition to race-mixing by telling me they were only against it because they felt it wasn't fair to the children.

I would hear them out, partially because I enjoyed the Socratic exercise of it all.

"Well," one of them, let's call him Mike, would explain, "It's just not fair to the kids because they're not white and they're not black so they grow up not fitting in anywhere."

"That's not exactly true," I would say, "Mixed kids are accepted as part of the black community."

"So why would you do *that* to your kids?" Mike said.

"Why would I give birth to kids that would grow up as part of the black community?"

"Yeah."

"Oh! So I see what you're saying, you're saying I'll be forcing them to have a black life when they could have had a white one. Right?

"Right!" Mike said.

"Wow. That does make sense. And what about Ira's kids?"

"Huh?"

"What about Ira's kids? What kind of life are they supposed to have?"

"Well, they would be black, just like Ira is."

"Do you wish *you* were black?" I said.

"What? No!" Mike said.

"If you were black, do you think you'd wish you were white?"

"Of course," said Mike.

"So let me get this straight. You think I should make a choice not to have black children because if I mate with someone suitably pale, my children will get to be all-white. How great that is for them. But Ira can't make that choice. You're saying that if I just marry the right person, my white husband and I, and our pallid offspring, can thank our lucky stars that we aren't black. We can pretend racism doesn't exist."

"That's not what I said," Mike protested.

"But it's what you *meant*. You think I'd be stupid to choose to have black kids when I can have white ones, instead. If I have children with Ira, I'm not going to be able to put my head in the sand about the racism that persists. I won't be able to escape the fact that it still affects people, because among those it will be affecting, will be my own children. You think I should make the same choice you plan to make which is to marry white, have white children, and spend the rest of your life claiming racism is a thing of the past."

One day, when I was pregnant with Leah, and William was locked up, I walked out my front gate to the bus stop and saw a man waiting there that I hadn't ever seen before. He had a cross-body messenger bag and was wearing the familiar Colorado business-casual uniform of khakis and a polo collared shirt. I introduced myself and learned his name was Darius. He explained to me that he, his wife Lisa, and their two kids had just moved in across the street from me.

"Where?" I asked, certain he was confused, either about where I lived or where he did.

He pointed at the three-story Victorian that was, in fact, across the street from my own (but three houses down). His new home was the crown jewel of our block. The Victorian was fully renovated inside and painted a triumvirate of whimsical colors on the outside. The lawn and landscaping were perfectly manicured and it had one of those security company signs posted near the front porch. It was a white, late-Yuppie or early-Gen-X family's wet dream.

As Darius and I boarded the bus that day, I spoke in rapid-fire sentences intent on getting him up to speed on what our block was truly like. I had decided that when William was released from jail, I wanted all the other crack smokers and dealers gone.

I was certain Darius, in light of his recent home purchase, would be easily swayed to my way of seeing things.

When I finally paused to suck in a breath of air, Darius interrupted me.

"Crack addicts have to live somewhere," he said.

"What?" I said.

"They have to live somewhere."

"Yeah," I said, "I guess that's true."

"And I'm going to go out on a limb and guess that they arrived in Cole long before you or I did."

"Yeah," I said, "That's for sure."

"So what right do *we* really have to ask them to leave?"

"What's your worst fear for Leah?" I ask William one Sunday as we drive back from my parents' house. Leah is in the back seat, asleep after an exciting day playing with her cousins.

"That someone will try to hurt her," he says, "And I won't be there to stop them."

We drive in silence for a moment, then William turns the question around to me. "Why? What's yours?"

"I thought I knew," I say, "but now mine seems so bourgeois."

"Tell me."

"No," I say, "It's dumb."

"Tell me."

"I worry that she will struggle to find her purpose in life. I don't want her to take forever to get her life on track. I don't want her to waste as much time as—"

"As me?" William says.

"No, as me" I say.

We laugh.

"I took longer than you," William says, "I'm *still* not on track."

"I took long enough. I wasted junior high, high school, part of college..."

I turn in my seat, looking to confirm that Leah is asleep, then I say, "I want her to be amazing every day. I don't want her to be like I was, never reading anything other than teen fan magazines. Sitting in my bedroom trying out various eye shadow combinations. I was such a waste of space."

"Oh, you mean when she's older?" William asks, "I thought you meant my worst fear for her right now."

"Do you have different fears for when she grows up?" I ask.

"I worry that I'll be dead and she won't be able to defend herself."

"She's not growing up under the same conditions you did. I mean it's not like someone's gonna challenge her to a fight." I say.

"What if something happens to you? We'll have to move back to the East Side. That's the only place I'm gonna be able to rent an apartment. If she ends up at East High School she's gonna have to drop somebody on the first day if she ever wants to see peace."

"It's *never* occurred to me that she would *ever* be in a fight," I say.

"It's never occurred to *me* that she wouldn't."

I am silent. My stomach is in my throat. I'd never considered how significantly her life would change if he had to raise her alone. It wouldn't matter how much life insurance we took out on me, without my daily presence in her life, she would have to toughen up pretty quickly.

Modern middle class parenting is about deciding every day which challenges we will allow our children to face and which ones we will conceal from them a little longer. Poor parents don't get to make those choices. Whatever crises arise are the ones the children will face, right along with their parents.

William never learned to plan ahead. He's spent a lifetime finding what he needed, right when he needed it— not before. The twenty-five-roll pack of toilet paper from Costco had never had a place in his life until I came along.

When we'd first met I'd understood his mindset and I'd respected it. Somewhere along the way though, I'd decided he had nothing of value to contribute to our daughter's upbringing.

Now, upon considering my own death, I was recognizing his skillset as valuable again. What if we someday found ourselves living in the aftermath of a natural disaster like Hurricane Katrina? How would our little family get by? Not by listening to me, that's for sure.

He had so much knowledge, strength and ingenuity that had been rendered less valuable since he'd married me, but that didn't mean we'd never need it again. Under the right circumstances his skills were more valuable than a hundred bars of gold bullion sitting in a safety deposit box in the Caymans. He wasn't using his skills on a daily basis anymore, but why wasn't I allowing him to pass them on to Leah?

He's looking at me, looking at the road, then looking back at me.

"Okay," I say, "What do we need to do to make sure she's tough and independent like you were at her age?"

He stares out at the road ahead of us, collecting his thoughts. Then finally, he presents them. "She needs to take martial arts classes. She has to learn to take a punch and keep fighting."

"Okay," I say, "What else?"

"She's old enough now to understand what I'm trying to teach her. When she cries and I tease her instead of running to her rescue, you have to let us be. "

Tears are streaming down my cheeks, "Okay," I say again, "What else?"

She needs to go to the East Side with me more often and spend time with her black cousins in the projects. You can't go with us."

"Why not?" I croak.

"Because when the grinning white lady shows up, people change how they act. And you won't be able to stay out of it if she gets into an argument. You can't intervene to make everybody feel good. You can't hover over her and protect her all the time. I know you, Kristl. You'd lose your mind wanting to make her and everyone else feel better but she has to learn how to stand on her own."

He looks over at me, checking in. I nod without speaking and he understands my signal, encouraging him to continue.

"You said yourself you loved how confident your little black friends in Texas were. How do you think they got to be so strong? It wasn't by having their mommas make everything better for them all day, every day. You have to let her become as strong as they were. That way, if anything ever happens to you, she'll be able to survive on the East Side since that's where we'll have to live."

"You're beautiful. You can find happiness," the woman at the dinner party says to me.

Wait. What?

Dammit. I've done it again.

In the eight years I've been married to William, I've made this mistake only a handful of times. I forgot *not* to tell a near stranger that my husband struggles with a crack addiction. I wasn't looking for sympathy—at least not any more than *she* was. We were talking about man caves and she was complaining that her husband had just bought yet another video game system. I told her that my husband has to sleep in our garage whenever he makes a series of choices that are too selfish. I thought we were having a wife-to-wife, my-husband-drives-me-crazy moment.

"It's true," I had said, "He has to live in the garage whenever he's making terrible choices because we have to protect our family's few electronics from growing legs and dashing off to the pawn shop."

Suddenly, this woman has appointed herself my counselor. She's stroking my upper arm. She's telling me to believe in myself.

"You deserve so much better and so does your daughter," she says, "Be a good example for her. You have the strength within you. Reach deep and make it happen."

"Make what happen?" I say, scowling at her.

"He should be in rehab and you and your daughter should be long gone."

"He's been to rehab. Twice," I say. "He's also been to jail, which, surprisingly, is every bit as good as rehab, but at a much lower price. We've had our share of jail visits, believe me."

"That's horrible. Why would you put your daughter through that?"

"Through what?" I say.

"No child should have to visit a parent in jail," she says, "You don't *owe* him a relationship with his daughter."

"I'm sure I *do* owe them *both* that," I say, "Listen to me— Listen to me—" then, I yell, "Stop talking!"

She closes her mouth and her eyes pop wide. Everyone in the room is looking at me now.

"You think I should abandon my crack-addict husband I guess just to prove to you and Dr. Phil that I'm not co-dependent. But what if he weren't my husband, but was my brother instead? Or my son? Then would my loyalty be understandable?

"You seem to be saying that if I just divorce him and re-marry the right person, my new, non-addicted husband and I, and my daughter, can pretend he's just someone *less fortunate* instead of recognizing that racism, the criminalization of addiction, mass incarceration, and the felon sub-caste are what made him quote-unquote *less fortunate*."

"That's not what I said," my new self-appointed therapist protests.

"But it's what you *meant*. Crack addicts have to live somewhere. They have to belong to someone. He belongs to us. When did abandoning family members become the *strong* thing to do? Do you know how much easier it would have been to cut and run? I could have saved myself so much stress, so much money and so much upheaval by just kicking him out. *That* would have been the super easy way for *me* to escape his problems, but it wouldn't make them go away for him.

"And once I've arranged that life for my daughter and I, the one where we pretend that people like him don't exist, then we can become like all the other the CandyLand citizens who, once a year, feel enough guilt to buy a boxed turkey lunch at Whole Foods. Is that how you think my husband's problems should be dealt with? Or wait, maybe we could schedule some volunteer hours at a homeless shelter so that we could ladle out soup. What if Leah's father happened to come through the line while we were volunteering? Awkward, right?

"Okay, so no ladling for us, right? Oh, I know! We should hold a fundraiser. We can all get dressed up in beautiful clothes, hire a guest speaker, and pay a thousand dollars a plate as admission."

No one is talking. Everyone is staring directly at me. My SSRI medication is really supposed to keep me from getting *this* worked up. I decide that as long as I've already alienated everyone anyway, I may as well make just make one last point.

"I don't want my daughter to grow up pretending no one is hungry, that no one has parents in jail, no one stinks because they didn't have a place to shower this morning, no one has a felony record holding them back, and no one struggles with addiction. I don't want her growing up in a subdivision of a subdivision where people know, to the nearest fifty-thousand dollar mark, how much each other's houses are worth. I don't want her to become adept at the social jostling that hyper-segregation forces today's subdivision-of-a-subdivision dwellers to participate in.

I change my voice to a vapid falsetto:

"Oh you live in Piney Village? Or Piney Creek? Or Piney Lakes? Or Piney Rolling Hills Estates?

Do you go to the Piney Lakes pool? Or the Piney Creek pool? We live in Piney Lakes so we can choose to go to the Piney Rolling Hills Estates pool but if you live in Piney Village can only go to the Piney Creek pool.

Can you believe the houses in Piney Creek only have two-car garages? Where do they park their third cars?"

People aren't looking at me anymore. Everyone has averted their eyes. They're looking at their shoes, the carpet, the walls – pretty much anything, to avoid looking at me..

A warm, peaceful, feeling sinks in. "Look," I say to everyone and no one, "This dinner party has been lovely but it's time for me to go. Thanks for inviting me. It was wonderful."

PRIMARY SOURCES AND USAGE NOTES

In the 1930s, President Franklin D. Roosevelt funded a project whereby writers were sent to find former slaves and record the experiences they'd had over the decades since they'd become Freedpeople. These former slaves talked about slavery, the Civil War era, and Reconstruction. Some also talked about the Jim Crow era, even though they were not specifically asked about it, because they were still living within it at the time of their interviews. These collections are known as the *Slave Narratives,* and are available online, free of charge, as well as in various curated collections.

Much like the *Slave Narratives,* during the 1990s, a group from Duke University set out to record the recollections of those who had lived through the Jim Crow era. The project was called *Behind The Veil,* and included recollections of all facets of black life during Jim Crow. The recordings are available online or within a book and CD set called, "Remembering Jim Crow." When referring to these recordings I will call them *Jim Crow Narratives.*

I have made use of these narratives as I attempted to understand the experiences of the black side of our family.

Anyone familiar with African American Vernacular English (AAVE) knows that its speakers often use a hard "D" sound in place of a "Th" at the beginning of words. Some transcribers tried to represent the dialect by transcribing "Dem" and "Dey" etc. I have converted the spellings (e.g. "Dem" back to "Them") back to standard "Th" spellings because I believe it allows the reader to focus on the speaker's meaning, instead of forcing them through the exercise of a mental dialect translation.

Conversely, when the dialect is reflected in word choice or sequence, such as the use of "was" instead of "were," I leave that usage intact.

I also substitute "black people" or "Freedpeople" when the original speaker uses a word that can be considered offensive. Blacks during the 1930s referred to themselves by a variety of labels. Among those labels: "coloreds," "darkies," and, of course, *that* n-word.

The majority of the people interviewed and presented in the *Slave Narratives* seem to have been those who had not received advanced schooling, and therefore spoke using a version of AAVE strongly associated with the Deep South.

It's important to keep in mind that while the *Slave Narrative* voices might be considered quaint and somewhat endearing, there were plenty of blacks who skillfully used what is known as American Standard English (ASE) back in the 1930s as well.

To view the writings of educated blacks who chose to write in American Standard English during the same time period that *the Slave Narratives* were captured, look into the 1930s archives of *The Crisis*, a publication of the NAACP.

The Duke project that produced the *Jim Crow Narratives* had a more diverse mix of interviewees. Some spoke AAVE and others spoke ASE.

As for the black members of our family, since they were poor and uneducated, the dialect used in most of the *Slave Narratives* can be assumed to be an accurate reflection of how they would have expressed themselves.

It's worth noting that my white great-grandparents were also uneducated and did not speak ASE. Of my grandparents featured in this writing, my grandfather spoke ASE, but my grandmother often used a more working-class grammar. My parents spoke ASE, but they both went to college.

My husband speaks AAVE. My daughter is free to speak either ASE or AAVE. Our hope is that she, like most blacks in the United States today, will learn to switch from one dialect to the other as necessary (or whenever she feels like it) and will love using both.

ACKNOWLEDGEMENTS

While I paid for two rounds of copyediting, I followed up both rounds by adding, deleting and re-arranging my words. I'm certain I re-introduced all kinds of errors but I couldn't resist making what I thought had to be improvements. I apologize to readers if my errors made reading frustrating. I ran out of (wheat) money before I ran out of ideas.

Amy Benson May was the closest thing I had to an editor. Her degree in a social justice related field, her marriage to a black man, and her status as the mother of a biracial child gave her insights that no one else was able to provide to me. The book is better because of her input.

I constrained the narrative of the book to focus on the single ancestral line that was the source of the wheat money. That meant I largely ignored my father's side of the family. Their absence in the book does not reflect an absence in my life. I am very indebted to my father and paternal grandfather for their role in my anti-racist upbringing. While they were poor and white, they never participated in racist acts or used racist language. Their compassion and moral compasses had deep effects on the person I became.

They did not feel the need to step on others to raise themselves. My father picked cotton in Oklahoma, side-by-side with blacks he'd known his entire life. He befriended blacks in college as he ran beside them on college track teams in the late 1950s. I could tell twenty stories of his adventures along the color line that make me proud that he is my father. Perhaps those stories are for another book.

A black man named O.J. Odom taught my grandfather, Chet, to play guitar and he so cherished that relationship, he refused to sing the "n-word" in a song that O.J. taught him. He certainly never used the word for any other purpose.

I have to thank Ben Wilkinson, my husband's cousin, for providing me with the information he'd gathered on Tolliver and Jemima. This book wouldn't exist without his contribution.

I'm grateful to Jason Cuerdon, my husband's lawyer, for putting up with my grand ideas about poetic justice and for the tether of practicality he provided us as we fought the mass incarceration machine.

Thanks to Noelle Roe for being such a good friend to me, especially during the last week of each year as I struggle trying to find a lighthearted-dead-serious way to teach Leah deep cultural pride. No matter what I've asked of her, she has been there for me, smiling and cheerful.

Thanks to Soniah Kamal for introducing me to the world of writers, writing workshops, and writing friendships. As an introvert, I don't make friends easily. Writing friendships feed one dimension of my soul. I wouldn't have writing friends if Soniah hadn't been my first.

Thanks to Toni Morrison, Alice Walker, Maya Angelou, Zadie Smith, Chimamanda Ngozi Adiche, and bell hooks for their writings. The words they've put on paper have bettered me immeasurably.

Thanks to all the people who allowed themselves to be interviewed for the *Slave Narratives* and the *Jim Crow Narratives*. Without the excerpts of those narratives I would not have been able to bring my daughter's black ancestors' experiences to life. In all my quoting of sources I've been careful to stay within the bounds of the fair use clause of the Copyright Act and therefore I should not be subject to lawsuits claiming infringement. However, if any readers are direct descendants of those I've quoted I welcome those interested parties to contact me about the quotes I've used. I would never want to carry the burden that I've exploited a Jim Crow or slavery survivor by using their words to enrich myself while leaving their descendant's wanting.

Finally, I owe a great debt to all the authors I have quoted within this book, without their research and writing, I would never have understood the true history of these 150 years.

A NOTE ABOUT RICH PEOPLE

In this book I write about "rich whites" and "white elites" and I accuse them of manipulating the poor to serve nefarious ends. Because of that, I understand that I can easily be accused of demonizing rich people or encouraging class warfare.

Right or not, it's true that when it comes to rich people, I consider them guilty until proven innocent.

I often explain it this way, "I don't judge people by how much money they make. I judge them by *how* they make it and *how much of it* they keep."

If you are rich, I'm curious as to whether someone in the Philippines made next to nothing so that you could scrape another quarter-percentage point of profit margin into your pocket. Have you hidden money in Bermuda because you believe you need it to pay for gardeners at your sixty-five million dollar estate? Do you have forty cars?

Worse, do you employ strategies that exploit last place aversion or use the racial bribe to encourage hatred so that you can make more money?

The choice to use thinly-veiled "colorblind" language to turn poor whites against poor blacks is not without consequence.

In modern times, rich television personalities foment divisions without ever needing to mention race. That colorblind language whips up poor whites who can easily de-code the messages back into racist diatribes. Those people's children then feel encouraged to run over black men for sport, or drag them behind trucks until their heads are ripped off.

Under these circumstances it would hardly seem right to accuse me of encouraging class warfare when the accuser's alternative is clearly a hundred-plus years' waging of a race war.

ABOUT THE AUTHOR

Kristl Tyler lives in Aurora, Colorado with her daughter, Leah and her husband William.

In an effort to continue growing as a *Good Human Being* she reads everything Ta-Nehisi Coates writes, watches Melissa Harris-Perry religiously, and is subscribed to the blog of Abagond, as well as the websites Colorlines and ColorOfChange.

The Wheat Money website at **TheWheatMoney.com** contains errata, references to all books cited in this work and other relevant resources.

Made in the USA
San Bernardino, CA
16 May 2015